COURAGE *to* STAND

COURAGE
to STAND

TIM
PAWLENTY

an American Story

TYNDALE HOUSE PUBLISHERS, INC.
CAROL STREAM, ILLINOIS

Published in association with the literary agency of Alive Communications, Inc., 7680 Goddard Street, Suite 200, Colorado Springs, CO 80920, www.alivecommunications.com.

Library of Congress Cataloging-in-Publication Data

Pawlenty, Tim, date.
  Courage to stand : an American story / Tim Pawlenty.
    p. cm.
  ISBN 978-1-4143-4572-7 (hc)
  1. Pawlenty, Tim, date. 2. Governors—Minnesota—Biography. 3. Minnesota—Politics and government—1951- 4. Minnesota—Biography. I. Title.
  F610.3.P38A3 2010
  977.6'053092—dc22
  [B]   2010047426

Printed in the United States of America

16   15   14   13   12   11
7   6   5   4   3   2   1

To Mary, Anna, and Mara,
and in memory of Gene and Ginny

CONTENTS

★ ★ ★ ★ ★ ★ ★ ★ ★ ★ ★ ★ ★ ★ ★ ★ ★ ★

INTRODUCTION

A crushing deficit. Runaway spending. A rocky economy.
A broken health-care system. Big government out of control.

AMERICA IS IN TROUBLE.

People I talk to in every small town and big city across this great country of ours recognize we're headed down a dangerous road. Here's what I mean.

In the spring of 2010, the world watched in horror as Greece's financial system suffered a near-total meltdown. There were protests and riots in the streets as a populace so addicted to entitlements and living the good life off the government dole faced the harsh reality that they might have to sacrifice what the government had promised them—because the government simply had no more money to pay for it. An entire population seemed horrified that they might have to work past the common retirement age of sixty-one. Imagine.

My family was eating breakfast one morning, discussing Greece and its financial trouble because it was in the newspaper. Mara, my then-thirteen-year-old daughter, completely unprompted, with simplicity and clarity, looked at me and said, "That will be America soon."

That's a quote. I didn't prompt her. A thirteen-year-old

recognized America is spending blindly toward the edge of a cliff. "That will be America soon."

If a child can see it, why can't the Washington establishment? And yet here we are, faced with leadership at various levels of government—especially the national level—who are unwilling or unable to tackle the real issues of our time.

For years, politicians in this country have only been rewarded for saying yes. That's a basic, undeniable truth. Yes to more spending. Yes to big bailouts. Yes to finding new ways to bring the bacon back home to their states and districts and towns and friends, no matter what the cost to everyone else. Yes to the funding of big-government programs that sound like a dream come true for many Americans but wind up costing every one of us so much that they damage our economy. And in the long run, these programs damage something much more important. They damage the American spirit.

Whatever happened to the power of *Enough*? the power and the guts to say, "No"?

I'm hopeful we've reached a turning point in America's history. A point where it's no longer acceptable to complain while doing nothing to actually make things better. Let's stop admiring the problem and start proposing the solution. It's no longer okay to look backward, unless it's to find inspiration or recognize the errors of the past so we can be certain we don't repeat them.

More than anything, right now, at this moment in history, I believe it's time for America to square its shoulders and get about the business of fixing our problems ourselves. It's a difficult job. But it's an essential job. It must be done. And it's a job that will serve us well.

For the past eight years, I've tried to inspire just that kind of pull-yourself-up-by-your-bootstraps reform in my home state of

Minnesota. I took the job of leading Minnesotans through one of the most trying and difficult periods of change the state has ever known. And guess what? We did pretty well in what is arguably the most liberal state in the nation. In the spawning ground of Eugene McCarthy, Hubert Humphrey, Walter Mondale, Paul Wellstone, and yes, even Al Franken, we've managed to cut spending, reform health care, reduce big government, and set Minnesota on a better course for the future. And we did it without raising taxes.

It wasn't easy. Political fists were bloodied. A few teeth got knocked out. There were even moments when we shook hands across the aisle and joined forces. I believe we succeeded because I was willing to do whatever it took to get the job done. The people of Minnesota deserved nothing less, and I believe the American people should demand the very same commitment from their leaders in Washington.

The political reward system needs to change. We must become a country in which we respect leaders who are willing to stand up, draw a line in the sand, and say no to the never-ending demands for more spending while saying yes to a future that makes sense not only right now, but for the America our children and *their* children will inherit.

Spending our way out of recession? Spending our way out of the health-care crisis? Spending our way out of debt? Does that really make sense? Runaway spending in Washington certainly isn't new, and many Republicans in recent history haven't exactly adhered to the "fiscally conservative" promise that the Republican Party is supposed to live by.

So there's plenty of blame to go around. But the fact is, the current administration, through the smoke-and-mirror effect of bailouts and big-government spending, has taken America's future and leveraged it into a mountain of debt so large it's nearly impossible for anyone to wrap their heads around. It pretends more spending will help our problems go away. That's fiction.

When the rain started to fall on America's picnic, Washington hung up a big old plastic tarp to protect us from the deluge. (Ever wonder why they call some of these things "TARP funds"?) Good intentions? Maybe. But a bad decision. The problem was, the rain just kept coming. The tarp started sagging in the middle and filling up with water. Poke it with a broom handle all you want, try to drain some of that rainwater over the sides, but the blanket below is getting awfully wet in the meantime. Everyone can see the tarp's starting to tear at the seams, and we've run out of duct tape. This whole thing's going to collapse—and the picnic will simply be over. Time for a new plan.

When it comes to big-government spending and the future of our economy, we've reached a point where politics must be set aside and new solutions must be found. This is no longer a dispute between Republicans and Democrats or conservatives and liberals. It's a matter of junior high math.

You simply can't have a spending graph that goes sharply up, coupled with a revenue graph that's nearly flat. Anyone who has ever balanced a ledger—scratch that—anyone who has ever balanced a checkbook at their kitchen table should be able to see the problem. Mercifully, Americans are beginning to see this. They're smart, and they get it.

Here's the breakdown: The federal government takes in approximately $2.2 trillion per year, in total, from all sources. They—rather we, since it is our money after all—spent $3.7 trillion last year. So we spend more than we make. It doesn't work.

But that's not the half of it. We have $14 trillion of debt and a $65-trillion liability in front of us if we include Social Security, government pensions, and all of the various entitlement programs that are considered "off the books."

The math just doesn't work. No reasonable amount of revenue will ever offset that liability. Ever. The truth of the matter is, just as we've done in the formerly free-spending state of Minnesota over the last eight years, we're going to have to change, to reform our ways. The problems we face now loom so large, and the citizens of this country are so well-informed and aware of what's at stake, that I think most Americans are increasingly willing to take difficult but reasonable steps to fix them.

The bigger question, the question we all need to ask, is, "Do our politicians have the political will to do it?" Can the new breed of politicians that are making their way into Washington actually lead us through? I sure hope so. I mean, we have to find the resolve, the political backbone to stand up to the status quo, to say, "No. Enough's enough. We have to do this. Right now."

We did it in Minnesota, and we have to do it in Washington.

I don't claim to have all the answers, and I certainly haven't done everything perfectly in my time as Governor. But I have learned some things along the way and accomplished some things that are instructive for the country right now. Lessons built from experience. Lessons that could be instructive for the federal government and for those individuals now settling into Washington who care about the future of this great nation—who have what it takes to move us forward.

It won't be easy. It never is. But America was built on grit and courage, on the backs of men and women who have been willing to shoulder the weight of the seemingly impossible tasks laid out before them, and who have only grown stronger in the face of obstacles and opposition.

Every one of us has that courage inside us. The courage to do the right thing. The courage to say, "No" when everyone else says "Yes"—because we know it's the right thing to do; and the courage to say "Yes" to what's right, even in the face of staunch opposition. It comes down to the courage to stand up for what we believe in, as well as the courage to simply stand up—no matter how many times we're knocked down.

Calling upon that courage when it's needed most is the American way. It's that powerful resolve that we all recognize as the American spirit.

That's the spirit I was raised with here in Minnesota, the spirit I hope I can impart in some small way by sharing my story, sharing my views, and sharing a few insights I've gained on this journey—a journey that started on the streets of South St. Paul and led me through the end of my second term as Governor of the great state I call home.

As I left my time in office behind, I couldn't predict what the future would bring, but I left the Governor's office knowing I had worked hard and given my best. I used my best judgment and applied plenty of good old American common sense to the decisions I made. Most of all, I left being open to whatever might come next. A Christian friend gave me a reminder years ago to put things in perspective, not only in my political career, but in my life more broadly. *Although we're in charge of the effort, some things are out of our control. We need to trust that the future lies in God's hands.*

There is much work to be done, and I have the will and desire to do my part, whatever that part may be. If I can help to shape America's future for the better in any small way, then it is my duty, and my honor, to serve in whatever capacity I can.

The funny thing is, through all of the debates and battles, triumphs and losses, I haven't become tired—of any of it. In fact, after all these years, I find just the opposite is true: I'm more energized every single day. With every person I meet, every hand I shake, every eye I lock, every speech I give across this great country, I'm more inspired by the possibility of what lies ahead for America.

Now we need to get it done.

1

★ ★ ★ ★ ★ ★ ★ ★ ★

GAME FACE

FOR ALL THE POMP AND CIRCUMSTANCE that comes with the changing of the guard after any big election in this country, there is one detail that someone along the way seems to have overlooked: No one hands the incoming Mayor or Governor or President a playbook. There's no instruction manual. Despite the plethora of people who want to offer advice and the memos that cover logistics, when it comes right down to making important decisions, you're on your own—and you'd better have the experience, faith, strength, and composure for whatever might come your way.

Never was that made more clear to me than in the first few days after I was elected Governor of Minnesota in 2002.

My election was hard fought. I got into the race pretty late, I had far less money than my opponents, and despite serving as Majority Leader in the Minnesota House of Representatives,

I didn't have much name recognition. In the back of my mind, I'm not sure I ever fully expected to win. Running on a truly conservative platform, promising not to raise taxes in the bluest of the blue states? My chances of becoming Governor of Minnesota could best be summed up as more of a remote possibility than a foregone conclusion.

The morning after the election, I remember waking up in our family's suburban home, the same house where I'd slept nearly every night since 1994, and looking out our bedroom window to find the surreal new presence of State Troopers milling about my driveway. *What will the neighbors think of all this?* Despite having served ten years in the legislature, this clearly marked a major transition for my family.

And that word, *transition*, loomed incredibly large. I would have only about sixty days to build a team and set everything in place before the inauguration in January. How would I start the actual work of fulfilling the promises I'd made to the people of Minnesota? I tried to wrap my mind around it all over breakfast. That's when I received a phone call reminding me of a meeting with Governor Ventura.

Jesse Ventura, the ex–professional wrestler with the larger-than-life personality (and the stature to match) had served four years as one of the more colorful Governors in Minnesota's history. Being a bit of a wrestling fan myself and having watched matches including masters like Hulk Hogan and Jesse Ventura, I respected Governor Ventura's intensity as well as his willingness to enter public service.

Jesse "the Body" Ventura had not been my election opponent; he'd decided not to seek a second term. My DFL (that's the Democratic-Farmer-Labor party, generally the prevailing party in Minnesota and fully aligned with the national Democratic party) opponent was Senate Majority Leader Roger Moe, a thirty-plus-year veteran of the state Senate. Former Congressman Tim Penny was the Independence Party candidate.

From what I could tell, Governor Ventura was ready to move on. Life in public office had taken a toll on his family, and after reaching a high point on the bell curve of national and international prominence, he had decided it was time to step off the mat.

The meeting was a way of passing the symbolic baton, and a press conference was scheduled to reinforce that point.

Even though I'd served in the legislature for years, stepping into the Governor's office, that physical space in the southwest corner of the capitol, still inspired a great deal of awe for me. There's a kind of confusion about how you get to the office itself, through a series of doors—one door leads to another, and another, to the point that the uninitiated might feel like they're caught in a carnival mirror maze.

By now I know my way, of course, but I remember stepping into the room that day thinking how remarkable it all was. I had just been elected Governor of the state and would have to carry all the responsibility that came with the office. There are 5.3 million people in the state of Minnesota, and no matter how many of them had actually voted for me, all of them would be turning to me for leadership and guidance at the highest level.

Now it was time to take that first step.

Governor Ventura and I had weathered our share of run-ins through the years and had actually grown to know each other quite well. I was conservative, and he was famously Independent, so while we were on the same team in serving the people, we were periodically adversaries on some pretty big issues. And when the administration was doing something I didn't agree with, it fell to me as House Majority Leader to engage the issue in the press.

Sometimes it was even fun—a good sound bite helps draw media attention to your cause.

I recall one particular instance when something I said publicly turned out to be more provocative than I could have imagined. Responding to an increase in state taxes, I said in an interview, "In the cause to cut taxes, Jesse Ventura has left the taxpayers behind enemy lines."

Ventura, a former Navy man, apparently heard my comment on the radio and was deeply offended by it. As I returned to my office, the phone rang. It was Ventura's assistant. "The Governor's going to be in your office in five minutes." He was driving all the way in from his house in Maple Grove, she told me. If he was driving twenty-plus miles to see me instead of just calling, clearly he was intent on delivering his message in person.

The next thing I knew, Governor Ventura appeared in my office in casual clothes, shut the door, and started shouting. "I was in the military, and we don't leave anybody behind enemy lines, you blankety blank-blank!" It was loud. The Speaker of the House had an adjacent office and later told me he could hear the shouts through the thick, old walls.

At one point we were both standing, and my back was against the wall as he moved toward me. I thought, *He's gonna hit me!* Truly, I thought for sure it was coming. *He's gonna smack me.* He was the kind of guy who could get agitated quickly, and I'd seen it often, but I'd never seen him take it to a physical level. I realized that as dramatic and bizarre as this whole situation was, we needed to de-escalate. Without shouting, I calmly told him that I had used the phrase "behind enemy lines" as a rhetorical device, a metaphor, and I never meant for it to reflect on his military service or commitment. He was owed an apology, and I apologized.

The hockey player and wrestling fan in me would have taken

some pride in surviving a Jesse Ventura smackdown. But the apology felt better. And that was all it took to let the air out of the balloon. He went from enraged to reasonable and graciously accepted the apology. The meeting ended well.

Sometimes an apology is itself a sign of strength.

That's just one of many meetings I had with Ventura that were colorful, to say the least, but over the years I've come to like and respect him. He has been fair-minded about my work as Governor, and we've even played golf a few times. I see him as different from his public persona. He is engaging, has a great sense of humor, and is a strongly devoted family man.

So walking into his office that November day in 2002, I kind of hoped he would share some insights on what lay ahead for me, maybe tell me a few things that a Governor needs to know or share some practical steps that I ought to take to get ready for January. Something. When he wasn't forthcoming after a bit of small talk, I came right out and asked him, "You got any advice for me?"

"Nope," he said.

That was it! Minutes later we stepped out into the reception room for our press conference. He was decent. He was kind. He didn't try to tell me what to do, and I respected that, and his team turned out to be very helpful during the transition.

I would soon need all the insight, wisdom, and guidance I could draw upon, because I was about to get hit harder than any blow Ventura could have laid on me.

★ ★ ★ ★ ★ ★ ★ ★ ★ ★

A FEW WEEKS into the whirlwind of pulling together my transition team, planning an inaugural celebration for January, and figuring out that I could turn to the National Governors Association for advice while preparing my family for this strange new world in which State Troopers were staking out our house in order to keep us all safe, I was called to another meeting to receive the official November budget forecast.

Minnesota is on a two-year budget cycle, and budget forecasts are put together twice a year—in February and November—in order to give everyone a heads-up on how things are looking. In an election year, the November forecast is typically shared with the Governor-elect just before it is announced publicly, and that was exactly what this meeting was all about.

Back in February of that year, the forecast had predicted something close to a $2 billion deficit. In a state in which spending had been out of control for decades, that didn't actually sound so bad. The only problem was, the economy in Minnesota had been deteriorating all year.

As I sat down with some of my transition leaders in a nondescript government conference room in a nondescript government office building that served as our transition headquarters just down the street from the capitol, I remember thinking that surely the deficit would have grown. *Okay, it could get as high as two-five, two-eight. . . . Huge problem? Yes. But we can handle it.*

So we settled in, and the state finance officials dimmed the lights a bit and threw a slide up on the screen, and right off the bat they let us have it. The projected deficit had ballooned to nearly $4.6 billion.

For a moment, it was as if all the oxygen had been sucked out of the room. Everyone went silent, and I noticed a few eyeballs glancing my way, anticipating a reaction.

To put into perspective just how big this problem was, the entire Minnesota state budget back then was around $28 billion. We were overextended by about 17 percent.

Hearing a number that big, no matter who you are and how

well you think you're prepared to handle the job of Governor, you can't help but feel challenged. You can't help but think, *This is awful.* I mean, I wasn't even sitting under the capitol dome yet, and here I was faced with what seemed like a nearly insurmountable economic challenge, in an economy that was already in decline.

In that moment, the weight of my new position took hold. It's one thing to be a legislator when the state is hit with bad news. As Majority Leader, I could have made a comment or held a press conference or responded as part of a larger process. But in that moment, I realized, *This team of people is looking to me for leadership. They're looking to me for strength. I need to be their Governor— right now.*

Over time, organizations tend to take on the tempo, characteristics, and personalities of their leaders. It's something I've observed in practice, and it's been written about by an endless parade of business experts and leaders from all walks of life. In any moment—but especially in moments of crisis or stress—what you project truly matters. It matters in terms of emotion, character, strength, perspective, values, and vision. This was just such a moment, and it was an early test for me.

Luckily, it was only a small group of people in that conference room, because I'm pretty sure a couple of those staffers caught a glimpse of my pale-faced horror at the size of that deficit—even if only for a second before I pushed that feeling of shock and dismay aside. I remember thinking, *I can't project this as a knockout blow. The team needs to see we can handle this.* So as much as I wanted to show my frustration, I held my reaction at bay.

Thinking and acting like a true leader in times of great difficulty is a huge responsibility. It takes discipline and focus. It's a switch that flips more naturally for me now, after eight years in office leading Minnesota through all of the ups and downs and challenges we've endured. Yet one of the things I find most remarkable about leading is the leeway it affords you to recognize opportunity in even the most dire of circumstances.

The fact is, leadership takes optimism. Not blind optimism. *Informed* optimism. Imagine what would happen if a leader emerged from behind closed doors in the midst of a crisis and told the American people, "Well, folks, I've got some bad news. We're in some hot water here, and I don't know what to do about it. Basically, we're hosed. Things just aren't looking good for the future, and we may just have to throw in the towel."

It seems like common sense that no leader in his or her right mind would ever say such a thing. And yet it takes more than common sense to see beyond the dire circumstances that are sometimes laid before you. It takes thoughtful optimism and courage and the ability to recognize that those challenges may actually create opportunity.

As the budget-office gurus continued to lay out the details of the dismal financial situation I was about to inherit as Governor, I quickly began throwing coal on the engine of a whole new train of thought. *This isn't a disaster; it's an opportunity, because it's going to force change. Positive change. Change that will set this state back on the right track, and finally—finally!—force state government to accept some fiscal responsibility.*

Forcing fiscal responsibility on a government that had been overspending for forty years wouldn't be easy, of course, even in the face of financial disaster. It's tough to make anyone eat plain old potatoes when they've grown accustomed to pouring on boatloads of gravy for decades. But when the battle came, and it would most certainly come, I knew I had a powerful weapon in my arsenal. I had a platform that I had just successfully stood upon to win the election. A key plank in that platform was that I absolutely refused to raise taxes.

I realized as I sat in that conference room that there was a line in the sand here—a promise I had made to the people of Minnesota, a promise I intended to keep with all my heart and soul. I knew I had to maintain that position as a matter of credibility and integrity, in addition to the fact that it was something I wholeheartedly believed in.

Minnesota at that time was already one of the top five most highly taxed states in the country. The thought of adding to that burden, which already heavily weighed on the hardworking people of the state, was unfathomable to me. So while this budget crisis was a major problem, and it definitely worried me, I also immediately knew there was only one way forward. We would have to cut spending. We would have to cut back on the big-government promises and programs of the past. We would have to find the strength to move Minnesota in a new direction.

That moment when the budget news slapped us all in the face was the first chance I had as Governor to demonstrate the calm, steady demeanor that effective leadership demands. My team needed to see it, just as the people of Minnesota would need to see it when this problem came their way in the morning news reports.

We see the effects of steady leadership all around us. We recognize great leadership in many walks of life. When something goes wrong, people either get nervous or they gain assurance from their leader's strength. Often, it's not even anything that's said. Sometimes it's in precisely what's not said. And sometimes the message is conveyed simply by the way a leader holds himself when confronted with a trying and difficult situation.

By the time I left that conference room, I knew that tackling the tasks that lay before me would take all of my strength, faith, hard work, and commitment. But I also knew the people of Minnesota would be up to the challenge and help me lead the state down an entirely new path.

A few weeks later, in my very first State of the State address, I did my best to distill the essence of my newfound resolve into words my listeners would be ready and willing to hear. It's been eight years since I've gone back and looked closely at that speech, but I clearly remember the simple message: "Sure, we've got a problem, but this is Minnesota. And let me tell you about Minnesota strength, and Minnesota people, and Minnesota resolve, and Minnesota commitment and service. Let me remind you how we've overcome these challenges historically."

It's funny, thinking about it now. The highlights of that speech could very well serve as a road map for the life that led me to the Governor's office in the first place. A life in which I was surrounded by Minnesota strength and Minnesota people. A life filled with examples of Minnesota resolve and commitment and service. The fact is, I would need to lean on every bit of my upbringing, my family, and my faith in order to stand up to the opposing forces and unexpected twists of fate that would pummel our state over the course of the next eight years.

After all, that personal experience and history made me the person I am today.

2

★ ★ ★ ★ ★ ★ ★ ★ ★ ★

STOCKYARDS AND STABILITY

WHO WE ARE depends in part on where we come from.

From our hometowns to the challenges we rise above, from our families to the fabric of our growing up years, our roots—like it or not—have a way of shaping us. Anyone who really knows me will tell you pretty quickly that my roots are firmly planted in the city of South St. Paul.

Nestled along the Mississippi River, South St. Paul isn't a neighborhood within St. Paul, as some folks incorrectly presume. It's a separate town of about twenty thousand people.

Driving through the main streets and neighborhoods in the residential area of South St. Paul today brings me right back to my youth—in part because the landscape hasn't really changed that much. The humble, single-family homes that popped up in the fifties and sixties are still there, side by side, row by row—though the trees in the neatly mowed front yards have grown a whole lot taller. Dogs and kids' bicycles lie on their sides, lazing in the sun on single-car driveways. American flags hang on the posts of wooden fences, fences that were built not to keep anyone out but just to define the yards and look nice with the flowers. Small boats rest on trailers in side yards, just waiting to see some fishing action on the weekend.

The street signs are all marked with *SSP*—a sign of South St. Paul pride. Holy Trinity Church still stands strong, along with two other Catholic churches, Saint John and Saint Augustine (one of the few Catholic churches I know of that still hold masses in Latin). The old Croatian Hall hosts meetings and dances and occasionally cookouts on the lawn, and folks can gather over beers and games of bubble hockey down in the basement bar. The Dairy Queen is one of the few big chain restaurants you'll find, in the very same spot it stood when I was a kid. And down toward the end of Southview Boulevard, just up 3rd Avenue from the library, the police station, the old courthouse, and the Historical Society Museum, sits the Coop, a family-owned fried-chicken joint with a take-out counter and three tables inside, where in the year 2010 you could still buy a fried-fish dinner on Friday for a grand total of $5.62.

When the weather's nice, the owners of the Coop place a little sign out on the sidewalk. The sign refers to the restaurant as "A SSP Landmark." I suppose the Coop is just about as good a landmark as any in South St. Paul today, because the industry that once served as the anchor of my hometown no longer exists there. The meatpacking plants and stockyards that once thrived along the western bank of the Mississippi—once the biggest stockyards in the entire world—are gone.

What used to serve as the center of employment and life for

so many residents of this town was swept into history, seemingly overnight, at the dawn of the 1970s. It's something anyone in America who lives in a one-industry town, whether it's an auto factory town or a shoe-manufacturing community, can relate to. When that one industry starts to close up shop, it leaves decades of unease and heartache in its wake.

So as much as the residential portions of South St. Paul remain the same, the side of my hometown along the mighty Mississippi is a faded ghost of a once-glorious past. A drive down Concord Street—formerly the main thoroughfare outlining the stockyards—now feels sadly empty. What used to be a landscape rife with more saloons in the course of a few miles than just about anywhere else in America, all stretched across the floodplain of the Mississippi like a bridge between the Wild West and my childhood, is now a mostly quiet, nondescript industrial park.

The thing is, it's impossible to convey any understanding of South St. Paul *without* talking about those stockyards. The city was home to both the Swift and Armour processing plants, and the Union Stockyards were a hub at which millions upon millions of cattle, hogs, and other livestock were delivered, sold, processed, and shipped out across America. Those stockyards were at the core of just about everything in South St. Paul. The high school mascot is a steer. The sports teams are called the Packers (short for Meatpackers). Skipping over this part of my city's history would be like trying to describe Moscow without mentioning Communism or giving a tour of Hollywood while ignoring the movie industry. South St. Paul isn't nearly as big as those places, of course. But the stockyards loomed that large.

I might not even be here if it weren't for the stockyards. Jobs from those yards drew my grandparents to South St. Paul in the first place.

Like millions of Americans, I'm a descendant of European immigrants. In the late 1800s, my great-grandparents on my father's side, Joseph and Mary Pawlenty, emigrated from Poland to Little Falls, Minnesota, where they tried (unsuccessfully) to be mink farmers, among other things. They were tough and worked tirelessly, as so many immigrants from that generation did. The story, as it was passed down to us, is that Great-Grandpa Joe was seriously injured in a farming accident later in life and died of a broken back.

Joe and Mary's son, John, married a girl named Rose, the daughter of another Little Falls–based Polish immigrant family. When it came time to look for work, the two of them moved to South St. Paul, where the stockyards offered opportunities for anyone willing to work hard in conditions that weren't always optimal.

* * * * * * * * * *

THE UNION STOCKYARDS received all manner of livestock, but the primary three were sheep, cattle, and hogs. In 1911, more than 700,000 sheep were sold in the yards, along with 900,000 hogs and more than 500,000 cattle. By 1918, the numbers rose to 1.5 million cattle and more than 3 million hogs. Stop for a moment and imagine how many trucks it took, driving in from farms in North and South Dakota, Wisconsin, and all over Minnesota, to transport those animals. Imagine how many men were needed to unload those trucks and move the animals into their pens—pens that were stretched out side by side over hundreds of acres, squares and rectangles that when seen from above looked like a giant patchwork quilt covering the earth. Try to envision how many men it took to make sure all of those animals—millions of them—had food and water. Think of the daily grind to get the job done under the hot summer sun and through the bitter Minnesota winters. And just imagine the conditions in the bowels of the meat-processing plants in the days before air-conditioning.

The Dakota County Historical Society Museum (just down the street from the Coop) has a fantastic panoramic exhibit that details all of it, including a station where you can try your hand at one of the less-glamorous jobs those plants provided: stuffing pigs' feet into Mason jars. The museum has a timer set up so you can see just how fast you can do it. Workers were expected to fill four jars every minute in order to earn $8 per day. The best of the best pig-foot stuffers could fill seven jars every sixty seconds, earning bonuses that would kick them up to $11 per day. Imagine the feel of those hacked-off feet in your hands. The museum uses plastic feet, but those workers were grasping the real things. Think of the stress on your hands, on your back, filling a jar every fifteen seconds, day in and day out, week after week.

This is the kind of stuff my grandparents were doing when they moved to South St. Paul. It was a hard life, but it was a way to scrape by and support their family. Together, John and Rose had ten children, one of whom, Eugene, would turn out to be my father.

My dad was born in 1923. Gene, as everyone called him, grew up to become a truck driver. He, too, would build his life not far from South St. Paul's main industry after growing up in the middle of the Great Depression.

The stories of how tough times were and how much people had to scrimp and save to survive are endless. There are history books for that. But one story sort of says it all. There was one point in the early 1930s when the federal government, in an effort to help shore up prices and stabilize the economy, decided to pay farmers to slaughter their livestock rather than bring it to market. That act caused more than 600,000 hogs to be shot and killed in the course of a few days at the Union Stockyards—to be buried in trenches just a mile or so from the little house my dad grew up in.

Just imagine the smell.

Yet somehow, the old-timers remember those days as a glorious time to be alive. I've always found that inspiring—how all that hard work and effort and struggle gave people a sense of pride; how family was held in such high esteem; how budgeting for ten kids on roughly eight bucks a day was somehow doable.

Work and life were intertwined in South St. Paul in those days. Whole families, including the youngest children, got involved in livestock shows and 4-H competitions. One local radio station, WCCO (an AM station that's still thriving today; I hosted a one-hour radio show on WCCO each Friday morning during my time as Governor), had a broadcast studio in the Stockyard Exchange Building—a historically protected brick structure that still stands across Concord Street from the old stockyard site. A guy named Al Smeby used to broadcast daily livestock market reports from a little booth there, and people in town would listen. People like Tom Kaliszewski, the stockyards' most prolific salesman and a legendary figure in South St. Paul history, a guy who personally sold more than 3 million head of cattle in his fifty-year career.

This is the world my dad was living in when he met Virginia Oldenburg, the sister-in-law of his good friend Tommy Stanek. The woman who would become his wife. My mother, Ginny Pawlenty.

★ ★ ★ ★ ★ ★ ★ ★ ★ ★

PEOPLE SAY OPPOSITES ATTRACT, and Gene and Ginny couldn't have been more different. My dad was six-foot-four; my mom, just a little over five feet. Although my dad was slim as a young man, he put on a few pounds over the years; my mom couldn't have weighed 110 pounds soaking wet. He was of Polish decent; her family was German. Somehow they were the perfect match.

My parents married in 1948—the same year the meatpackers union went on strike and sank South St. Paul and the entire state of Minnesota into a state of turmoil for sixty-seven days. The meatpackers complained that they hadn't seen a wage increase since 1941, and had they held out, they might have won themselves a raise. But the Governor at the time stepped in, closed the streets, and allowed hundreds of so-called "scabs" to cross the picket lines and take those union positions on a temporary basis, essentially pulling the rug out from under the meatpackers and taking away their advantage in any ongoing negotiations. Eventually, it all just fizzled, and everybody went back to work.

Gene and Ginny would have five kids: Peg, Steve, Rose, Daniel, and me. They lived with the first four in a little white house on Park Street, just up the hill from the stockyards. But when an interstate highway came pushing through a few hundred yards from their little slice of the world in the months before I was born, my parents decided it was time to move. They invested their life savings in a brand-new house in a brand new development on 12th Avenue South.

I was born in St. Paul on November 27, 1960, and that three-bedroom, one-bathroom house on 12th Avenue would be the only home I knew until I was an adult.

The way my parents and siblings tell the story, it was as if they were moving on up. The idea that they could live in a brand-new house a little farther from the stockyards and a little closer to the stores and "uptown" area was just the bee's knees.

I took a drive by that house recently. The gray exterior, the white trim—it's still just as it was. Almost frozen in time. The single-car garage-under design looks small now, but it sure didn't seem small then. I guess everything seems bigger when you're a kid. It's a reminder that as time goes by, perspectives change.

Looking at that house, I can remember when, later on, my parents finished the basement with wood paneling, giving us some extra room. But before that, everything was on one level—three very small bedrooms, along with the kitchen, living room, and one bathroom. I don't recall ever thinking that sharing a bedroom with two older brothers was a burden. It's just the way it was. Before Steve moved out, we had a single bed and a bunk bed in there. Steve got the single, Dan was up top, and I slept on the bottom bunk. I know a lot of kids these days would complain about having to share space, but I don't recall it as burdensome at all. I remember it being fun.

Behind the house was a nice backyard, where my mother did some gardening. She always planted flowers back there, and she grew a few vegetables. She loved gardening. A little farther back, we burned our trash in a metal barrel. Cardboard, plastic, cans, and all forms of trash—everything you can think of would be thrown into that fire. I remember thinking burning the trash was fun duty, especially the part where we used lighter fluid to get the flames going.

The stockyards provided enough of a tax base that we had two community pools and our own hospital, and the public schools were some of the best around. But when I was a kid, it seemed everything we really needed was right there on our block. We rarely ventured even over to 13th Avenue, at least until we were older and my brother Daniel had his eye on one of the girls on that street. It was only a block away, but there just didn't seem like much reason to go over there.

Our neighbors included the Bruggemans, the Kellys, the Bojanoviches, the Marschinkes. They and other neighbors were hardworking people who held jobs like mailman, cop, cement layer, and handyman. And of course, many people in town worked at the stockyards. We kids would play endlessly in the street right in front of the house. It was sloped, so sometimes we'd go up top to the flat area for games of street hockey or touch football at a moment's notice. Often families had five or six kids. You could whistle, and fifteen kids would come running out looking for fun.

At the end of the day, we'd sit on top of a nearby hill and wait to see our dads drive up the street. Often families had only one car, so while our dads were at work, it's not like our moms were running us to activities all over town. If we wanted to go somewhere, we either walked or biked, or we were stuck right there after school until our dads came home with the car. Kids on our block would wave and run to greet their fathers even before they hit the driveways.

Life on 12th Avenue was filled with simple pleasures. People seemed to make the most of whatever they had. For instance, it was pretty common to have a milkman back in those days, but on 12th Avenue we also had a beerman—a neighbor with a pickup truck loaded with cases of beer from the local brewery— who came around every Friday night. It wasn't really his job; he was just being friendly and helpful since he worked at the brewery. Apparently he was able to buy those cases for cheap because they were "damaged" goods—although no one seems to remember any visible damage to any of those beer cans. If your dad was home, the beerman would stop in and have one with him. In fact, he'd do that with each neighbor along the way.

In the evenings and on weekends, families seemed to spill out into the streets and patios. People sat on stoops or in lawn chairs on driveways, having a cold one while the kids played. Even the terribly cold Minnesota winters didn't keep us indoors. For years my dad set up a little ice rink in the backyard so the neighborhood kids could come over for games of hockey. Sometimes the game was boot hockey, sort of like ice hockey but without the skates, usually played with a tennis ball instead of a puck. A few different rules applied, but the full-contact nature of the sport was fully intact. Even without pads. Even when your sisters were playing. It was a tough game, and you got to know it fast because everyone got in on the action.

From everything I saw as a child, the city of South St. Paul was a place where neighbors mattered, where family mattered, where church mattered, where respect for things mattered. Everywhere you turned, you saw hardworking, fun-loving people, doing whatever they could to get by, most all of them living by the rules and trying to do the right thing.

3

★ ★ ★ ★ ★ ★ ★ ★ ★ ★

STRONG COFFEE

MY MOTHER'S MOTHER died before I was born, and her husband had abandoned the family when my mom was a kid, so I didn't have a connection to the previous generation on my mother's side. My father's father passed away by the time I was four, which left me with little memory of him, either. So the only grandparent I really remember from my childhood was my paternal grandmother, Grandma Rose.

In many families of that generation, the grandfather garnered great reverence. He was the man who made it through the Depression, fought in the military, built a career outside the home, and worked hard, raising a family in Everytown, America, making it possible for all his sons and daughters and grandchildren to lead successful lives. In my family, I watched that reverence directed to

Grandma Rose. I'll always remember the deference my dad and his brothers and sisters showed her. She was not well educated or outspoken, but she seemed to command an inherent respect from her children. It was clear she was the matriarch. It was also clear to me, even as a child, that her children loved her, nurtured her, doted over her. And she doted right back.

Grandma Rose was every bit the Polish matron. She was a joy-filled, round-faced, elderly Polish grandma. She lived by herself in a very modest home on Concord Street, just north of the stockyards. She and my grandfather apparently chose that house because neither of them ever learned to drive. Back when they were working, there was a streetcar that ran down Concord Street, and that made their house about as convenient as could be. The house has long since been torn down, just as the streetcars have disappeared and the tracks have been paved over.

Grandma Rose always dressed in a flower-print dress and an apron. I can hardly remember a time when she didn't have an apron on, and she seemed to always have her hair up in those big, oversize rollers, held in place with plenty of Aqua Net hairspray. She wore glasses and Dr. Scholl's–style shoes with the thick platforms. You get the picture—just the quintessential grandma.

Sundays after church, some combination of my dad and his nine brothers and sisters and their children, my cousins, would gather at Grandma Rose's. I can still smell the coffee she served. Strong coffee for the adults. For the kids? Strong coffee with lots of sugar and milk. That was the only choice we were given! Long before Starbucks and Caribou ushered in the coffee craze in America, there was coffee with my grandma. The adults would sit around the kitchen table and talk politics, religion, life, heartbreak, joy. The children, at the periphery, either listened in or slipped away to play.

Grandma Rose's house backed up to a hill that led to a large sand and gravel pit. The property was surrounded by wire hung with signs reading, WARNING, WARNING, WARNING. But it was always vacant on Sunday mornings and well worth the trek up the steep hill to get there. Ignoring the signs entirely, we would squeeze through the fences and go into the gravel pit and climb on the huge sandpiles, which I realize now was horribly dangerous. There are air pockets in those piles, and if you hit an air pocket, you could become entombed in sand. But we didn't know that.

When we weren't risking our lives on sandpiles, we enjoyed safer fun right in Grandma's backyard in a little wooded area with a rope swing. A lot of times, though, we would wind up just sitting and listening to the grown-ups talk. Many of my Sunday morning memories from when I was eight or nine years old involve listening to the adults' discussions and drinking the strongest cups of sugar-laced coffee imaginable.

Back then, I'm sure it seemed boring. Likely we complained. Now? It lives in my memory as a glorious family experience.

Grandma Rose always had cookies or treats at the ready. It seemed as if the measure of her love for others included how much food she could force into every one of us. Mostly sweets, of course, unless you were there for lunch or dinner, when you'd get some form of potato, or some form of sausage or other affordable meat. And she dispensed matronly advice with every plate.

Some days I visited her by myself. I'd sit in her oversize grandma chair with the reclining feature, where you could pull the lever and get your feet up in the air, and the two of us would read and talk. Grandma Rose was really big on reading. She insisted I take time to read while I was there and always asked about my schoolwork. She loved me unconditionally, and her love and support helped shape me. We talked about God, too. Her steadfast belief in her heavenly

Father was as powerful a part of her presence as the cookies she doled out, the dresses she wore, or that ever-present apron.

Over the years, I've often thought about what it would take to raise ten kids, most of them boys, on a modest budget. I've wondered what it would take to keep that ship afloat and on course under challenging circumstances. Mary and I have two kids, and we often feel completely maxed out. I can hardly imagine multiplying that by five, and on a shoestring. But God provided for Grandma Rose, and I don't remember her ever being anxious or expressing worry. A trusting heart and a confidence that God would provide were not only reflections of her personal strength, but an affirmation of her faith.

* * * * * * * * * *

HARD WORK AND FUN. Discipline and love. These things didn't seem at odds in the 1960s of my youth. They went hand in hand. And while I hate to reflect on it like some old man reminiscing about the good ol' days, the world just seemed to work in a way that allowed the people of South St. Paul, my family included, to live a pretty great life.

In those days, a few thousand bucks could buy a plot of land on one of Minnesota's ten thousand lakes, maybe a two-hour drive north of the Twin Cities. Once you had some land, you could build a cabin on it, and suddenly you had a perfect escape for your family on the weekends. Even everyday guys who carried lunch buckets to work might be able to afford a little lake cabin. My family didn't have a cabin until my dad bought one much later in life. But one of his brothers had one. So in the summer, when invited, we'd pile everyone in the car and drive up to a peaceful Minnesota lake and spend the weekend fishing and swimming to our hearts' content.

My mom didn't care much for rustic cabin life. If it involved an outhouse, pumping water by hand, and kerosene lamps, she was less than totally enthusiastic. She was the sort of woman who preferred electricity. But she loved my dad enough to indulge his affection for those trips, as well as his passion for fishing. One year, she scrimped and saved and bought a little outboard motor for my dad. I was pretty young, but I can still remember how my dad beamed over this thing. He didn't have a boat of his own, so he would store it in the garage and throw it in the back of the car so he could take it up to my uncle's cabin and hook it up to a rented or borrowed boat. For the fisherman in him, that outboard motor was like a little piece of heaven. His pride and joy.

Unfortunately that pride and joy led to one of my first memorable mistakes in life. I can't remember exactly how old I was, but I was evidently old enough to take a boat out myself. Or so I thought. During one of the trips up north, the minute we arrived, I ran down to the dock, threw the outboard motor on whatever boat was available, started her up, and hurried myself out toward the middle of the lake. My dad came out and watched from the dock, just as I was pulling away. He didn't mind my using the motor, but he did mind the fact that I didn't use good judgment. He was standing there looking right at me when suddenly I realized I hadn't taken the time to clamp the motor on properly. In the blink of an eye, the motor popped off the back of the boat and dropped like a stone down to the bottom of the lake.

I could hear my dad yelling from the dock, but there was absolutely nothing I could do. I was out too far, and the lake was far too deep at that point for anyone to swim down to recover it. All I could do was row back to shore, guilt-ridden and humiliated. My dad gave me an earful, telling me to *think* first next time. But the thing I remember more than his aggravation is that he sincerely hoped I had learned a lesson.

Boy, did I ever. Although that event now seems small and long ago, the experience taught me to take the time to do things right. Skipping steps to get ahead, failing to carefully think through the process, and rushing through things all lead to mistakes or worse. That's just one of the many life lessons my father taught me.

* * * * * * * * * *

MY DAD EVENTUALLY MOVED from being a truck driver to a dispatcher, and even later he became a manager of a little trucking company with its very own lot on the fringe of the stockyards. At one point, part of his job was to make sure that the refrigeration units attached to the front of trailers, called Thermo Kings, were working and keeping the trailers' contents cold. There was product stored in those trailers all weekend, and they needed to maintain a certain temperature, otherwise the load would go bad and there would be a big problem.

On weekends, Dad would take me down to the truck yards and put me to work. Even though it was an easy thing for him to do himself, he'd hand me a clipboard with the numbers of the trailers and give me the job of going around the lot and looking at all the temperature gauges for him. The Thermo Kings were beyond my reach, so if an adjustment was needed, I'd tell my dad, and he'd get a big yardstick to reach up there and hit the reset button.

I thought I was doing the most important job in the world, and I took it incredibly seriously. The fact that he would trust me with such a responsibility seemed like a big sign of confidence.

That working role started in grade school and continued right into junior high. And as I grew up, the fun and responsibility my dad passed on to me kept growing.

Because nobody was around on Saturdays and Sundays, my dad often let me drive on the lot. Sometimes I drove our family car around as I performed my inspections. Other times it was the company van. Sometimes, after the work was done, he'd let me just drive the van around the lot—for hours. I wasn't even close to sixteen. Here I was in this van working a "three on the tree" shifter, imagining I was going in and out of intersections as my dad did paperwork inside. Occasionally we'd bring my minibike. It wasn't a commercially made bike like one of these mini hot-rod motorcycles you might see today; this was a homemade minibike that he'd throw in the back of the truck and take down to the yard to keep me entertained, endlessly.

Now that I'm a parent, I look back on that long rope, that trust to do real work, to drive around when I was so young, and smile. I think about it often when measuring the length of the rope Mary and I give our daughters. Though it's much shorter than my dad gave me, we nevertheless try to allow room for them to find their own confidence and to grow and blossom along the way.

A lot of the lessons I learned from my father came through simple observation. He wasn't the type to sit down and say, "Here are five life lessons; take notes." Instead, he would teach me just by the way he lived. I didn't think of it as picking up life lessons back then, of course. I just looked up to my dad and the way he always made me feel like I was on top of the world.

In some ways, my dad might have made a great politician. People liked him. He was an outgoing, gregarious guy. He enjoyed people, and everywhere he went, people seemed to enjoy being around him. They were drawn to him, I think, because he was open and friendly and joyful and fun loving. A more modern term to describe his personality might be *transparent*. He let people in, and I think people were attracted to that. People want to be around positive, joyful people. That was a characteristic I tried to embody as I began my career. It sank in through osmosis, through spending time with my dad, more effectively than it ever could through reading some management book or trying to digest *How to Win Friends & Influence People.*

On some of those weekend afternoons after we left the trucking lot, we'd stop at one of the saloons on Concord Street, and my dad would buy me a grape pop and some snacks. He and his buddies enjoyed a cold one while I listened in on their conversation, and I thought I was living large. I really looked forward to those times. It was like getting a chance to walk into the teachers' lounge at school, where no student was supposed to go. It was a glimpse into the adult world. Everything was different in there. A saloon was so far from everything else in a kid's environment. The beer-and-cigarettes scent in the air. The way the bottom of your shoes sort of stuck to the floor. The mirrors and lights and signs everywhere. The Naugahyde stools. These were Saturday and Sunday afternoons, so it wasn't raucous. It was five guys sitting around talking. And my dad clearly enjoyed it too. I realize it all sounds very simple, yet back in those days, I thought we were living the high life.

Bruce Springsteen has a song called "My Hometown." It's not an exact parallel to my life growing up, but every time I hear that song, it takes me right back to those childhood years. The innocence of it all. I love those lines about the "big ol' Buick" and running to the store "with a dime in my hand." My dad had a big ol' Buick in real life, and a big ol' Chevy Impala—always these big ol' used cars. And just driving through South St. Paul—my hometown—with my dad seemed like a really big deal. He genuinely seemed to enjoy my company, and he always found something fun for me to do. I appreciated that. "You got nothing to do? Let's hop in the car and go look at minibikes," or "Let's go see your Uncle Delmer," or "Let's go down to the airport and watch the planes come in," or "Let's go down to the Coop for some fried chicken."

This was years before psychologists and experts started talking about spending "quality time" with your kids—something my dad and I certainly shared. But the thing I think I appreciated most about my dad is that he also shared *quantity* time with me. He was around.

My dad came home for lunch most days. Since we didn't have school lunch programs back then, I walked the seven or so blocks from school back home for lunch every day too. And Dad (Mom, too, of course) often made me lunch. It wasn't fancy. Maybe a fried bologna sandwich or a can of Campbell's soup. But I could tell that he loved doing it. It wasn't a chore or a duty for him.

It's funny how the simplest things can leave the deepest impressions. Like when Dad and I watched television at night. I remember the two of us setting up those rickety old television trays to eat something and watch some show. I can't even remember what we watched. But my dad would break out the braunschweiger (sort of a poor man's liver pâté—a squishy, spreadable sausagelike concoction; some would call it just plain foul, but he loved it) along with some Ritz crackers and cheese. Quite the hors d'oeuvres! He'd sit in his La-Z-Boy with the leg-up option, and I'd sit in my chair, and we were the kings of the world!

My dad and I were connected. It's as simple as that. We had a fun, open relationship. I loved him very much, and he loved me, and we weren't afraid to show it.

Of course, his love for me certainly wasn't exclusive. He loved all his kids. Even if you were just a friend of a friend, often the first time he met you, he'd give you a big bear hug. Affection flowed from the man. When we were sick, he'd take care of us. He'd tuck us all into bed at night. My mom would, too; it's just not as often that we hear about dads. I can't really imagine what my life would have been without that simple time spent with my parents. I realize it's not as common for kids today, and I cherish those memories. In fact, the overwhelming thing I remember about my childhood is that my mom and dad were *both* there.

* * * * * * * * * *

IF YOU WERE TO DRAW UP a spreadsheet on my dad—laying out his whole personality, his stature, his attitude, everything—and then flip over to the other side of the ledger, there you'd find my mom. Gene's polar opposite, Ginny.

My dad was gregarious, fun loving, outgoing, and laid-back. My mom, on the other hand, was organized, scheduled, energetic, focused, and intense. As casual as my dad was, that's how cranked up my mom was. Always moving. Never sitting down. Always busy. Always doing something while simultaneously gathering up ideas about what needed to be done next.

My mom was a homemaker for much of her life, so in most of my memories of her, she's dressed in pants or simple dresses. She took a job as a bookkeeper when I was a little bit older, and I recall her dressing up in business attire for work. But if we were just hanging out, she was casually dressed.

That was about the only thing she took casually.

Because of her, our little house on 12th Avenue was neat and orderly to almost military standards. We ate at the same time each day, we picked up after ourselves, and everybody had a chore after dinner. Somebody did dishes; somebody swept the floor; somebody took the trash out to the burn barrel. We each had a job. The house wasn't big, and with five kids, I understand now why my mother demanded a sense of order. Shoes belonged in a certain spot. Jackets had to be hung up. Every kid had to take a bath, every night. Not a shower, a bath. And my dad was right there backing her up. "Timmy, get in the bath!" A few minutes later, "Daniel, get in the bath!" My dad wasn't much of a disciplinarian. My mom was the one we had to worry about. But my dad was huge, so all he had to do was raise his voice or rattle his newspaper and we'd react. We sure were a clean bunch of kids!

My mom was a hard, hard worker. Her work ethic was off the charts. It boggles my mind to think that some people didn't consider being a homemaker a "job" back then. Nothing is farther from reality, then or now. Watching my mom at work in that house, it was clear to me that her organizational skills were extraordinary. I soaked in her example as much as any of the life lessons my dad passed on. In order to be efficient, you have to be organized.

I always had the sense that my mother had strong convictions, strong beliefs, strong values—and that she was willing to back them up if challenged. Later in life, through some discussion with my siblings, it became apparent to me that she had a conservative streak in her—which was remarkable considering that in those days there were probably ten Republicans in all of South St. Paul. I've been told that she was a Nixon supporter at one point, in '68 or '72. I can only imagine how much fun it would have been to discover that we shared some mutual political interests as I grew older.

By far the strongest lesson my mom imparted was the importance of my getting an education. "If you're going to be able to make your own way in life and pursue your dreams, or even get by, you're going to have to get an education." She just pounded that ethic into me, repeating it often. There was no way she would let me go through life without having that education seed firmly planted in my young brain.

Whatever I wound up wanting to do, she knew education was the pathway. And she did everything in her power to make sure that pathway was cleared for me.

Mom's efforts must have paid off, because I took my education seriously from a very early age. Beyond my doing well in school as a child, I'm not sure what it was my mother saw in me that made her so fiercely certain I would go to college—a first in our family.

My sisters have also mentioned that Mom had some fun because of my date of birth. She was pregnant at the same time as Jackie Kennedy.

Everything about Jackie was iconic in 1960, from the clothes she wore to how she cut her hair, and the anticipation of the birth of her child in November of that year captivated the entire nation. My sisters recall sitting around the Thanksgiving table, discussing who might have her baby first, Jackie or Ginny. As it turned out, my mom lost that race; John F. Kennedy Jr. arrived two days before I was born. There were surely thousands of women all across America who were pregnant at the same time as the fashionable soon-to-be First Lady, and my sisters' impression is that the parallel experience was interesting for my mom.

My mother had a tough life growing up. When she was very young, her mother was diagnosed with tuberculosis and was separated from the family to recover. In those days, a TB diagnosis meant the whole family was quarantined from society. So my mom and her sisters, Winnie, Jackie, and Mary, were sent away, which was rendered that much more painful because their father decided to divorce their mother, simply packing up and splitting for another part of the country, leaving the children behind. Eventually my mother and her three sisters were sent to live with foster parents but were split up into twos. As it turned out, my mother and her sister Mary were placed with two school-teachers. As tough as the situation must have been, it was likely a good fit for my mom, because she was an excellent student and studied hard. Against terrible odds, when any young girl could have understandably shut down or gone down the wrong path in life, my mother chose education as a way forward. She graduated high school at the top of her class and planned to become a nurse . . . before she met and fell in love with my father and decided to start a family instead. She would have been a great nurse.

My mom's foster parents gave her piano lessons. She truly enjoyed music. At some point I recall we had an upright piano in the basement that she would occasionally play. I never took lessons myself, but the sound of music playing in the house was a steady part of my childhood. She especially loved all the old crooners: Engelbert Humperdinck, Frank Sinatra, Dean Martin, Elvis Presley, Mario Lanza. She played those records so often, those sounds are ingrained in my head. That music would always be on in the background if my parents had friends over for a visit. And the tones and melodies from those old 33 LPs would filter through the house as she was cleaning. And she was always cleaning. With a house full of kids, the work seemed to never end.

Sunday afternoons were Mom's break time. With five kids, I can imagine she truly needed that break too. My memories of this don't really begin until Peg and Steve had moved out, but I can remember my dad gathering Rose, Dan, and me into the car and taking off to give my mother a few hours to herself. I think she deeply appreciated that time.

Occasionally there were other times during the week as well when my mom dropped Dad off at work and kept the car for the day. Then she would take the younger kids along to go visit and have coffee with her sisters, particularly her sister Jackie, who lived the closest. For me, it wasn't unlike tagging along to Dad's chats over a cold one with friends. Beer chats for dad; coffee chats for mom.

* * * * * * * * * *

MOM WAS A FULL-TIME HOMEMAKER throughout much of my childhood, but I later learned that she had worked as a bookkeeper for a car dealership before I was born. Those bookkeeping skills were valuable because my mom was the one who handled our family's finances. I have memories of her sitting at our kitchen table with a pile of bills and the checkbook open, fretting over the balance and puzzling over how to make it all work out. Sometimes during the holiday season, just to do her part, my mom would take on seasonal work at Van Arsdell's department store. I think that was her way of making sure we didn't fall behind—and for Mom it was especially important to make ends meet at Christmastime.

Christmas was a really big deal to my mom. Maybe it's because of her own family situation growing up; I'm not sure. But she outdid herself every year. The decorations. The lights. The baking. She truly poured herself into Christmas each year, and despite the fact that we didn't have a lot of money, she always managed to shower us with gifts.

Besides the requisite clothing, my favorite gifts were games. My siblings weren't very big into playing, but I loved to play board games with the adults. Or cards. Whatever games I could get my hands on. If the siblings did join in, I'd always have to contend with my older brother Dan's hypercompetitiveness. He simply could not take a game lightly, whether it was Monopoly or boot hockey or some made-up game that we invented while running around outside with other kids from the neighborhood. I definitely learned about competitiveness from watching him in action.

Dan was relentless. He hated to lose. And he would do everything in his power—physically, mentally, or otherwise—to win.

Throughout my childhood, both of my parents worked hard, and they instilled their work ethic in their kids, too. As far back as I can remember, my parents taught us, through acknowledgment and example, that hard work brings great rewards.

The kids in the family worked hard beyond just the chores in the house. The boys all had a paper route. It started with Steve, who eventually brought Dan alongside as a helper before passing the baton to him to carry when he moved out after high school. Dan then brought me alongside as a helper and passed the torch to me when he was too old for the task.

Back then there was a morning paper and an evening paper: the *Pioneer Press* in the morning, and the *St. Paul Dispatch* at night. There were people on the route who insisted on having their paper on their doorstep at 6 a.m., so at 5:30 we'd have to go down to the corner to get the papers. When it was really cold outside, my dad or mom would drive. We'd fold the papers up and put them in the backseat of the car. Then I'd pitch them out the windows or run them up to the houses.

Having your own paper route, which I wouldn't fully inherit until I was maybe fourteen, was a really big deal. Kids would talk about it: "You got a route? So do I! Where's *your* route?" And performing that duty, no matter how much you didn't want to get up at 5:30 in the morning or hated to stop everything you were doing in the middle of the afternoon, was mandatory. There was no way around it. It had to get done, and we didn't have the kind of parents—mom *or* dad—who would let us slack off.

I have to say, I was extremely proud to be making my own money at a young age. What kid wouldn't be? After all, what value does money have if you don't work for it? A gift is nice once in a while, but money and hard work went hand in hand in the South St. Paul of my youth. As far as I'm concerned, money and hard work are meant to go hand in hand. That sentiment forms the very root of capitalism. The very root of America, for that matter. I know there are people who have money in their pocket that they never had to work for. I know there are people who feel entitled to get paid whether they actually work or not, as if it's the government's job or simply someone else's duty to provide for them. I just don't understand that way of thinking. If you don't want to work hard and accomplish something every day, what's the incentive for getting out of bed in the morning? Attribute it to my parents or my South St. Paul upbringing, but I've felt that drive to work hard for just about as long as I can remember. Work ethic is not a particular political ideology. I consider it a basic truth of life, something God wants us to value. The Bible says, "Whatever you do, work at it with all your heart, as working for the Lord, not for human masters" (Colossians 3:23).

I believe it comes back to the notion that *we're in charge of the effort*. Although God holds the future, He does not expect us to sit idle.

4

★ ★ ★ ★ ★ ★ ★ ★ ★ ★

LESSONS

IN ADDITION TO THOSE GLORIOUS WEEKENDS when life in the shadow of the stockyards was relatively subdued and there was space for a kid to ride a minibike or drive a van around without fear of colliding with a semi, there were other times when my dad would take me down to Concord Street during working hours. To me, it felt like a bustling avenue in Manhattan but rich with an ambience more reminiscent of the Wild West cowboy shows that were still all the rage on television. While the true heyday of the Union Stockyards and the Swift and Armour meatpacking plants came before I was born, I had a brief chance to witness part of it for myself, in all its remaining glory, before I'd grown taller than my father's waist.

On those days with my dad, I absorbed up close the sheer

size and magnitude of the impact that industry had on my hometown.

First of all, the smell was overwhelming. It was pungent and powerful. It would waft right up the hill into the streets where we played. The city had a stigma because of that smell, but we were all so used to it that we hardly noticed it most days.

The wooden fences and pens of animals seemed to stretch out as far as my young eyes could see. Beside and behind them, the processing plants cast shadows as big as neighborhoods. I can't overstate how large these plants were. Seven stories high, they were some of the most massive structures you've ever seen. Swift and Armour, right next to each other, surrounded by pens full of thousands of animals that had been brought in from all over the Midwest for sale and processing and slaughter. The *moo*s and *baa*s were a cacophony you had to shout over just to be heard. Everywhere were gritty men in big rubber boots, walking in manure, carrying yardsticks, and chewing tobacco. Thousands of people from all over the region worked in the yards, carrying out all the tasks that come with slaughtering animals and processing the meat.

Sometimes the meatpackers worked outside in their bloody smocks, carving up meat on metal tables near open back doors in the summer sun. My brothers remember being down on Concord Street at lunchtime when those same guys would run across the street to the saloons, still wearing their bloody smocks, to grab a burger and a couple of beers for lunch before heading back to work. The visceral realities of life and death and the food chain were everywhere, right down to the big red and white signs by the cattle pens that read, *Enjoy BEEF Every Day!*

Plenty of people do enjoy beef every day. So you might wonder how that industry could suffer. It's hard to imagine how an industry so entrenched in a place could up and move or shift direction or simply disappear. But that's exactly what began to unfold just as I was about to turn nine years old.

In 1969, Swift & Company closed its plant. They decided to decentralize, in part to combat the power of the unions, and move to smaller processing plants at a variety of locations. I would figure that out years later, of course. At the time, all I knew was that they were shutting down. It was all anyone talked about. It was devastating news—I could tell by the seriousness in the grown-ups' faces. Even at the age of nine, I felt this palpable sense that the bottom was dropping out of everything. It wasn't just a few dozen workers who were laid off. The whole plant closed its doors. Hundreds, maybe thousands, of people were left with no work, with what seemed like no warning.

For a nine-year-old boy, the seriousness of the situation directly revealed that bad things do happen in the world and that those bad things happen to people you know and people you care about. I saw firsthand that they could happen in my own hometown.

Watching how that plant's closing affected the adults around me made something very clear to me: a job is not just a job. I suppose that's why I can't stand when jobs are reduced to nothing more than numbers and statistics. A job is, in many ways, an identity. Most people's lives revolve around their work. Think about it this way—if you spend eight hours sleeping and eight hours at work, it's simply a matter of math—your job takes up about half the waking hours of your life. Add in a couple of hours commuting, and it's more than half. Of course, for the people of South St. Paul, it didn't take an hour to commute to the stockyards. Most moms and dads were home in time for dinner and to catch the 5:30 news on television. But when you think in terms of the importance work holds in people's lives, how it shapes the choices people make about where and how they live, and combine it with the sense of loss that comes when a whole industry disappears, the loss is immeasurable.

The Swift building was demolished by 1972. For anyone still clinging to hope that the industry would come back, that mammoth demolition dramatically drove the permanence home.

The city of Chicago was suffering a similar, simultaneous loss. The Chicago stockyards closed up in 1971 as part of the same decentralization. Their closing actually made what was left of South St. Paul's stockyards, briefly, the largest stockyards on the entire planet. But by the end of the 1970s, Armour & Company would close its South St. Paul plant too. Failed revitalization projects kept the building around until 1989, but finally it, too, was wiped off the landscape. Gone forever. There are photos of the demolition that make it look like a war zone. Offices with papers and typewriters and calendars hung on jagged walls, blasted open, exposed to the sun, frozen in time. Rubble everywhere. By the mid-1990s, 107 acres along that waterfront would be redeveloped as an industrial park. Even so, a small stockyard clung to life where the great Union Stockyards once stood. It wouldn't be until April 11, 2008, that the very last livestock auction was held on the last tiny plot of old stockyard land.

I'm skipping ahead here to make a point. In fact, I want to flash forward all the way to 2010, when I happened to be touring South St. Paul on a little reminiscing mission while preparing to write this book. On a fine spring day, I stopped into Holy Trinity Church—the church I attended nearly every Sunday with my parents before heading over to Grandma Rose's house, the Catholic church built of sturdy beige brick where I sat on those hard wooden pews, where I first learned about the meaning of faith and absorbed God's presence in my life. I wasn't expecting to speak to anyone, but no sooner did I step inside than a volunteer who was setting out candles in the otherwise-empty church approached me.

"You look a lot like the Governor," he said.

"I'm the weatherman on Channel 4," I told him. He looked puzzled. "No, I am the Governor. Nice to meet you." He chuckled at my attempt at humor as I shook his hand.

It turned out he knew my family, and I knew his. South St. Paul is a small town, and just as the landscape hasn't changed much outside the stockyards, many of the old families have stayed put. So it's not uncommon to run into acquaintances whenever I'm back for a visit. He and I got to talking about various relatives—he lived a few doors down from my uncle Del and had lost his wife a few years ago. We reminisced about some of the folks we both knew. He asked me how I was weathering the current legislative session, and we shared a laugh about the antics of a rival politician.

Then, right in the middle of all that, he said something that really struck me. "It's dying here in South St. Paul." I asked him how so, and he said there didn't seem to be anyplace to go anymore. "The stockyards took years to build up to number one, and then they just left us."

All I could think was, *That happened forty years ago.* Four decades later, it was just as fresh and painful for this man as it had been in the 1970s. He had worked for a while in one of the hide cellars, by all accounts a terrible place to work, yet he reminisced about Concord Street, calling it Boomtown, USA, and talking about the cattlemen who used to come in and close deals at the saloons over poker games. "It was great," he said.

"It was something else," I replied.

He was right. It *was* great. And I'll forever be grateful that I had a chance to glimpse some of that firsthand as a young boy. But the frightening reality that it could all disappear so quickly was a lot for a nine-year-old to absorb. And that wasn't my only worry. Another not-so-hopeful possibility—the possibility of nuclear war—was something many children in the fifties and sixties were taught to consider.

* * * * * * * * * *

IT SEEMS LIKE SOMETHING out of an old movie now, but in 1961, just a year after I was born, President John F. Kennedy actively urged families all across America to build fallout shelters. Right next to the stockyard exhibit at the Historical Society Museum in South St. Paul, there's a glass case showing off some of the Cold War–era brochures that once circulated around town. Brochures with titles such as "Ten for Survival: Survive Nuclear Attack" and "Facts about Fallout Protection." They even have an old Family Radiation Measurement Kit, comprised of a little Geiger counter–type device called a ratemeter to tell you "how fast the radiation is bombarding your body at a given moment" and a dosimeter "to record the radiation you have been exposed to . . . just as a mileage indicator tells how far your car has gone." I don't recall my parents ever owning one of those kits, and the sort of matter-of-fact language on those brochures seems almost humorous now. But the Cold War was no laughing matter in the 1960s.

Like most kids my age, I was impacted by the images and reporting about tensions between the United States and the Soviet Union in my formative years. I didn't understand the situation fully, but I have vivid memories of bomb-raid drills at school. We'd all go into the hallways in the basement by the boiler room, presumably to get out of harm's way in an air attack. Above and beyond the standard fire drills, where we'd all move outside in an orderly manner, we also practiced the "Get under your desk!" exercise. As strange as the experience was, there were some practical applications to those drills, seeing that tornadoes are a regular occurrence in Minnesota. But fears of a nuclear attack, and especially some sort of Soviet invasion, were part of my childhood learning. We were taught to be prepared. I thought there was a legitimate chance the Russians and the Americans were going to have some kind of conflict. I imagined what it might be like for the Soviets to be in our country.

Those are troubling thoughts for a child. Drills that attempted to prepare my classmates and me for an attack, combined with the effects that the closing of our town's economic core had on families, not to mention life's usual challenges, taught me early on that things might not always go well. Which is true. Things don't always go well.

The question is, how do we deal with adversity? When things go wrong or threaten to go wrong, the way each of us responds is as important as the challenge itself. To whom do we turn? Where do we find our strength, our courage?

Although I could not have described it as a child, my parents, along with the lessons I learned those Sundays at Holy Trinity Church, gave me a foundation. I was fortunate to be introduced by my parents and by my church to a loving God. A God who is trustworthy, who is omnipotent, and who is in charge of the final outcome. Jesus, teaching in parables, did a beautiful job of taking the complex and making it simple so we could understand how He wants us to live.

In Matthew 7:24-25, Jesus said, "Everyone who hears these words of mine and puts them into practice is like a wise man who built his house on the rock. The rain came down, the streams rose, and the winds blew and beat against that house; yet it did not fall, because it had its foundation on the rock." That's pretty simple—even for a child.

★ ★ ★ ★ ★ ★ ★ ★ ★ ★

I CAN UNDERSTAND how some people get to the point where they feel discouraged. *"My troubles are too great, my circumstances too far beyond my control, so why should I care about anything anymore?"* But that sort of thinking just wasn't present in South St. Paul. Grinding it out day after day was expected. Caring for family and neighbors, working hard, doing the right thing, getting the job done, trusting that God would handle the outcome—all of it mattered, and all of it was drilled into my head on a daily basis, whether I realized it or not.

Occasionally, the lessons were drilled into my head in ways that weren't so subtle.

I think I was about twelve when my dad picked up a side job to earn a few bucks one weekend—a side job that required my help. It was a sweltering summer day, the kind of day when outside work is the last thing anyone wants to do. But my dad clearly needed me, and I always wanted to lend a hand if I could. I didn't ask a lot of questions, and he didn't give me very much information about the task at hand—until we got down to a parking lot beside a warehouse.

The side job involved yanking meat hooks from large wooden bins that were stashed in a couple of truck trailers on the lot. Tangled meat hooks that once held whole sides of beef were tossed in those bins, in trucks without Thermo Kings to cool down their trailers. Hundreds of thick, heavy meat hooks, covered with discarded remnants of sinew and fat, all rotting in the blistering heat. It was up to my dad and me to pull out every one of those hooks and hang them up—presumably to be power washed and used again.

Have you ever opened up an expired or rotting pack of hamburger from the bottom of your refrigerator and given it a big whiff? Yeah. Multiply that by a thousand, and you'll get the idea. You could smell that rotting meat as soon as we opened the doors of those trailers. Then, when we hopped up there, we could hear the buzzing. My dad reached in and grabbed his first hook, and I held my breath and leaned in through a swarm of flies to grab mine—and I lost it. I tossed my cookies next to one of the bins, only adding to the mess and the stench.

My dad didn't say much to me. I looked up at him, hoping for an out. *He isn't really gonna make me keep doing this, is he?* My dad's face was steady. He wasn't having an easy go of it either. But he looked at me and said quietly, "We have to do this."

It was all he needed to say.

"We have to do this." We may not want to. We may not like it. It may be messy. But there are times in life when we have to. We keep moving forward, regardless of the challenge. Our family needed the money, and my dad needed my help. So I wiped my mouth on my short-sleeved shirt, pulled my gloves on a little tighter, and stuck my hands back into the hooks. Over the course of a few hours, we got the job done.

"We have to do this." It's impossible to count how many times I've applied that lesson in my life, especially in the political arena, where the tangled mess often seems insurmountable. When a job needs doing, get it done. Plow through; never give up. Keep moving forward. When it's right, when it's necessary, just do it.

My parents taught me countless lessons in those early years, many of which slipped quietly into my subconscious. I'm forever grateful to both of them for all they did for me, for all of us kids. They were the constants in my life. The two of them, together, were my pillars. My double-walled foundation. I never fell into rejection or rebelliousness like some kids do. I loved my parents unconditionally and couldn't conceive of any part of that love and support ever going away.

I could not imagine that one of them was about to leave this earth.

* * * * * * * * * *

MY MOTHER SEEMED VERY CENTERED. Maybe that's true of most moms. But I always remember being impressed by what I saw in her. She was a woman who was well-informed, who listened to the news and read the newspaper, who managed to stay involved with her kids' education, right down to serving as secretary of the PTA. Whenever I saw her in an apron with her hair up in rollers, zipping around the house making everything perfect for PTA meetings or other gatherings at our house, she seemed fully in charge of her surroundings. Cutting the grass when it needed to be cut, tending the garden until every single weed was vanquished, ironing clothes—not to mention sheets and pillowcases—everything had to be just so, and she knew how to accomplish all of it not only through her own efforts but by directing her children (and her husband) to act as extensions of her never-settled hands in keeping the house in tip-top shape. Uncle David, Mom's sister Mary's husband, used to tease Mom endlessly about how neat and orderly she was. At a family gathering once, he walked into the house wearing a white glove and jokingly began testing all the surfaces for cleanliness.

I'm not sure how much she loved being teased, but she certainly loved being with family. It wasn't just holidays and special occasions. We often visited my mom's sisters and their families. Aunt Jackie's place was a favorite destination—not only for coffee but for the adults to enjoy an occasional glass of wine. Sometimes the whole brood would show up to watch a Twins game on television.

My mother had a great relationship with all her sisters, but she and Aunt Jackie were about as close as two sisters could be. So it was difficult for my mom when Jackie became ill. I didn't understand what was happening at the time—I was too young—but Aunt Jackie had suffered from breast cancer for some time. She had beaten it to some degree initially, but it seemed she was never fully cancer free. I was about twelve when we received news that she had ovarian cancer. It was really bad. They discovered it too late, as they often did back in those days, and by then the cancer had spread all over her body, including her brain.

My sister Rose recalls Jackie's final days vividly. She describes it as a horrible, painful death that just tore my mother apart. I remember how sad my mother appeared. While things eventually returned to normal in our home, my mother really never got over Jackie's death.

And then, the summer after my sophomore year in high school, my mother started complaining about abdominal pain. It would strike when she was going about her normal routines. She'd be washing the floor or ironing clothes and suddenly grimace. My sister Rose, who was a senior at that time and as close to Mom as a daughter could be, would see it and ask what was wrong. The way Rose recalls it, Mom would dismiss it and say it was nothing but then look terribly sad. It's almost as if she didn't want to know. Or perhaps she did know instinctively but didn't want to face the truth or didn't want to place that burden on her children.

My memories from that summer are scant, but from what I do recall, my mother didn't seem sick at all. She seemed to be every bit the loving, doting mother she had always been—attentive in every way to our family and our chores and managing the household.

I was fifteen years old in the summer of 1976, so perhaps I was off in my teenage world and too distracted to notice. But I really thought everything was fine.

My mom refused to go see a doctor at first. She insisted it was nothing. But as summer stretched on, the pain became unbearable, to the point where it was truly debilitating. One day, she couldn't get out of bed. That's when my father finally insisted she see a doctor.

In August 1976, three months before my sixteenth birthday, my mother was diagnosed with ovarian cancer—the same disease that had taken her sister Jackie. The pain of that loss was still fresh, and here she was facing a similar circumstance. My mother must have been terribly fearful when she learned her diagnosis.

I remember that word, *cancer*, startling me. Gradually I developed an uneasiness about her prognosis. No one told me what to expect, but I slowly began to worry that things might not turn out all right. I had learned by then that sometimes they didn't.

Rose, who had just graduated from high school at the age of eighteen, suddenly became a major force in our family. She looked after me. She looked after my dad. She was the one who made sure the bills got paid while my mother went through treatment, a combination of radiation and cobalt in those days before chemotherapy. Rose cooked, alternating with my dad, and helped keep the house in order. She bravely stepped up at a time when our family needed it most.

My brother Steve and sister Peg were both married by then and had long since moved out. So it was just my dad, Rose, Dan, and me at home. With the tables suddenly turned, the four of us tried to become the chief caretakers to our caretaker.

As if my mom's cancer wasn't stressful enough, my father, who had been promoted from truck driver to dispatcher and manager, was in the middle of dealing with a truckers' strike at work. Looking back now, I'm amazed at the strength it must have taken him to face every morning with that kind of pressure piling up on him all at once. He exemplified the quiet, persistent strength of character that was so consistently present in his generation.

My mother, through it all, was predictably resilient. Her hair was thinning from the treatment, and she suffered from severe nausea. Still, she tried to do the dishes. She tried to tidy up. She tried to go about her duties as the master of her home. My dad and Rose would have to gently tell her to sit down. For the first time in her adult life, she was no longer fully in charge of her surroundings.

That loss of control was particularly painful for her. She'd worked every moment to keep up our home. It was more than a point of pride; it was her gift, given freely to the family she loved so much. But now the ability to do even simple daily tasks was slowly taken away from her.

Her treatments, however, wouldn't last long. She was terminally ill.

When the radiation and cobalt weren't working, Rose tells me, she rode in the back of an ambulance with my mom to get an MRI, or something similar, at a nearby hospital. This was a fairly new diagnostic tool at that time, and not every facility had one. But the results of that test were awful: My mother had a tumor that started in her abdomen and spread all the way up into her back. She also had cancer in her lymph nodes.

So in January 1977, my mother went in for surgery with the intention of having at least part of that massive tumor removed. But apparently, there was nothing they could do. It was simply too big and too entwined with her vital organs to safely extricate.

My sister describes that as the beginning of the end—an end

that would come more quickly than any of us, including her doctors, realized.

Rose has memories of sitting on the windowsill in my mom's hospital room, along with my sister Peg, talking about life and how everything was going to turn out. She says that my mom was pragmatic, engaged, and full of her usual organizing and planning right to the end. She even told her girls what she wanted to wear at her own funeral.

She did not talk of such things around me. While my two sisters spoke in such matter-of-fact ways with her, I was still left to wonder how truly severe the problem was. If I knew in my heart that she was likely not going to make it, I'd concluded that on my own. No one told me directly.

I later learned that in her very last hours, she pulled my two brothers and two sisters together around her hospital bed and told them directly, "Whatever you do, you get Tim to college." She made each of them promise to follow through. It was her dream for me, a dream she had instilled in me herself. She could not go peacefully without knowing that her dream would be fulfilled.

I don't recall the details of that final February day in 1977 when I sat talking with my mom in her hospital room. Rose remembers more than I do. "You had green tennis shoes on, and she didn't like those shoes for some reason," Rose tells me. "'Why are you wearing those shoes here?' she said. I remember that to this day! And she told you to get a haircut. She was still trying to parent. She was just a spitfire!"

The whole family had been in to see her that day, everyone except one of her sisters, my Aunt Winnie. She and her husband had planned a trip to Florida, and they spoke to the doctor before they left. "Go," he told them. He didn't expect any big changes in my mother's condition.

But Rose recalls leaving the hospital with a bad feeling. "I knew we were in trouble," she remembers. "She was having trouble breathing. They were gonna take the tube out that night and take her off of the oxygen to try to get her breathing on her own, and when they did that . . ."

What happened next I do remember, very well. We were all sitting at home. The phone rang. We all knew it was the hospital. My dad picked up the receiver and listened, and the three of us watched as his expression changed and our father broke down.

As a boy, I had this image of my dad as a strapping, strong, invincible superman. Somebody who could protect us and bring home the bacon for the family. There was always a clear sense of strength and courage about him. To watch that hero sob, seemingly vanquished, broke my heart in a way I will always remember. And my heartbreak would only grow as the realization of that phone call's true meaning sank in. I'm not sure of the precise words that were spoken. I remember it was difficult to comprehend what was happening.

Suddenly, forcefully, it hit me.

My mother was gone.

* * * * * * * * * *

THE DAYS THAT FOLLOWED ARE A BLUR. My sister Peg and my sister-in-law Corinne swept in to help. Rose and my father, who had both been so strong throughout my mother's illness, were devastated. As were Dan and Steve, of course, and so was I. Yet somehow Peg found the strength to push through her own sorrow and lead my father through everything that needed to be done. Phone calls to loved ones. Funeral arrangements. Things no man would ever imagine having to plan or prepare for just days after his wife's fiftieth birthday—the same age Mary and I are now.

Many of the specifics of what went on in those days after that phone call have now faded from my memory. What's left is a series of impressions and feelings that linger to this day. I do remember a lot of prayer in our house. I remember the family gathering around, not only for the funeral, but constantly—circling up as a way to protect us, to shore us up, to push us through.

The pain of losing your mother at a young age diminishes over time but is ever present in your heart. My sadness stemmed from more than losing my mom, though. Watching the deep emotion that beset my father was a life-altering experience; it taught me that every one of us will face difficulty and sorrow, heartache and heartbreak—no matter who we are or how invincible we may seem in our own or anyone else's eyes. I learned, simply by seeing my hero besieged by such grief, that whether it's a dad or a Governor, there will always be challenges along the way, however old or strong or good or resourced a person might be. Everyone goes through it. It's the stuff of life. I learned that courage is the will to move forward in a positive direction even in the face of life's most difficult circumstances.

I quickly realized I had a choice. I could turn down a dark path filled with self-pity, or I could choose a positive path, one with hope and a purpose. I leaned heavily into my decision, and with clarity I chose to focus on the positive path. I knew I could draw upon the example of my parents, two people who lived lives of hard work, strength, joy, perseverance, and faith. I was convinced that despite my mother's death, God loved me deeply and had a plan for my life. Jeremiah 29:11 says, "'I know the plans I have for you,' declares the Lord, 'plans to prosper you and not to harm you, plans to give you hope and a future.'" I didn't want to let God down by failing to put in my part of the effort.

That sense of resolve did not diminish my sadness overnight.

I spent the better part of the next two years under a cloud, but one thing that helped was focusing intently on schoolwork, as it was the one measurable step I could take down the path of purpose. I've heard the pain of loss described as a cloak of sadness, something so heavy that it feels as if it will never go away. All I could do was take one day at a time. And then the next and the next.

As it turned out, life wasn't quite done doling out its series of hard lessons for my family; some time after my mother passed away, my dad got laid off from work.

I remember feeling a new and heightened sense of worry. *Mom's gone; Dad's unemployed. This isn't going to go well.* How would we pay the bills? How on earth would I afford to go to college?

But it's incredible how dependable God is. Trusting God is not just a matter of hearing words in church and hoping they're true. For me, it's been a lifetime of experiencing a faithful God who always provided what I needed, when I needed it, according to His will. He doesn't promise a pain-free or trouble-free life. But He does promise to be present if we reach out to Him in prayer. I know beyond a doubt that God has walked every step of the pathway with me.

Although it is far easier said than done, Jesus taught us not to worry. "Seek first his kingdom and his righteousness, and all these things will be given to you as well," He said. "Therefore do not worry about tomorrow, for tomorrow will worry about itself. Each day has enough trouble of its own" (Matthew 6:33-34).

The part about each day having enough trouble of its own I fully understand. Daily troubles are a constant in life. Mercifully, God sends angels, or at least people who seem like angels, when we most need them. One of my favorites was Dickey Johnson, who clearly qualified as a godsend. He was the produce manager at Applebaum's grocery, where my brother held a job. Dickey didn't know he was part of God's plan; he was simply a good guy who heard about our family's situation and offered me a position in his department—sight unseen. Not just any job, either—a job in the produce department, loading and unloading, cutting, wrapping, packaging, and displaying produce. A good job with good pay.

Dickey's job offer was an act of raw kindness—reaching out to help someone during a time of great challenge. *"You're in trouble? Here's how I can help."*

Mr. Johnson didn't go easy on me. He worked me hard and made sure I was up to the task. I was still a student, so the work was part-time. But that part-time job would help me earn enough money to take care of some of my own expenses. More than that, it allowed me the freedom to realize that going to college might just be possible.

I kept that job for the next seven years or so, working part-time, year-round, to help pay my way through college and the first year of law school.

I felt fortunate in the wake of my mother's death for the emotional support system my family provided and the much-needed financial support that the job provided. It didn't make my problems go away, but it lightened the load and helped me on my path. Yet the most important support system I needed was with me all along. God was present, consistently demonstrating His faithfulness. He was and is the firm foundation upon which I rely in times of trouble, and the one to whom I offer praise and thanks for the many ways He's blessed my life.

The loss of my mother marks the first time I remember asking fervently for God's help. I always considered myself a believer in God, but like most young boys, I wasn't thrilled to sit in church every Sunday. Quite simply, it seemed boring, and although I was learning truth from the Bible, I didn't understand how that was actually relevant to my "real life." Most Sundays I couldn't wait to get over to Grandma Rose's so we could go outside and play. But I now realize that sitting in those pews, listening to the stories from the Bible, following the rituals of respectfully kneeling, standing, and praying, and greeting friends, neighbors, and strangers around me created a quiet impression in my soul that grew powerful and was available and familiar when I needed it most.

My parents instilled that seed of faith in me. They certainly followed Proverbs 22:6, which says, "Train a child in the way he should go, and when he is old he will not turn from it."

It would take years before I fully understood the power and meaning of faith in God, before I fully absorbed the importance of what Christ has done for me, for all of us, before I would study the Bible on my own and accept God's grace with the full intentions of an adult mind.

But at sixteen years old, I needed and felt God's presence like never before. With the loss of my mother, I came to understand that God was still there and always would be, both present and in control. Trusting Him to be in charge was my best hope.

5

FISTFIGHTS AND ICING

THERE ARE MANY THINGS I take seriously in life. Family, friends, God, and hard work are a few of them. But there's one other thing I'm passionate about that deserves some special attention here: hockey.

For most Minnesotans, the sound of blades and sticks on ice is as glorious as any gospel choir. It's a game filled with life's finest lessons and greatest joys.

I realize that if you didn't grow up in a northern state (or Canada), you're probably tilting your head thinking, *What?* Although it pains me to admit it, hockey is a bit of a niche sport—an all-consuming niche sport beloved by millions of devoted players and fans. It is difficult for hockey fans to understand how anyone else *can't* be a hockey fan. Hockey was a big part of my childhood, my teen years, and my adult life, and it even played a role during my time as Governor.

Watching games on television on weekends in the winter months was a family ritual for us when I was a kid. We spent hours memorizing key facts about the Minnesota North Stars and the Chicago Blackhawks. And of course we spent loads of time playing hockey, traveling to and from hockey games, or playing street hockey in boots. We were competitive about it too.

The Minnesota high school hockey tournament is as big or bigger than the Stanley Cup in my state. At state tournament time, we would have brackets taped up on the door in the kitchen, and we'd have little family wagers on which team would win. My brother Dan played in the tournament in high school in 1972, and it was a big deal.

Today, the high school hockey tournament (recognized as one of the biggest high school tournaments in the country for any sport) draws huge crowds to the Xcel Energy Center—an eighteen-thousand-seat stadium. The Minnesota Wild, our NHL team, is enormously popular with Minnesotans and has a history of selling out its games. Our University of Minnesota Gopher hockey teams, men and women, are among the best in the nation. Most people in Minnesota have either a family member or a close friend who plays hockey. It's hard to be a Minnesotan and *not* be involved in hockey as a player or a fan.

To provide just a flavor for the intensity of it all, consider some of the lyrics of our Minnesota Wild theme song:

We were raised with the stick and a pair of blades
On the ice we cut our teeth
We took our knocks in the penalty box
Our mother was the referee

This sport was here before we came
It will be here when we're gone
The game's in our blood and our blood's in the game
Lay us down under a frozen pond

We will fight to the end; we will stand and defend
Our flag flying high and free
We were born the child of the strong and Wild
In the state, the state of hockey

I was skating almost as far back as I can remember. When I got into inline skating for exercise in the summertime, later in life, I would do it with a hockey stick in my hand because skating without it felt unnatural. Incomplete.

Having played the game makes watching it as a fan even better. Hockey is a sport in which there's a lot constantly going on. It's fast paced. And much better to watch live. I'm a partial season-ticket holder for the Minnesota Wild, and watching those guys play is completely engaging—there's an elegance and strategy to how the game plays out and how it's designed to come together. I love watching the finesse and skill of players at the elite level. The way they handle the puck, passing and shooting, is exquisite. It's almost an art form as far as I'm concerned. And it's extraordinarily demanding from an athletic standpoint.

But it's a gritty sport—not for people who don't have guts. At the professional level, some players are finesse athletes, but many of them are just "grinders"—they're the ones who go into the corners, take the hit, take the elbow, dig out the puck, and do the hard work of setting up a marquee player or breaking up the other team's play.

South St. Paul has one of the oldest indoor hockey rinks in

the state, Wakota Arena. My dad used to take me to old-timers' games or semipro games. We would stand in the corner and watch and create our own play-by-play commentary and analysis. Other times, we would sit in the stands with the whole family and watch my brother play. Dan's 1972 team championship banner hangs in that big old warehouse-style arena to this day.

When I'm at that rink now, I'm the one playing in those old-timers' games. I've tried to set aside an hour a week to head down to that old rink, strap on the gear, and hit the ice with players at least somewhat near my age.

Unlike baseball or soccer or football, the overall tempo of hockey is fast. That makes the game a true escape. If you play golf or softball or any sport that doesn't require 100 percent concentration, your mind can easily wander back to work or the problems of the day. But when you're playing hockey, things are happening so quickly and continuously, you can't help but fully concentrate on what's going on right in front of you. You have to stay in the moment. It's a great way to erase your worries for an hour. It's an all-in experience.

Hockey doesn't lie to you, either. A middle-aged guy with a few extra pounds on him can play golf or maybe tennis and walk away thinking he's still got some game. But if you try to play hockey with a little bit of age and lack of conditioning, the game lets you know quickly that you're out of shape. Forget about getting out on that ice with a group of eighteen-year-olds or twentysomethings. You'll see in real time how the years have marched on.

I was never a great hockey player; I never made it past junior varsity in high school. I played varsity soccer, even played on a team that went to the state championship. But playing soccer never held a candle to the fun of lacing up the skates and putting a stick on the ice.

From the outside, there is one part of hockey tradition that seems barbaric. I'm referring, of course, to hockey fights. Yet from those fights I've learned lessons that have applied, surprisingly, to my career in politics.

Watching two guys, gloves down, helmets off, pounding each other while the ref stands back and lets it happen is understandably unsettling to some. But what most people and even many fans don't realize is that there are unwritten rules and traditions at play in those fistfights on ice. In a book titled *The Code: The Unwritten Rules of Fighting and Retaliation in the NHL*, Minnesota author Ross Bernstein reveals the time-honored system that exists among even the game's most notorious thugs.

For example, generally speaking, hockey fights don't just break out without warning. If you want to fight, you ask, "You wanna go?" That's the usual phrase. Or sometimes you hook or jab the other guy with your stick to let him know you want to fight or you've got a score to settle. Sometimes there's a second question: "Do you want to get squared up?" In other words, should we drop our gloves first, get set, and then fight . . . or are we just going for it, chaotically, right now?

Another unwritten rule relates to not taking unfair advantage. If someone is hurt or fought the night before or is at the end of a shift and really tired, that's not necessarily a fair time to fight. If one player is fresh and the other is gassed, that fight will usually wait until next time. You also don't pick on someone who's substantially smaller than you, and you generally don't throw punches if the other fighter is down. If someone is guilty of some previous discourtesies that deserve more of a beat down than he's already received, you can certainly pick the guy up and get him back on his feet and then start whaling on him again. But generally, if someone's down, you don't hit him again. The fight's over.

There are "enforcers" on most hockey teams—guys who are in charge of striking back when a player on the opposing team does something that's out of line. These enforcers don't always get to do their enforcing in the course of a single game; sometimes they're looking for payback for something that happened last night— or last week. Or a fight may relate to events that the onlooker wouldn't even recognize.

See what I mean? It's somewhat civil, in its own way. But like I said, hockey is a gritty game. There are always exceptions to this "code," when an enforcer will just launch on a provocateur as payback. But that's the exception. And even then, it's almost never a sucker punch. There's always at least some brief warning or indication that an enforcer is about to strike. Otherwise that enforcer will face payback next time around!

So there's an order beneath the chaos. I like to think a similar order exists in the political arena. I apply some of the unwritten rules of the "code" in negotiations and dealings with political opponents. Think about it. In the legislature, there are no contracts. Deals are made in meetings or sealed with handshakes across negotiating tables, and if you give your word, you've got to keep it. When agreements are reached, you have to live up to those agreements, and sometimes it's up to you to enforce those agreements. You need to hold people to account if they violate those basic rules, if they're mischievous or harmful—on a playground, in a hockey game, under a statehouse dome, or in international affairs. Bad behavior needs to have consequences; otherwise, it will continue. That's not to say the consequences should be overly harsh, and you never want to punch when somebody's down. You want to win, but you don't want to destroy your opponent. And if you're the one getting pummeled, you also don't want to show your weakness, because if people see you being pushed around, they're going to know you're someone who can *be* pushed around, and it won't stop.

Want another measure of how much I love hockey? Occasionally, if I really need a good mental break and I can't get out on the ice for one of those old-timers' games, I'll sit at the computer when I'm home at night and pop over to hockeyfights.com to watch a few of the latest videos. I'll drive Mary nuts, calling her over when there's a really good one. "Mary, Mary! Come watch this!" I know she has zero interest in watching those fists fly, but it's interesting to me.

I love hockey. It's a great disappointment that the older I get, the less time I have to play. I realize I'm fifty now, and hockey is not exactly tennis or golf. Time marches on, and I'm not sure how many more years my body will be able to take the game. With any luck, I'm hoping I can keep playing hockey for another ten or fifteen years. But while I may not always be able to play, I'll always enjoy the sport. It has always been there, like a backdrop to everything else. And its lessons, I've discovered, have crossed over into many areas of my life.

6

★ ★ ★ ★ ★ ★ ★ ★ ★ ★

THE GREAT DEBATE

AT SOME POINT IN HIGH SCHOOL, I did something I realize now was pretty unusual for a teenager. I subscribed to *U.S. News & World Report.*

At the time, it seemed like a natural addendum to my education. I loved my high school history class. A lot of kids thought it was boring or irrelevant, but I couldn't get enough, and that love of history poured over into a desire to better understand America's place in history in the 1970s. Some of my desire to read up on current events and politics today traces back to that early curiosity.

Where else was I supposed to gather that information in 1976? This was obviously pre-Internet. I wasn't getting the information I needed from the local shopper. I could get some of it from newspapers, and I would often sit down and watch the news with my parents. But the local news was just that—local—and even the national news on television seemed to skip over most of the important international news of the day. *U.S. News & World Report* was a fairly efficient, quick news source with a global component to it, which I liked.

A remarkable thing happened once that magazine made the journey into our 12th Avenue home. Whenever I left an issue lying around, my father would pick it up and read it. My dad was a regular television news watcher, but he never would have subscribed to a news magazine. It just wasn't his cup of tea. Still, once he got his hands on it, he couldn't wait to jump into a discussion with me about whatever he had read that week.

I don't recall my parents ever arguing with each other about politics or issues, but I have vivid memories of my extended family, or chunks of it, having raucous discussions about all sorts of things. My dad, his easygoing demeanor notwithstanding, would jump in with great enthusiasm and passion and sometimes anger over Social Security reform or what was going on in the Middle East.

Something changed, though, when my dad started reading those magazines. He would pick something out of that week's edition, knowing I had read it, and then he would open a full-on debate with me on the subject. It was clearly designed for sport. He wanted to debate. He liked it. It didn't seem to matter what the issue was.

When I was growing up, my family was largely apolitical. Yet as my brothers and sisters moved into early adulthood, because of their upbringing or life circumstances, I discovered they were largely what's been called "lunch-bucket Democrats." Why I became a conservative so early on is anyone's guess, but my steadfast views were on display immediately through the course of those kitchen-table debates with my dad or others. For some reason, it never mattered to me that my views were at odds with those of most members of my family at that point.

My siblings were in a starkly different place from me politically during their early adult lives. My brother Steve was a union steward, an organizer who passed out union cards, got union authorization for workplace representation, even picketed. My other brother, Dan, was a union member at an oil refinery. Later he went to work for a city and was part of the union there, too. Over time, both of them saw the shortcomings of the liberal agenda and started to be open to other arguments. My sister Rose, to the extent she had political views, was a bit rebellious and embraced liberal arguments as a way of striking out on her own philosophically; these days she's more of an independent. And my other sister, Peg, has spent forty years as a secretary at the same company. She has a world-class work ethic; when the alarm clock goes off, she gets up and gets right in the game. She's a dependable, slug-it-out kind of person. She's never had time for politics.

Today, *The Economist* has taken over as my summary-form weekly publication of choice. Still, I have a hard time letting go of the magazine that first brought the world right into my mailbox. Even though I'm disappointed with what's become of *U.S. News & World Report* in recent years, I've been a loyal subscriber now for going on thirty-five years.

* * * * * * * * * *

MOST OF MY DEBATES WITH MY DAD were good fun. But every once in a while we'd touch on a topic that hit a little too close to home, and we would really get into it, verbally.

There was one time when the two of us started arguing over Social Security reform. For me, at that young age, it was all a matter of black-and-white policy, mathematics, and idealism. I was trying to demonstrate to him that Social Security was in trouble and needed reform. Even back then, it was clear Social Security was on a trajectory toward insolvency, and I was trying to explain to him what you pay versus what you get out and how it didn't add up—and he got really mad. I mean *really* mad. He was deeply offended by it, to the point where I had to apologize because I had let the quarrel go too far.

The thing I had overlooked in making my argument was the emotional impact. The issue was more than math, more than reform, more than the need to examine the system. My dad had received a promise from our government. In his military service, he put his life on the line for his country. He served in the Air Force in World War II. To him, just as it was to so many other members of his generation, Social Security was something the government both promised and owed him for all the sacrifices he had made for his country.

I wish I could remember the details of more of our debates, but I can't. They've slipped away like so many conversations in life. All I'm left with is the memory that those debates and conversations existed and grew more frequent in my late teen years, and that at times they were very intense. I never participated in high school debate competitions. I never needed to—I had all the coaching and practice I needed right at home. But I always respected my dad. He had strong views on many subjects, and he was one who could hold his ground. He demonstrated that not just in our discussions but in his refusal to get involved in things he didn't agree with. He always did what he felt was right. I never forgot that, and I always respected it—now more than ever.

* * * * * * * * * *

THE YEAR 1976 WAS A TURNING POINT for me, in many ways. That summer not only marked the start of those debates with my dad and the news of my mother's declining health, but it seemed to be a period of awakening for me regarding our country's place in the world.

It was the bicentennial that summer, and every town in America celebrated in one way or another. Hometown festivities around the Fourth of July in every corner of every state seemed more meaningful and full of life than usual. Everywhere you turned, houses and municipal buildings were decorated with red, white, and blue.

It was also an election year, and it marked the first time I became aware of a new, hopeful presence in American politics: a two-term Republican Governor from California named Ronald Reagan.

I suppose it was fairly unusual for a fifteen-year-old kid to pay attention to the primaries and caucuses. None of my friends really cared about any of this stuff, but I did. Perhaps it grew from that unease I felt about the Soviet Union and my thoughts about how America should be reacting to the threat of Communism. When Reagan stepped up to challenge incumbent President Gerald Ford for the Republican Party nomination, I remember thinking, *This guy's got it right.* What initially drew me to him was the idea of projecting strength internationally. I resonated with the concept of America being great and of bringing the values and traditions that made us great forward into the modern era.

Ford eked out the nomination, of course, which meant I'd have to wait a few years to see Reagan really emerge as a national political figure. But he certainly piqued my interest at that young age.

As it turned out, 1976 was a turning point for the country as well. The American people elected Jimmy Carter.

Carter's election may have seemed like a liberal victory. But sometimes wins can turn out to be losses, and that election marked the beginning of the end of a weak and unstable period for our country. We had already gone through the lackluster, ineffectual years of the Ford administration. By the time we had moved through the first couple of years of the Carter administration, America was finally fed up. People from all walks of life were waking up to the fact that we needed a change. Real change. A return to American values and strength.

Carter's election and disappointing performance finally gave Ronald Reagan his chance to shine nationally. And the prospect of Ronald Reagan becoming President inspired me to get involved in politics—in the most grassroots fashion imaginable.

But first I had another important decision to make—whether to follow through on my mother's dream that I would go to college.

* * * * * * * * * *

IN MANY WAYS, my mother's death forced me to grow up faster than my peers. It was a crash course in some of life's biggest concepts, from the importance of faith and family to the fragility of life itself—concepts that some people don't start to grasp until much later in life. But it also meant I needed to become resourceful if I was going to make the right choices and move forward in a positive direction. Part of that came with my desire to go to college. But first I had to figure out how to do it.

No one in my family had earned a college degree before (though Dan attended classes briefly), so my family had no institutional memory on the subject. What colleges were even an option? How would I find out about financial aid? What did a year's tuition cost? Would I have to live on campus, or could I commute? Was my GPA good enough? Was there testing? Where did I apply?

I was on my own. Yet once again, a member of the broader community of South St. Paul helped pull me through.

There was an industrial arts teacher at my high school who knew my situation and helped me obtain a scholarship worth a few thousand dollars just before high school ended. That scholarship was presented at a program in the school auditorium, and I swear I couldn't have been more thrilled if I'd just won the lottery. It was such a tremendous relief and help. My father had vowed to do everything he could to help pay for school, and I applied for financial aid as well. And slowly but surely, the maze of this brand-new world that the family had never before ventured into opened up. I was off to college.

7

BIG MAN OFF CAMPUS

I GRADUATED HIGH SCHOOL in 1979 and fulfilled my mother's greatest wish: I enrolled at the University of Minnesota that fall . . . with the full intention of becoming a dentist.

Growing up, I was mightily impressed by our family dentist, Dr. Vogel. He had his own parking spot, occupied by what I remember as a glistening Buick Riviera. I thought, *Dentists! They must have it really good! This is my ticket!*

So as the first person in the history of my family to pursue higher education, I began my college career as a pre-dentistry major.

I didn't make enough money working at Applebaum's grocery store to afford to live on campus, so I stayed at home and commuted to Minneapolis for classes in the red and white Buick

Century I inherited from my parents and drove until it died. I pretty quickly developed a routine of waking up at the crack of dawn to drive in for morning classes, splitting by midafternoon to work several nights a week, and studying in between with the occasional party. There were more than fifty-five thousand students enrolled at the university in those days, and two-thirds of them were commuters. So school itself wasn't much of a social opportunity. For me, like many others, it was all about learning. I attended classes, I absorbed as much information as I could, and I left.

But I did spend enough time on campus to learn just how liberal a university campus can be—especially once I started campaigning for Ronald Reagan.

By the fall of 1979, Reagan had burst back onto the scene with his compelling, positive vision for America. It was a vision based on strength, a willingness to confront the Soviet threat, and an appreciation for some basic things in our society that we had drifted away from—things like faith, private-sector economic growth, and the need for government to be limited and effective. He projected an absolute fortitude but presented it by reflecting stability, decency, grace, and an overall positive personality. I would finally be old enough to vote in the 1980 election and had spent years reading not only *U.S. News & World Report* but various policy and history books as well. By the time I hit that college campus, I was more than ready to jump in. I joined the College Republicans and said, "I want to help Reagan." They said, "Great, here you go," and handed me a stack of brochures to pass out around campus.

The west bank of campus was where the political and social science buildings were located. The busy pedestrian bridge that spanned the Mississippi River, connecting the campus's east and west banks, seemed like a perfect spot for me to stand and hand out these brochures.

Today, looking back, most people remember Reagan as a truly great President and leader. But in 1979 in Minnesota, he was, to say the least, a provocative figure. My simple act of offering pro-Reagan brochures was viewed by many on campus as politically intolerable. People shouted at me, and one student actually spit at my shoes!

It was a good introduction to politics. I was certainly taken aback, yet I felt strongly that Reagan was the person we needed for the job. So I didn't give up. I continued to work with the campus Republicans (what few there were) to play my minuscule part and do what I could to help get Reagan elected in 1980.

* * * * * * * * * *

BY MY SOPHOMORE YEAR, I started to realize that maybe dentistry wasn't going to be my thing after all. One of the required pre-dentistry chemistry classes—I can't recall if it was organic or inorganic chemistry—put me over the edge. I didn't like the class, and I wound up with something like a B-minus. Not the end of the world, but not the kind of grade I expected of myself either. And it wasn't a subject I enjoyed.

So I made my way over to the career services office on campus one afternoon. The so-called "career counselor" was most likely a graduate student, all of maybe twenty-five, who had zero real-life experience that would actually qualify him to be giving "career counseling" advice. But in his defense, he asked one of the most important questions he could ask a student, one no one had put to me directly before. "Well, what do you really like?" I told him I liked current events and history. "So," he said, "go do what you like. You will do well at what you're passionate about."

It was good advice, and I followed it. I dropped pre-dentistry and enrolled as a political science major. I also decided to expand on my experience handing out brochures during the Reagan campaign and signed up to work with U.S. Senator David Durenberger's 1982 reelection campaign.

My experience was pretty much what you'd expect for a young field staff member on a senatorial campaign. There were lots of long days and long nights. Still, I enjoyed the excitement and energy of the campaign and the great friendships I developed, and I was energized by the idea of supporting Dave Durenberger. He had spent part of his life in South St. Paul and was one of us. A real Minnesotan. What I liked about working for Durenberger's campaign was the sense that what I was doing could have a real effect on who might vote for him in '82 and further the important work he could do for Minnesota.

Working for that campaign also afforded me an unforgettable brush with the man whose successful campaign I had supported two years earlier. President Ronald Reagan came to the Carlton Celebrity Room in Bloomington to speak at a Durenberger fundraiser. I helped out at the event and observed President Reagan as he made his way from the backstage area to the auditorium. I didn't have a chance to interact with him, but it was meaningful to me just to be in his presence. This was someone I greatly admired, and seeing him in person, off camera, left an impression. It also gave me the opportunity to watch him deliver his speech from a different and better vantage point. What struck me most as President Reagan spoke to that crowd was his smile. He seemed genuinely happy and joyful and pleasant—even when he spoke about serious topics, such as national defense. That's the lingering impression I have. That, and how the crowd was noticeably respectful of him. He was the President, of course, but at that point I'd never witnessed such a large audience so completely engaged in any politician's speech. It was powerful to experience. I left the event in awe of him and inspired.

* * * * * * * * * *

AS I APPROACHED THE END of my undergraduate years, it became increasingly clear to me that not many employers would be impressed by, much less particularly interested in hiring, a political science major. Working on a senatorial campaign was all fine and good, but when I left school, what I really needed was a degree that would land me a job. So I considered a path that many political science majors end up following: law school.

I didn't have any innate desire to become a lawyer, but I thought the training could prove valuable, and I figured a law degree could help me land a real job. It wasn't a lengthy analysis, but I concluded that whatever sort of job I could land with a law degree would probably be a better career for me than whatever I might be able to get with just an undergraduate degree in political science. So I went for it. And conveniently, the top law school in the state—one of the top twenty in the country—was right across the pedestrian bridge on the west bank of the University of Minnesota campus.

So began my University of Minnesota Law School education. Better stated, my law school *experience*. An odyssey like no other.

The change began with the physical surroundings. The law school is all in one building. It's more navigable, in some respects, than many large high schools. The library, the classrooms, the lecture halls, and the lounge areas are all under one roof. Our entering class was only about 250 students, so even combined with the other two years of students, it was tiny compared to the overall size of the university. I saw the same people over and over again.

Faces became familiar. The whole experience was more social, by default, than it was for me as a commuter on the sprawling undergrad campus.

Our first-year class was divided into five groups of fifty, each called a section. Ours was section C, a terrific group of men and women with varied backgrounds. All our classes were together, either as a single section or combined with others. In part, the purpose of a section was to become much better acquainted with that group of students, supporting one another in various ways through the unique experience that is the first year of law school.

There was one woman in my section with whom I most definitely wanted to become better acquainted. Although we'd spoken periodically during orientation and at other section gatherings, I remember seeing her in the library in gym shorts, a T-shirt, and running shoes. I thought, *Wow. She's beautiful.*

I had seen her other times in those first weeks too, and each time she walked by, my heart jumped. Her name was Mary Anderson, and it turned out that she was as kind and intelligent and engaging as she was pretty.

We were both dating other people when we first met, but the attraction was undeniable. We gradually formed a friendship. Our assigned study carrels weren't far from each other on the second floor of the library, and when you're a law student, the library is a place where you spend countless hours. Mary occasionally helped me study; she was a great help, and studying with her made law school that much better. Eventually, we began dating.

In the meantime, the ups and downs of life continued. In the fall of that first year, I broke my finger badly playing a game of touch football. I really did a number on it. I wound up needing surgery, and the doctors had to implant pins to put it back together. The worst part? It was my writing hand, and note taking was an essential component of classwork and studying. It seemed impossible to navigate law school without the use of my writing hand. I quickly grew frustrated and actually considered taking some time off law school or even dropping out altogether by the middle of that very first winter.

The thing is, I was worn down even before that touch football accident. Working at a job, going to school full-time, and juggling homework with commuting to and from the university had been exhausting. But I had never been a quitter, and for all of my blustering about it, I knew I'd find a way to press through.

In every difficulty, there is opportunity. My inability to take notes in class led to a more directed study plan for me. Every class had a syllabus, and every professor predictably stuck by that syllabus. I found that if I used the syllabus and study guides and read all the class material, I could learn even without taking notes. It wasn't ideal, but somehow it worked out. I studied more efficiently and found it created time in my day I didn't think I had.

Between my first and second year of law school, I landed a clerkship at a law firm in Minneapolis. Normally clerkships weren't offered to students until after the second year of law school, so I was fortunate to get the job. I felt like I'd just signed a Major League Baseball contract. It was a job that paid what at the time seemed like great money, and the hours were open-ended. I could work as much as I could manage in a twenty-four-hour day.

I said good-bye, with gratitude, to Applebaum's after seven years in the produce department. And before summer was out, I convinced the law firm to allow me to clerk during the school year as well. I cut class to a radical degree, relying primarily on study material instead, as I went head-to-head with one other clerk at the firm to see who could bill the most hours. There were many nights when I'd come back after school to pull a late shift, even after working earlier in the day. I was passionate about it, and I needed the money.

But with all the hard work, my law school years were a hard grind. Work competed with studies and any notion of a social life—again. Still, there was one professor from my very first year of law school who left a particularly significant impression on me. His teaching skills were excellent, but just as important, it was apparent he cared about the toll that law school, and legal training more broadly, could take on its students. His name was Steven Block. He taught a class called Civil Procedure. Under Professor Block's instruction, our section learned the detailed process by which civil cases are brought to trial. Pretty dry stuff on the surface, but he made it interesting.

Professor Block was one of the only openly gay professors at the University of Minnesota Law School in those days, and later he would become the first person I knew who died as a result of HIV/AIDS—a new and very frightening disease in the early 1980s.

On the very last day of class that first year, rather than give another lecture or cross-examine us on rules of civil procedure, Professor Block faced our classroom and began to speak about something entirely different. Carefully and thoughtfully, he encouraged us to always maintain perspective. To hold close that which is truly important and resist law school's unfortunate tendency to choke a lawyer's ability to perceive the best in the world. With care, he read a remarkable passage from Mark Twain's *Life on the Mississippi*, a passage that was particularly poignant to all of us who sat quietly, recognizing the truth of what he was conveying.

The passage came from chapter 9, a section in which Twain's protagonist describes the process of becoming a riverboat pilot. There was a time when he noticed the beauty of the river. He reminisces about being completely transfixed by a glorious sunset—

"the dissolving lights drifted steadily, enriching it, every passing moment, with new marvels of coloring." But once he became trained as a riverboat pilot, he forever saw the sunset as a reflection of storms to come, and swirls in the water as dire warnings of what hazards lay in wait beneath the surface.

> Now when I had mastered the language of this water and had come to know every trifling feature that bordered the great river as familiarly as I knew the letters of the alphabet, I had made a valuable acquisition. But I had lost something, too. I had lost something which could never be restored to me while I lived. All the grace, the beauty, the poetry had gone out of the majestic river!

The broader passage, read more fully as Professor Block did that day, was written by Twain in part to doctors. The blush on a woman's cheek becomes a sign of a fever instead of a sign of loveliness, "all her visible charms sown thick with what are to him the signs and symbols of hidden decay." Twain warns against losing that which is truly valuable in the quest for professional knowledge.

Professor Block's thoughtful reading made an impact. Forever viewing the world through the lens of legal analysis presents the danger that a lawyer will lose the ability to care about people as individuals. Empathy will give way to dissecting life's problems as legal issues rather than human struggles.

Mary and I were both in the classroom that day. We consider ourselves fortunate to share that common memory and the lesson Professor Block taught us. I've since referenced it in my own speeches at graduation ceremonies, trying to pass on to other students what Professor Block so thoughtfully passed on to us.

He died that fall. A memorial was held at the law school, and that Mark Twain passage was read aloud in his honor. There isn't a law student who attended his class that last day of our first year who will ever forget it.

* * * * * * * * * *

WHEN MARY AND I STARTED DATING, I was still driving the old Buick I had inherited from my parents. When it was new, with its cherry red paint and white vinyl top, that car was pretty sharp. But nearly ten years after my parents purchased it, and especially after I had banged it up in a couple of accidents, that car was not exactly a first-class mode of transportation. First of all, the passenger-side door wouldn't open. That meant friends, family, and even my new girlfriend, Mary, had to crawl in through the driver's door whenever we'd hit the town.

When I say I "inherited" this car from my parents, I mean it had basically lived through most of what one might consider its useful life before they passed it on to me. But that V6 engine just kept going and going, so I kept the car on the road. By the time Mary and I were cruising around in that car, the floorboards had rusted out to the point that you couldn't even trust the floor mats anymore because they'd sag right through the holes in the floor. My solution was to cut some thin sheet metal, lay it over the holes, and then put the floor mats down on top of that metal. Genius. Plus, if I recall correctly, the heater had stopped working.

Mary made no comment.

Seriously, I don't know what she saw in me. She certainly didn't stick with me for the money and fancy cars!

All kidding aside, I think she saw in me the same thing I saw in her: a true companion; someone who, for reasons that are never fully clear, you feel completely connected to on a heart level; someone full of life and energy and the promise of a fantastic future. A future that would turn out even better because we were together—assuming we could figure out how to get over the physical distance that was about to be put between us.

* * * * * * * * * *

BETWEEN OUR SECOND AND THIRD YEAR of law school, Mary accepted a clerkship offer with Vinson & Elkins in Houston, Texas. I was disappointed that she wouldn't be around that summer, but it was only a short time. A much bigger test came after our graduation in the spring of 1986, when Mary took a permanent position at that same firm, a thousand miles from home.

It was a great job, and she was happy to have it. At that point, the future of our relationship was uncertain, but the two of us committed to still seeing one another. I flew down every few weeks so we could spend long weekends together—going out to eat, taking in a movie, and going for runs together. Between visits, we talked on the phone every chance we could. Of course, airfare wasn't exactly cheap in those days, and this was long before all-inclusive nationwide cell phone plans; long-distance calling was billed by the minute. It was expensive, and we hated having to constantly say good-bye.

After many months of this routine, we decided we'd had enough. We wanted to be together, full-time. So I began to pursue work in Texas and actually got as far as receiving a job offer from Bracewell & Patterson (now Bracewell and Giuliani), a well-respected law firm that would have been a terrific place to work. I thought I was ready to leave Minnesota—yet something about that decision just didn't feel right. It was purely a gut call, and when it came right down to the wire, I turned the job down.

I wanted to marry the love of my life, but Minnesota was my home. And it was Mary's home too.

Mary was raised in Edina, a suburb of Minneapolis. Her mother was a homemaker, and her father was an electrician who eventually became a home builder. He was a tough Scandinavian, the son of immigrants, who never had the opportunity to finish high school. His father, Mary's grandfather, immigrated to the United States from Sweden through Ellis Island but suffered a workplace accident and became partially paralyzed. So to help make ends meet, he pulled Mary's father out of school after eighth grade to serve as his electrical apprentice. The two together could do what one could not. The silver lining was that Mary's father learned firsthand how to become an electrician. But he was heartbroken that he hadn't been allowed to finish school, and he insisted—much as my mother had insisted—that each of his daughters value education. All Mary's education had been in Minnesota. High school, college (Bethel University), and law school.

In her heart, Mary was still a Minnesotan.

So in April of 1987, when Mary was up for a visit, we took a walk around a local lake, Lake Harriet in Minneapolis. It was a beautiful spring day, and I asked her to marry me. It wasn't a total surprise. We had talked about marriage, and we knew it was what we both wanted. But she didn't know that this would be the moment, and the thrill of the question, and her answer—"Yes"—would mark the start of our new life together.

8

* * * * * * * * * *

FAITH AND POLITICS

I NEVER EXPECTED or planned to leave the Catholic church.

Throughout my childhood, I attended Mass nearly every Sunday. Even when I was a little bored and anxious to get out to Grandma Rose's house to play, I took my faith seriously. I went through my first Communion, catechism, and confirmation. When my mom died, my faith only deepened, and my belief in the existence of a loving God carried on into college and law school.

But meeting Mary helped me look at faith in a whole new light.

From the outset of our relationship, Mary and I spent time talking about faith, God, and the church as part of our discussions of life's big questions. I appreciated her willingness to talk so openly about her faith and her encouraging me to be stronger in mine.

Mary was a student of the Bible. I thought it was amazing that she could recall so many passages so well and could apply them readily to life's circumstances. I was intrigued by her ability to say, "Just a minute," while flipping through her Bible. Moments later she'd say, "Here's a passage that might be instructive" and put the Bible in my hand. Although I later understood that type of Bible knowledge is not uncommon, it was uncommon for me to see. And her enthusiasm for it all was infectious. As I studied with her, I came to recognize the ongoing, dynamic relevance of Scripture to my life. How could something written so very long ago continue to be so helpful and so relevant? Truth, clearly, withstands the test of time.

Faith was intertwined with our courtship. Mary attended church with me, and I attended church with her—and as I fell in love with Mary, I also found myself increasingly drawn to her church, Wooddale Church in Eden Prairie.

In its early years, the church was called Wooddale Baptist Church and was part of the Baptist General Conference. It's an interdenominational church now, and its members, like me, aren't necessarily Baptist by upbringing. Regardless of background, they share a common belief in the life, death, and resurrection of Jesus Christ. They are committed Christians who believe in God, seeking to live lives that reflect that belief.

The church has grown and expanded over the years; today it occupies a thirty-two-acre campus. And it still fills up nearly every Sunday, a packed house full of joyful worshipers.

God has clearly blessed Wooddale's ministry, and the Christian men and women who have devoted themselves to this church have contributed to its great success. Those seeking to learn more about God have been drawn to Wooddale in part as a result of the ministry of the church's leader, a man who has been the senior pastor there since the mid-1970s, the Reverend Dr. Leith Anderson. He was, and is, an incredibly gifted teacher and speaker. The first time I heard him speak, I was inspired by his style and persuaded by his temperament, intellect, and wisdom. From day one I felt I was truly learning from him, and I benefited from his sermons. He drew me in, to the point where if I missed his message any given week, often I'd get a tape of it and listen to it later. His messages are substantive and grounded in Scripture. It's obvious that God has called him to this ministry. This wise man could have done anything with his life, but he chose to devote it to Christ.

I'm not the only one Leith Anderson has inspired; great leaders have many followers. In addition to his leadership of Wooddale, he also serves as president of the National Association of Evangelicals—comprised of forty-five thousand churches, forty denominations, and many colleges, seminaries, organizations, and individuals. But he'd be the first to underscore that his mission is not about him; it's about drawing others to Jesus.

I try my best to be a faithful follower of Christ. I believe in Jesus Christ as my Lord and personal Savior. I acknowledge and worship Him regularly through prayer, by reading Scripture, and by attending worship services. I also try, however imperfectly, to apply His teachings to my life and, when appropriate, to share them with others.

Those who question the Christian faith understandably hark back to the condemning, judgmental, finger-waving, sweaty, yelling-on-television preachers who turned out to be adulterers or involved in some massive financial fraud. Or any other in a long list of Christians who have fallen short. But in my experience, most Christians are thoughtful, loving people who try their best to live faithfully, every day.

My decision to join Wooddale Church was not about rejecting

Catholicism. Wooddale is a biblically based Christian church and is, as I mentioned, interdenominational. My spiritual life has been a journey, and I joined Wooddale Church as another step in that journey and to merge my faith and church life with Mary's. Our lives and faith traditions came together naturally. We never struggled over denomination or allegiance to a particular tradition. Rather, what Mary and I held in common was a shared belief in God. We believe that Jesus was and is exactly who He claimed to be. He came to earth not only to show us how to live but to become the ultimate sacrifice for our sins.

* * * * * * * * * *

IT WOULD REQUIRE a long journey to get Mary back home in that late spring of 1987. While most of her things were being loaded into a moving truck, she and I packed what remained into her car and made that long drive straight through the center of America along Interstate 35, which runs from Texas all the way to the Twin Cities and beyond. Riding that distance together, knowing we were soon to be married, was our own mini version of the great American road trip. We noted the subtle changes in landscape with every passing mile, sharing that journey over a wide swath of this remarkable country. It brought us even closer together as we headed for our home state.

On a picture-perfect, seventy-five-degree September day in 1987, at a beautiful little church in Mary's hometown of Edina, Mary and I married in front of about a hundred friends and family in a service officiated by Leith Anderson. The ceremony was in the afternoon, and a small reception followed. Throughout the day I considered not only how happy we were to have found one another but the true contentment we felt in being together. I've heard it said that deciding whom you will marry is one of the most important decisions you will ever make. It's true. I'm blessed to have a wife who has been everything I could have hoped for or imagined.

Mary has been a steady guide for me in many ways, including reminding me on more than one occasion that God cares deeply about even the smallest details of our lives. My tendency is to think of God as too big or too busy to be concerned with me. But I know that's not His nature, nor what the Bible teaches. In Luke 12:6-7, Jesus said, "Are not five sparrows sold for two pennies? Yet not one of them is forgotten by God. Indeed, the very hairs of your head are all numbered. Don't be afraid; you are worth more than many sparrows."

For all our shortcomings—and we have many—we know God loves us and forgives us. Because of that love, we're delighted to give Him our best in return, to use the gifts He's given us according to His purpose. Countless churches of all denominations throughout the country, big and small, share this belief. Mary and I could be happy in any number of different churches. So the question for us has never been whether we attend one church versus another but whether, as we live our lives, we're doing that which is God-honoring. In others words, what would Jesus think of our actions?

Come to think of it, that's a pretty good question to ask at any time.

* * * * * * * * * *

SHORTLY AFTER MARY AND I WERE MARRIED, we bought a small, split-level house in Eagan and commuted to our separate law firms each day. But in the summer of 1989, we both simultaneously received job offers from the very same law firm. Rider, Bennett, Egan & Arundel was filled with genuinely good people.

We enjoyed working there and spent the majority of our days, and many evenings, in the Lincoln Center building in downtown Minneapolis, where the firm was located.

Working at the same firm had several benefits. We were often able to commute together, working late, going to dinner late, driving home, and then starting the routine all over again. With the long hours it takes to get ahead as an attorney, that extra time we had together in the car was a good way to stay connected. Among our many shared experiences during those years was the daily routine of parking in the garage deep beneath the building in which we worked. It was there that Mary and I met a man named Lafayette.

There's a great old line that says, "The best sermons aren't preached; they're lived." That's a notion I readily embrace. Very few people are persuaded by someone flapping his jaws. Rather, people are most often persuaded by seeing examples of believers who walk the walk. Effective, informed, genuine, and loving teaching and preaching is wonderful and helpful, but there is no more powerful lesson than living by example.

Lafayette was a gentleman whose job was to keep the underground parking ramp clean and orderly and to assist people if they needed it. As predictably as the sun rising every morning, there he was every day in crisp, clean clothes, a big smile on his face. Day in and day out, he worked underground in that dimly lit garage with a genuinely positive attitude that any employer would appreciate in an employee. Rarely have I come across a more joyful, pleasant person. Years after I first met him, I finally asked, "Lafayette, what's the deal? I mean, you're kind, you're energetic, you're always joyful. . . . Where does this come from?"

His response was essentially, "Well, thanks for asking." Then he shared with me that his faith in God was the source of his inspiration, joy, and perennially pleasant disposition. In all the years I'd known him, he never said, "I'm a believer." He never handed me a Bible or a pamphlet. He simply demonstrated through his actions, through the way he conducted himself, what it means to be kind to other people, what it means to be generous, what it means to be thoughtful, joyful, helpful. In short, he showed love.

People convey their faith in different ways, of course, but Lafayette's was an unspoken demonstration of love to all those with whom he came into contact every day. He walked the walk. He didn't preach; he just lived a life that was God-honoring. Along the way, he influenced thousands of people who came and went and worked in and visited that building every day.

★ ★ ★ ★ ★ ★ ★ ★ ★ ★

THERE ARE SOME FOLKS in America who have lost sight of the fact that the founders of our country were deeply committed to God. Their reliance on God was apparent at the time they conceived of, debated, and ultimately created the documents that form the pillars of our nation.

A few weeks into the Constitutional Convention in 1787, Benjamin Franklin addressed George Washington and the other convention members, speaking to the bedrock importance of seeking God's guidance as they pursued the sacred task of creating our country.

> I have lived a long time, and the longer I live, the more
> convincing proofs I see of this truth—that God governs
> in the affairs of men. And if a sparrow cannot fall to
> the ground without His notice, is it probable that an
> empire can rise without His aid? We have been assured

in the Sacred Writings that "except the Lord build the house, they labor in vain that build it." I firmly believe this. I also believe that, without His concurring aid, we shall succeed in this political building no better than the builders of Babel.

I find this speech a vivid reminder that our founding fathers relied as much on God as on their own intellect and strength of character. Removing God from our conversations, our plans, and our actions is not in the best interest of our country. The separation of church and state means the government may not impose any religion on the people or prohibit the free exercise of religion; it most definitely does not mean that the best path forward for America is to strike God from the equation.

Inscribed on the walls of the Jefferson Memorial is a collection of words penned by our nation's third President. One inscription reads, "God who gave us life gave us liberty. Can the liberties of a nation be secure when we have removed a conviction that these liberties are the gift of God? Indeed I tremble for my country when I reflect that God is just, that his justice cannot sleep forever."

★ ★ ★ ★ ★ ★ ★ ★ ★ ★

THE IDEA THAT ALL EVANGELICAL CHRISTIANS hold a direct interest in politics or possess a desire to dominate the process in some manner is outdated and incorrect. They do not. Different churches and church leaders approach involvement with public policy in different ways.

I believe it's important and appropriate for the faith community to be involved in public issues. It is everyone's right to participate, and believers have much to offer. Good, concerned, faithful people are needed in the public square, whether running for office, passionately supporting a candidate or cause at the grassroots level, or simply exercising their right to vote. Christians can be a positive force for good—if we walk the walk. When that doesn't happen, when the involvement of faith leaders reflects hypocrisy or bad behavior, the effort is not effective; worse, it's counterproductive.

Christian leaders are deeply concerned about a wide range of national and global issues. Their ability to encourage committed Christians to demonstrate God's love in a tangible way by addressing topics relative to human suffering, like HIV/AIDS in Africa or hunger or poverty worldwide, is an inspiring use of the gifts God has given individuals. I believe the best approach is not to advocate for more and more government solutions but to encourage the effective work of communities, including communities of believers coming together to care for people's needs.

Pastor Rick Warren, author of *The Purpose Driven Life*, is a wonderful example of this approach. He has an enormous global following, and he urges Christians to help tackle the problem of poverty. Christians from all walks of life and all denominations are increasingly asking, "How do we turn our words into action to help others in need?" They're *not* saying, "Give me more government stuff." Today church leaders are saying, "Christians and believers, let's rally; let's organize; let's take inventory of our skills and gifts; let's get something done together."

Whenever Christian leaders try to influence social policy, it's important to remain good-hearted, measured, and loving. Tone and temperament matter. Today, two lightning-rod issues associated with social policy are abortion and gay marriage. When it comes to these debates, strong differences of opinion exist. Regardless of where people line up on these issues, nearly everyone appreciates and respects a constructive, respectful tone when the topics are discussed. I'm pro-life and in favor of traditional marriage, but when I talk about these issues, I watch my tone. Steady, measured speech does not diminish the strength of my views; angry outbursts convince no one.

People often ask how I reconcile my faith life and my public life and to what extent my Christian faith influences my decision making. For any public leader—or a leader in any arena, for that matter—our upbringing, life experiences, values, and beliefs inevitably influence who we are and how we approach the decisions before us. Faith is part of my experience, and it is the cornerstone of my value system. It is part of who I am and how I think. But there is a difference between believing in God and presuming God is on my side in matters of public policy. It matters more that I continue to search for wisdom, striving instead to be on God's side.

My faith in God gives me a sense of hope, comfort, and confidence, which then allows me to conduct myself in a more thoughtful, measured, and hopefully better way in public. Trying to live with grace and truth is part of my faith journey, and I try to project that publicly. Once in a while, someone will ask me in the middle of a crisis, "Why do you seem so calm?" Or occasionally a constituent will throw me the somewhat-backhanded compliment, "You seem like a decent guy for a politician. Why is that?" When that happens, I answer by saying, "I know where my help comes from." God's grace has guided me, and His love has sustained me.

I often think of Lafayette and am quietly grateful for his example.

9

★ ★ ★ ★ ★ ★ ★ ★ ★ ★

NEW BEGINNINGS

WHILE MARY AND I were starting our new life together, buying a house in Eagan, and working long hours to establish our legal careers, I also remained interested in public policy and politics. Six years after working for Senator Durenberger's 1982 campaign, I returned to help with his 1988 reelection campaign—this time as his political director. Working overtime in a law firm while trying to stay dedicated to the campaign was a bit much, though, and thankfully I was able to take a few months' leave of absence from the firm to focus on the campaign that year.

Having that time to dedicate to Senator Durenberger afforded me some incredible opportunities, including the chance to meet a man with whom my life would later intertwine—in ways unfathomable to me in 1988. He was a new Senator then, emerging on the national stage, backed by a personal military history that placed him firmly in the rarefied air of true American heroes. His name was John McCain.

Senator McCain came to Minnesota to campaign for Senator Durenberger on veterans' issues, and the campaign needed someone to drive him around for a couple of days. Mary and I, impressed as we were by McCain's life story and record of service, patriotism, and courage, were more than happy to volunteer.

I immediately liked John McCain. He was funny, irreverent, unorthodox, and personable. He spoke passionately, and I could sense immediately that he meant what he said. He was also gracious, inquiring about our backgrounds and making an effort to learn a bit about us. He thanked us for taking the time to drive him around. We told him it was our pleasure—and it was.

We didn't really strike up a friendship with McCain at that point. In fact, I wouldn't interact with him again face-to-face for more than a decade. But Mary and I were both impacted by his visit. Not because he was so funny or so courteous but because of his obvious and passionate dedication to our country and because of his epic experience as a prisoner of war in Vietnam. Although he didn't discuss his own story, he raved with enthusiasm about the heroism of his fellow prisoners. His life has been a powerful testimony to service, courage, and sacrifice. Mary and I were both appreciative of his continued public service and respectful of all he'd done for our country.

Over the years that followed, I sent Senator McCain notes from time to time. Congratulations on the way he handled a piece of legislation or words of encouragement as he campaigned for reelection. Occasionally he would send a note back, thanking me for my support. But we didn't actually speak in person again until I became Governor nearly fourteen years later.

As a footnote, Senator Durenberger was reelected in 1988 but some years later was admonished by the Senate because of the way he handled some reimbursement for housing. He chose not to run again in 1994. His marriage fell apart rather publicly too. It was one of those moments when you realize that even people you look up to are not perfect. When I first encountered Durenberger, he was a rising star, elected in his midforties, *and* he had spent some of his life in my hometown of South St. Paul. I respected the depth of his knowledge of issues and how studious he was. To see someone like that take a tumble leaves a pit in your stomach. He felt terrible about it, and his true friends rallied to his side. Their support helped him rebuild his life professionally, and I admire the way he relied on his faith to recover the joy I first saw in him in the early eighties. He is doing well now, and his story is one of redemption.

* * * * * * * * * *

OF COURSE, LIFE'S STUMBLES are not reserved for politicians. We all have limitations, and we all make mistakes. All of us have fallen short—no exceptions. Yet there are lessons to be learned from our shortcomings. For one, because of human frailty, it's important that leaders avoid the temptation to be self-righteous. Confidence and strength are one thing; a false notion of personal perfection is another. Anytime you see somebody stand up and claim to have all the answers or to be perfect, a warning bell should go off. None of us is perfect, and when that truth is revealed in someone who claims otherwise, especially in a leader, it appears in the form of hypocrisy. Whether in government or private enterprise, people will not tolerate or support you for long if you're saying one thing and doing another. It sets back the advances of everyone else who is trying, often at great personal sacrifice, to make a genuine effort for a particular movement or cause.

That desire, the drive to make a difference, is an intense internal pressure not only for the candidate running for office but for those who dutifully support the campaign as well. There was one night during that '88 Durenberger campaign when I was up in the middle of the night, working feverishly after what had already been a long day, or more likely a series of long days. Mary leaned into the doorway of our little home office and begged me to stop and get some sleep. She was genuinely worried about my health as she watched the long hours I was putting into the campaign. And I told her, "Mary, after this campaign is over, things are going to be different. It's gonna calm down. It'll be better—just after this campaign."

In the coming years I would find myself repeating that mantra often. "After this campaign," or "After this legislative session, things will slow down." Sometime in the late 1990s, in the middle of a similar late-night work session, I repeated a similar response to my wife's "you need to take a break" request, and she said, "Tim! You've been saying that for a dozen years!" We both had to laugh. It was true! That cycle of extremely hard work followed by a period of rest that would never quite materialize became the pattern of our lives—and that line of mine about things slowing down has carried on as a standing joke between the two of us.

* * * * * * * * * *

WHILE SOME OF MY EARLIEST INTEREST in public policy was sparked partly by a gigantic, global phenomenon—the Cold War and the threat of the Soviet Union—my first run for elective office grew from something much smaller. The issue in question was how a growing city should best develop.

Eagan is a beautiful Twin Cities suburb that had become one of the faster-growing communities in the country. Development concerns were front and center, and how they were decided would determine much about the future of Mary's and my new hometown. So I jumped into my very first election campaign and ran for city council in 1989.

Mary and I basically ran my campaign out of a shoe box in our home. We printed up some modest brochures and had a couple of friends help us out with the lit drops—dropping that literature into the slots beneath people's mailboxes according to a map of the city that we divided and conquered with a Sharpie or two. We did a little fund-raising to help cover the costs of printing signs and mailing letters to the lists we gathered.

My brothers and sisters got into the action too. They supported me as I walked in the Fourth of July parade. They held up signs and passed out literature. Then I went door-to-door, introducing myself to people and asking them for their vote. Hard work, perseverance, lawn signs, and shoe leather. I won.

I very quickly found that I truly enjoyed the work I was doing on the city council. Local politics is a remarkable and important endeavor. And I found I had an aptitude for it. Since the city council was comprised of only five people, including the Mayor, if I could persuade two other members that I had a good idea, it could be implemented.

My legal career was still moving full speed ahead at this point too. As was Mary's. I had the great fortune to get lots of time in the courtroom my first few years out of law school, working on assignment as a prosecutor for several municipalities around the Twin Cities. It was all misdemeanor-level cases—shoplifting, DWIs, domestic cases; just stacks of these cases—that left very little time for preparation and required a young attorney to be fast on his feet. I'd show up in court, and there were literally dozens of pending cases that all had to be processed that day. There were times when I had to absorb all the basic information about a case in a matter of minutes. The vast majority of them could be settled easily, but occasionally I had to take a case to trial more quickly than I thought imaginable—giving me a crash course in trial advocacy. Trying multiple cases, cross-examining witnesses, introducing documents, and understanding the application of the law—all learned at the speed of light.

Hard work was the norm. From the moment we got married, Mary and I put our heads down and worked hard. We had fun when we could. We loved going to the movies. We enjoyed taking walks together in the evenings; for some reason we've had some of our greatest talks while we walk. But for the most part, we both resolved to do everything we could to accomplish as much as possible in our careers while we were young. Why wait? We were both full of energy and had set our sights on building a solid future for ourselves and, hopefully sometime in the near future, a family.

Our "future" would arrive sooner than we expected.

* * * * * * * * * *

THE 1990 CENSUS resulted in a legally required redistricting process. That yielded an unexpected open seat in Eagan for the Minnesota House of Representatives in the 1992 election. Mary and I discussed at length whether I should run for that seat. On the one hand, we were busy with our legal careers, and it would be difficult to practice both law and politics. On the other hand, I seemed to have some ability and interest in public policy, and it was a great chance to serve others. Besides, the seat might not be open for another ten years. After much thought, discussion, and prayer, I got into the race.

Then we received the blessed news that Mary was pregnant with our first child. We were elated but had a lot on our plate.

In my experience assisting campaigns, it was very clear to me that the best way to win was to give it some shoe leather, pound the pavement, and drum up all the grassroots support I could. So Mary and I hit the campaign trail, again covering Eagan one block at a time. Lawn signs, literature drops, and door knocking became our daily routine. Even though she was pregnant at the time, Mary pulled out all the stops, riding along and helping put signs up wherever we could. Occasionally she'd say, "Ugh, I don't feel good," and go sit in the car. Orange Popsicles were the only thing that made her feel better, so we made sure they were in abundant supply. She wanted to be there, and her support helped push me through.

We knew victory wouldn't come easy. I faced a serious Democrat contender, plus a third-party candidate who was center-right. My platform wasn't exactly flashy or spectacular. It was based in common sense, conservative values, and bread-and-butter issues. I thought taxes in Minnesota were too high, and I wanted to do what I could to see them reduced. I thought St. Paul needed to get serious about holding the line on spending. I thought we needed to improve education in our state as well. I saw no reason to come up with anything flashy when the basics were what I cared about most. So I didn't. I just spoke from the heart.

Mary and I hit the town with that message in hand. I'd walk up one side of the street, and she'd walk up the other. At more homes than not, we seemed to find a pretty receptive audience. (I mean, really, are there many people out there who *want* to see higher taxes? Really?)

Contrary to what you might expect, most people are gracious and kind when you knock on their door—although strange things do happen. People would open the door in their underwear and stand there for a moment in plain view before saying, "Oh, let me go get my bathrobe on." Worse, there were guys who'd open the door and say, "What do you want?" and then stand there in their tighty whiteys listening intently the whole time I gave my spiel!

There were unpredictable moments, too, when people's dogs would unexpectedly come chasing around corners. Mary or I would wind up sprinting back onto the sidewalk or over to the next yard to get away from a territorial pooch. We quickly empathized with mailmen. One big dog actually lunged at me, and I defended myself by sticking my stack of brochures in his face. He ended up biting the stack and left teeth marks in the pamphlets! I didn't toss them; I just handed them out with apologies for the bite marks. My budget was limited—what else could I do?

Dogs aside, it was a hard fight, and that election could have gone either way. It wasn't a great year for Republicans. It was a presidential election year, the year Bill Clinton took the White House. There was high Democratic turnout across the state, and that third-party candidate, sure enough, ate into my votes. But I think something about my simple, straightforward message based on common sense paid off . . . because I won.

I would win that seat again and again, using much the same shoe-leather and door-pounding technique every two years for the next decade. And my message on taxes, cutting spending, and improving education always remained the same—bolstered each year by a few more ideas that I increasingly thought would be vitally important to the future of the state I called home.

10

UPHILL BATTLES

WALKING INTO THE STATE CAPITOL as a new legislator is a bit like the first day of school. But unlike school, in this case, there's the additional wow factor of walking into this fantastic building with its spectacular dome, marble pillars, and tangible history at every turn.

As with any new school or new job, most of that initial awe and sense of newness passed fairly quickly as I began to focus on the tasks at hand. The daily routines and details of the work itself became far more important than the surroundings. Like everyone else, I settled in. Still, every once in a while, to this day, I look around our beautiful, architecturally amazing capitol building, designed by the world-renowned Cass Gilbert, and take it in. Whether the work is as a legislator or as Governor, these aren't ordinary jobs. So much rests on the decisions elected officials make, and that part of the awe needs to remain.

In the beginning, my chair and small desk on the floor of the House of Representatives were located in the farthest back corner of the room. Mary came to the capitol that January day in 1993 when I was first sworn in. She was pregnant as could be at that point, just weeks from giving birth. We both squeezed into that back corner of the chamber and laughed at the placement. There was just barely room for two, but there were nearly three of us. That year would mark all kinds of new beginnings.

At 134 members, Minnesota's House of Representatives is one of the largest in the country. That size leaves lots of room for varying opinions on both sides of the aisle, and from the get-go, one thing I liked about the legislature was the debate. My willingness to wade in quickly brought me some early recognition from the old-guard Republicans as well. They noticed and seemed to value a new voice in the room, someone who could be a vocal advocate for our caucus's ideas, who was willing to stand up and lead the charge when it counted.

Right from the beginning, my rule of thumb was to be prepared. I never went into a situation without doing my homework and committing the important details to memory. I like to stay away from notes, and even more so teleprompters, whenever possible. I find using notes tends to slow down the repartee and verbal jousting that an active role in the legislature requires. But going without them does require an ability to memorize the essential points of a debate.

There were all kinds of characters among those 134 House members and the 67 Senators who convened just down the hallway. Some were big-name players who had held their seats for thirty or forty years. Many of those were hardworking and dedicated to the public good, but others were entrenched in their ways and couldn't see the value in a new idea if it whacked them right on the nose. Dealing with some of those old-time politicians would become a frustrating part of the process for me as the years went by. How can government move forward when some of its most powerful members cling to the past? In my opinion, it is not healthy for any politician to stay in one elected position for too long.

The members of the House worked long hours during the session. The debates, either formal or informal, could go on endlessly, almost without limit. I routinely left the capitol at midnight or one or two in the morning.

Other than sleeping (of which there was very little) and eating (which was often whatever you could grab on the fly), every moment was filled. Like many states, the Minnesota legislature is part-time, and I was still working at the law firm with cases to prepare. I wasn't dealing with misdemeanor shoplifting and DWIs anymore; now I was dealing with larger matters for some of Rider Bennett's big clients. It was complex work, and it consumed a lot of time as I prepared documents and sorted through byzantine legal arguments. I had to stay sharp, but the schedule was grueling.

I often drove in to Rider Bennett at 7 a.m. so I could get some work done before driving over to St. Paul for a 10 a.m. committee meeting. At the end of the day, depending on how late things went at the capitol, I sometimes drove back to Rider Bennett to finish up my work, continuing late into the night. Whatever it took. I couldn't afford to quit the firm and live on a part-time legislator's salary. Especially since we were starting a family.

* * * * * * * * *

FEBRUARY OF 1993 marked one of the happiest times of my life: the arrival of our first daughter, Anna.

The term *busy* is insufficient to describe a parent's schedule. Before 1993, Mary and I still had time to exercise. Mary got into aerobics in the eighties and wore the full outfit, complete with leggings. I even tried it myself (without the leggings). And in 1991, in between our hard work at the law firm and my role on the Eagan City Council, she and I actually found time to train for the Twin Cities Marathon—and finish it! As much as it felt like we were working nonstop those first few years of our marriage, we had plenty of time to go to movies and dinners.

Once we had a baby and turned our home office into a nursery and combined our already-full workloads with my legislative duties and the inevitable lack of sleep an infant engenders, our lifestyle became almost unbearable. We loved this little girl more than anything else either of us could imagine. But our schedules were grueling.

Once again, God had a plan in mind just when we needed it most. As I left the capitol one afternoon in the early part of 1994, I noticed a posting for a district judge vacancy that needed filling in Dakota County—the county where we live. I came home that evening and asked Mary, "Honey, you wanna be a judge?"

Mary said, "No."

Her knee-jerk reaction was understandable. She had a fantastic job at a big law firm where she was a rising star, a young partner with good friends and a bright future. But I knew from experience that judges operated on much more reasonable hours than either of us were keeping. The commute would be less than twenty minutes in no traffic. In general, the workday was 8:30 to 5:00, and other than periodically being on call, the job rarely included nights or weekends. Although she would earn less money, a predictable, stable schedule seemed like an appealing trade-off for our family. So even though she initially declined, I kept pitching her on it. I knew she possessed the depth of legal skill, the measured discipline, and the right temperament for the job.

The more I mentioned it, the more I could see her starting to come around. Eventually, the idea started to appeal to her. She was intrigued not so much by the prospect of an improved schedule as by the opportunity to do something meaningful. She applied.

When Mary and I look back at the course of our life together, we see a fairly clear path, but it wasn't always clear as events unfolded. When you're in the moment, it seems each concern and each problem is daunting. The way forward is rarely obvious. But in our experience, God has brought just the right circumstances or opportunities or people along at just the right moment to help us find our way. I've often considered Proverbs 3:5-6, which is one of those amazing passages that seems easier said than done: "Trust in the Lord with all your heart and lean not on your own understanding; in all your ways acknowledge him, and he will make your paths straight." What an incredible promise and source of encouragement.

It was far from certain that Mary would be appointed. She was relatively young, only thirty-three; surely more experienced candidates would apply. But the Judicial Selection Commission (the committee that recommends finalists to the Governor) recognized Mary's particular blend of strengths, and so did Governor Arne Carlson. Mary was appointed to the position.

Mary's appointment as a judge came at exactly the right time for our family, in terms of our ability to reasonably function—because my schedule wasn't about to let up. As she became available on nights and weekends, it stabilized our ability to care for Anna and put some sense of sanity back into our routines. Not that it would be easy to juggle being a judge and a mom. Mary could write chapter and verse on the challenges of combining those two roles. Parenting is its own full-time job, and with the fun part comes all the day-to-day work. Mary handled that, plus all the errands, grocery shopping, meals, laundry, and visits to the doctor for the inevitable childhood ailments, all while handling the sea of dysfunction that is the norm for a district court judge. She was still a working mother, like countless working mothers in this country, but at least now it seemed somewhat more manageable. What she discovered along the way was that the job was more complex, challenging, sad, daunting, and yet more rewarding than she had ever imagined.

★ ★ ★ ★ ★ ★ ★ ★ ★ ★

IN 1994, WE DECIDED TO SHOP for a larger home to accommodate what we hoped and prayed would be our growing, happy, healthy family. We wound up settling on a brand-new house in a brand-new development in Eagan. It was our little piece of the American Dream: a three-bedroom, warm, comfortable home that sat diagonally across from a little park with a pond. The house was set back just feet from the road in front, and before long we knew most of the folks who had bought houses in the development at the same time we did. We added window boxes in the front and planted trees in the back. It was a typical suburban home in many ways, in a typical suburban neighborhood. But it was ours. And it would serve as a wonderful home base for everything that was to come.

We still live in that house today. I'm proud to say we stayed put, at least part-time, even after I was afforded the great privilege of moving into the Governor's Residence on St. Paul's exclusive Summit Avenue. Eventually we finished off the basement. Over the years, the downstairs has been home to lots of sleepovers, not to mention a great storage place for my hockey gear. The coziness and comfort of that two-story home has always suited us just fine, even without much extra space.

In 1996, Mary gave birth to our second daughter, Mara. She came into the world every bit as happy and healthy as Anna. We were truly blessed.

When the girls started preschool and eventually grade school, Mary and I found ways to divide the drop-off and pick-up times. Somehow we pieced the schedule together with duct tape and chicken wire, just like all the other parents on our street. Somehow, together, we all made it work.

It's funny how fast time flies, though. After mowing the lawn recently, I sat down on the front steps of that house and looked out over our little patch of grass, and it struck me that we've been in that house for over sixteen years. *Sixteen years!*

As I sat on those steps, I couldn't help but think of that Kenny Chesney song "Don't Blink"—how it all comes and goes so fast. My musical tastes have always leaned toward classic rock and the songs of my adolescence: Springsteen, Bob Seger, the Rolling Stones, U2, John Mellencamp, and the like. But my two daughters—who just yesterday were babies and are now teenagers—fell in love with New Country and expanded my musical palate quite a bit. And that Chesney song says it all:

> *Trust me, friend, a hundred years goes faster than you think*
> *So don't blink*
>
> *. . . when your hourglass runs out of sand*
> *You can't flip it over and start again*
> *Take every breath God gives you for what*
> *   it's worth*

* * * * * * * * * *

I LOVED EVERY MINUTE of my ten years in the legislature. The ups and downs, the struggles, the fights, some disappointing losses, and some major victories—all of them taught me, all of them helped me to understand the ins and outs of the complicated system of checks and balances, including the unwritten rules that make our government live and breathe.

There is no way to understand it all without having gone through it yourself. It's impossible to explain—you have to live it to really get it. Serving in the legislature was like ten years of on-the-job training. In some ways, it was analogous to med students going through residency—including the sleepless nights. I don't mean to imply that it required the same level of skill or talent that's necessary to become, for example, a surgeon, but I do believe my time spent serving in the legislature was a kind of political residency. For doctors, residency means long hours in the field, working with patients, leaving textbooks behind to deal with the flesh and bones of their chosen profession. It's practical experience. For me it was a depth of expertise in public policy that an elected representative gets only by being actively involved in the legislature. And I was as actively involved as a person can get.

In 1998, for the first time in a very long time, Republicans won the majority in the Minnesota House. After six years on the job, I had made friends in the Republican caucus. I like people, which you'd hope would be the case for someone deeply engaged in public service. But just as important, I'm consistently fascinated by the stories of the people I meet. Each new description of someone's background or challenges, joys or opportunities, opinions or insights has taught me something. In addition, by that point I was known as a champion of conservative causes, and I had proven myself to be a good debater. To my delight and honor, my fellow Republicans selected me to be Majority Leader.

Six years after taking a seat in the far back corner of the floor of the House, I moved to a new desk. This time it was right up front, beside the main microphone, where my debating skills would continue to be put to the test—as would my ability to form coalitions.

As Majority Leader, I was the guy who had to pull our team together, yet now I was also the one to reach across the aisle when we needed votes from the other side—something that on occasion meant literally walking across the aisle that separated the right from the left, trying to persuade a Democrat or two or ten to join us in a vote. I was the one who often brought negotiations to a head and closed deals around conference tables that could deeply affect the citizens of my state.

Over the course of the next four years, our Republican majority accomplished a lot, but I think the thing I'm most proud of is that we cut taxes by the largest amount in Minnesota history. That was a major accomplishment in the state of Minnesota, which at that point was one of the highest-taxed states in the country.

My time as Majority Leader was incredibly meaningful, and we got things done. It gave me a chance to talk to the media, to share the Republican viewpoint and speak for my party, to begin to stand up against the long-standing left-leaning traditions that in my opinion had led our state in a terribly misguided direction. Local media pundits even started to buzz about the possibility that I would be well suited for higher office—the U.S. Senate, perhaps, or maybe Governor.

I thought about it too, but I wasn't sure it was the right thing to do or the right time to do it. I started to wonder if ten years in the legislature was enough. Perhaps it was time to move on. I had made a difference. I had left my mark. Perhaps it was better to quit while I was ahead rather than forge on into an even more demanding role. Not to mention, running for higher office would put a tremendous strain on my family.

Mary had shouldered the burden of most of the family responsibilities for so many years, maybe it was time I gave her a break. She deserved a normal life—with a husband who came home at predictable hours.

As I wrestled with whether to run for higher office, Norm Coleman, the popular Mayor of St. Paul and a friend of mine, announced his initial plans to run for Governor. He had run unsuccessfully for Governor in 1998 (when Jesse Ventura was elected), was well-known statewide, and had an established fundraising organization. It seemed like a good idea for him to run. So I went ahead and explored making a run for U.S. Senate, steering away from what was to be Norm's race for Governor.

The story was not a simple, straight line, though. As with all things in life, nothing is ever quite that easy. I couldn't have predicted that national Republican leaders, including President George W. Bush, would step in to persuade Norm that he should switch to the U.S. Senate race. Suddenly the pressure was on for me to stop my senatorial exploration and move over to the Governor's race instead. I received a call from Vice President Dick Cheney, politely suggesting that I support the better-known candidate, Norm Coleman, to run for U.S. Senate. It wasn't an easy decision, but I decided to defer to Norm for the good of the team and the cause.

After that, the original question I had posed to myself about putting an end to my political career suddenly seemed like a viable choice. To go back to the private sector full-time at the end of my current two-year term in the House made a lot of sense. So I made up my mind, thinking it was my final decision: I wouldn't be running for higher office.

I felt pretty good about my decision as I drove home. I pulled into the garage, and Mary met me in the entryway. I was so anxious to tell her the news that I didn't even wait to go in and sit down.

"I made my decision," I told her. "I'm not going to run."

"Really?" Mary said.

"We've been doing this for ten years. It's time to turn the page," I said. "We did what we could, and I think I made a positive difference. Now it's time to move on."

I fully expected her to be pleased. Instead, she grabbed me by the shirt and looked me dead in the eyes. "Tim," she said, "the state needs you." Then she launched into this Rocky Balboa–esque speech about how if I didn't run, everything I had worked for would be washed away. She had other inspiring words as well, and they gave me pause. I had come too far to stop now, she said, and on and on. "The state needs you! Get in there and fight!"

Ah, my very own Adrian. How could I turn that down?

That moment marked a turning point for me. It suddenly made sense to me that if I had something to give, it was worth the sacrifice to give it—and I truly believed I had a vision that could set Minnesota back on a much-needed course toward fiscal responsibility and a better quality of life for its citizens. I considered it for a while longer. Yes, I finally decided. I would run.

That inspired speech was the work of a wife who loved me. It was not the product of a political supporter or an activist, but of a woman who saw the best in me and hoped I'd use whatever gifts God had given me for good. What's funny is that sometime later, when our schedules were as challenging as ever, Mary told me that she'd meant it in the best possible way but hadn't really thought it through. She figured I needed a pep talk at the time, but she didn't think I could actually *win*. She told me she just wanted me to run and get it out of my system, thinking that when I lost, we could at last get on with our lives. The best-laid plans . . .

While all of this wrangling went on, another formidable Republican competitor for Governor had been campaigning for months. Brian Sullivan was a dashing entrepreneur with many millions in the bank and many party leaders lined up behind him. When Norm was still considering a run for Governor, I remember thinking that with Sullivan in the race, Norm would have his work cut out for him.

So here we were in 2001. Norm Coleman had dropped out of the Governor's race to run for Senate, and I announced I wasn't running for Senate. Instead . . . I wasn't sure. I had thought about it for quite some time—months, I think. Then Mary gave me that Rocky speech. Now that I had decided to get in the race for Governor after all, I needed to catch a multimillionaire opponent with a big head start toward the Republican endorsement. I found myself holding fast to Matthew 19:26, which helped me through the more challenging moments. "With God all things are possible."

Shortly after Labor Day in 2001—just a few days before 9/11, it turned out—I set up a rally at the old Croatian Hall in my hometown of South St. Paul. The space was standing room only, filled with friends and family, old neighbors, and a surprisingly big press turnout as well. I stood at that podium in those familiar, working-class surroundings, and I made the announcement that I was running for Governor. "A number of doors have been slammed in my face," I said, referring to the way the White House had recruited Norm Coleman and the way the Republican establishment had lined up behind Brian Sullivan over the course of that summer. "Now I'm gonna kick a few open."

* * * * * * * * * *

TO CALL THAT RACE AN UPHILL BATTLE is a bit like calling Mount Everest a hill. Even after grinding it out in the legislature for a decade, I had almost no name recognition; only true political junkies had any clue who I was. I had little money and no real network outside of the tiny legislative universe. But little by little, step by step, I resolved to keep climbing till I reached that summit.

I did most of my campaigning in my Dodge Stratus. Sometimes a volunteer drove me around, but I often just drove myself—all over the state. Most candidates use planes to get around Minnesota—there's a lot of ground to cover and a lot of lakes to drive around—but we didn't have enough money to do much flying in the early part of the campaign. We managed to pull together a small but dedicated staff, along with some incredible volunteers. We raised some money and just ground it out.

The 2002 Minnesota Republican convention was in June, and before that we campaigned through the spring caucuses—an unwieldy process that eventually winnows tens of thousands of people down to 2,200 convention delegates. At those caucuses, the attendees take part in a straw ballot. I was driving home from one of the caucus sites at nine or ten at night after a very long day when a staff member called me with the results of that early glimpse at my prospects. "Sullivan's whompin' ya pretty good," he said. He wasn't exaggerating; Sullivan beat me in that straw ballot two to one.

Discouraging, I thought. But I knew it wasn't over. I readied our troops, and we plowed ahead.

The toughest part of all of this, for me, was that one of my troops was missing. My General. Mary's role as a district court judge meant she couldn't take part in any aspect of a partisan election. She could love me and quietly support me at home, but that was it. She couldn't show up at my rallies. She couldn't do interviews with me. She basically couldn't lend her support to me anywhere other than in our home without violating the code of judicial ethics. Later many of those rules were tossed out as unconstitutional, but those were the rules at the time.

It was difficult, but we moved ahead as best we could. I missed having Mary with me, but on the other hand, I was on the road constantly, and I can't imagine how we could have done it had Mary not been home with the children. Everywhere I went, every time I connected with people and had a chance to share my ideas and hear their concerns about our state, it felt as if one more stone was placed before me, laying out a path to follow. And whenever I came home with doubts in my head, missing my family, Mary would reassure me that I had her support.

The dynamics of the race changed after that discouraging straw ballot in February. After that night, the election became a mathematical proposition. The process narrowed the field of delegates down to a reasonable 1,200 people. It was now possible for me to call or visit every one of them. And I did. In most cases, more than once. In addition, I had surrogates go out and talk me up to those delegates. Fortunately, I had many great legislative friends. Just about every Republican legislator supported me, which I was deeply grateful for. They reached out to friends and contacts in their local areas. I was slowly building momentum.

Up against such big money, I relied on making personal connections with people. My experience, my beliefs, my strong friendships, and the connections I made with the delegates were just about all I had. That, along with my personal story. Minnesota is an interesting place. People here appreciate authenticity and admire people who are genuine and who'll shoot it to 'em straight.

When they learn about my background, I think people can say, "Hey, this guy's experienced some of what I've experienced." My life was built on challenges and real-life struggle. It's a story that connects with what many Americans experience in their lives.

I hoped it would be enough to carry me through.

* * * * * * * * * *

THE DAY OF THE CONVENTION, I headed down to the Xcel Energy Center. Mary wished me luck and shared the sort of encouraging words she had throughout the process. It was tough to say good-bye and walk into that hockey arena to hit the convention floor, not knowing what my fate would be—what *our* fate would be—without Mary by my side. I'm not sure either of us ever quite got over how difficult it was to muddle through that experience, compelled as we were to be apart during the process. We were used to being by each other's side, supporting each other in important moments big and small. I didn't like the mandatory separation at a time like this, and neither did she.

The main floor of the convention was filled with all the hoopla you'd expect—stage, lights, sound system, delegates all packed on the floor holding signs for their chosen candidate. The place wasn't filled to the rafters, of course. The Xcel Energy Center is a hockey arena. It's huge. (To give you a sense of how big a crowd this place can handle, it's the very same hall where the Republican National Convention was held in 2008.)

The gubernatorial endorsement process started around noon. There are all kinds of rules and traditions to these things, but basically, someone placed the names of the candidates in nomination, and then we drew straws to see who would speak first. I don't recall if I won or lost the straw draw, but Sullivan went first that day. I went second.

My team didn't think it was a good idea for me to watch Sullivan's speech. So they shuffled me back into our waiting area—our war room, as it were, which just happened to be a place where I felt perfectly happy and comfortable—a hockey locker room. I wasn't accustomed to being managed like that, but I was content to hang out in the locker room, essentially by myself.

Even from that cement-encased room, I could hear the crowd roar now and then. I heard a few other loud noises as well, which I couldn't identify. When my staff came back, I asked, "How was it? How did he do?" I was surprised to hear their responses: "Oh, it wasn't that good. It was okay. I'd give it average marks." Much later, when I spoke with delegates and others who were in the arena that day, I discovered Sullivan had put on one of the biggest, boldest convention demonstrations anyone in Minnesota had ever witnessed. He had fireworks and confetti and a laser light show! But my staff apparently didn't want me to get discouraged, so they downplayed it. "It was fine. Just okay, really."

When our turn came, we went out there with a song on the stereo and a few relatives and volunteers holding up signs and wearing T-shirts with my name on them. That was it. Our entire "show."

But the real fireworks were only beginning.

Turns out, I had closed the gap since those earlier straw ballots. Our hard work and handshaking had paid off. Sixty percent of the delegate votes are required for endorsement. Sullivan and I were separated by only a thin margin by the time the first ballot results were announced.

Between ballots, we were both out there, talking to the delegates one by one, making our case all over again. As we walked around the floor of that hockey arena, it was clear the delegates were carefully considering their decision. The light show wasn't going to be a deciding factor. The convention stretched out through twelve ballots—each one taking time for counting. At one point, we were only separated by a twelve-vote difference.

As the convention stretched on past midnight, people started talking about calling a stalemate—which would have meant going to a primary in September. That, I felt, would amount to a concession on my part. I had raised and spent maybe a couple hundred thousand dollars that year for the campaign, which was very little to begin with, and it had already been fully poured into the effort. I had nothing left. The primary would happen in September. In order to run a statewide media campaign for the primary, I would need to have instant access to significant amounts of money. Sullivan would've buried me in media buys.

The day and night dragged on for so long that at one point I thought, *Well, maybe we should just be open to a stalemate and a primary.* Some key friends and advisers were encouraging me to take that deal, feeling we had to bring the convention to some kind of conclusion. But finally, well past midnight, one friend pulled me aside and said, "You came this far; it's been really hard; you clawed your way back from being down two-to-one in the caucuses—fight this to the end. *Fight it to the end.*" It was the kind of pep talk Mary would have given me had she been there.

Everyone had been in the same clothes since breakfast the previous day, and nobody had slept. But the delegates didn't want to go home without an endorsed candidate. So during the last round of speeches, I stood up and gave my best rallying message, my very best effort to persuade the assembled team of Republican delegates that I would fight for what was right for our party and for our state. Miraculously, the very next ballot indicated a clear shift in my direction.

In the end, I won the nomination.

It was far too late to celebrate. Everyone left the hall within a matter of minutes as the crew swept up and started packing the chairs away. I stopped for a quick bite to eat before heading home to Eagan, and by the time I walked out of the restaurant, the sun was coming up. It was the longest endorsing convention in the state's history. And I had become the Republican party nominee for Governor.

★ ★ ★ ★ ★ ★ ★ ★ ★ ★

THERE WASN'T MUCH TIME for celebration in the days that followed, either. We were now faced with the daunting task of preparing for a general election in November. It was already June, and we had blown through all of our campaign funds, so we were basically starting from scratch all over again. Only this time, we were running against the longtime Democrat Majority Leader of the state Senate, Roger Moe—a titan in Minnesota politics.

In any election, there's a basic principle that nearly always holds true. About one-third of the people are going to vote Republican, no matter what. And about one-third of the people will vote Democratic, no matter what. Elections are won or lost depending on how the remaining one-third looks at you. My approach to winning has always been pretty basic. From my perspective, that remaining third probably doesn't decide which candidate to vote for based on point five of your seven-point plan for health-care reform. Of course folks are going to take the measure of the times and the issues generally, but most of them also take the measure of the person. They want to know, would they like to have a beer with you? Are you approachable? Does your life story line up with theirs in a way that makes them feel like they're connected to you in some way? Can you communicate with them in a way that makes sense to them and that motivates them? Are you real? Are you who you say you are?

In that regard, I went about my campaign the way I always had—connecting with people one-on-one, any way I could. When you're dealing with a statewide election or any election that's larger than a single town or district, it becomes increasingly important to reach people where they live. I needed to talk with them in their cars as they drove to work and chat with them in their living rooms. In other words, I needed radio and television time.

The television route would lead to one of the first major missteps of my political career and an embarrassment that nearly cost me the election.

To give a little context, in Minnesota campaigns, you're only allowed to raise money in certain amounts, and if you agree to abide by a spending cap, you can receive some of your campaign money from the state government. We agreed to the cap. In addition, other groups are allowed to make "independent" expenditures on behalf of your effort. So the Republican Party or some independent organization could take out an ad and say, "Support Tim Pawlenty," but they essentially couldn't talk to my campaign about when and how they were going to do that. It had to be independent, and if it wasn't independent, that's a potential violation of campaign rules and laws.

In addition to doing some fund-raising and barnstorming around the state to attend every gathering, function, and fair I could, I hired a media consultant to help create some television ads. We went out and shot a whole bunch of footage—in my front yard, in front of the former Applebaum's grocery store in South St. Paul, at my old high school. Typical political-ad fare that told the story of my upbringing and life as a Minnesotan. What happened next is where the problem arose. The media consultant sold some of that footage to the Republican Party, which began airing ads with that footage included, claiming it as an independent expenditure that wouldn't count against my campaign limit. The party properly paid for the footage.

My media consultant thought there was nothing wrong with selling that footage to the Republican Party, as long as the party leaders were the ones who decided when and how the party was going to buy ads, how much would be spent, or what channels the ads would air on. But when the ads aired, one of my opponents said, "Huh? How can this be an independent ad if Pawlenty's *in* it?" The Independence Party and some others filed complaints with the Campaign Finance and Public Disclosure Board in Minnesota, which led to an initial probable cause finding indicating the campaign may have violated the rules.

I had supporters, including seasoned lawyers, calling me saying, "Fight this! This is completely wrong. The campaign board's finding is unconstitutional. You have a right to free speech, and so does the party. The law prohibits coordination between the party and the candidate on expenditures, but it doesn't prohibit selling material at fair-market value. You can win this!" But in many ways, we had already lost. The only message voters were getting was this terrible controversy on the front page. The story became a huge deal in Minnesota at the time—above the fold, top of the newscast, "Pawlenty accused of campaign finance violations."

I felt indescribably horrible, and so did my team. Nobody had intended to do anything wrong, much less illegal, and everybody felt awful about it. This wasn't just about my campaign. We represented the Republican Party, and this gubernatorial race was a definitive one for the future of the state. And now it looked like one questionable decision could derail our efforts. Because the issue cast a shadow over the integrity of my campaign, it spiraled to the core of my being in a way that was deeply unsettling and discouraging.

But I had a decision to make. If we agreed with the finding without further contesting the matter, the entire cost of those ads would count against my total allotment for campaign spending. And those ads came in somewhere in the range of $500,000. There would also be a penalty for this activity in the amount of $100,000 or $150,000. Combined, these would deal a nearly devastating financial blow to the campaign.

"Tell the campaign board to pound sand. Assert your constitutional rights. Litigate this. Even if you have to forgo winning the election, you'll be in favor of free speech and you'll help resolve a key constitutional issue." Much of the advice I was receiving fell along these lines. But I didn't go that route. Instead, I decided I was going to take responsibility for the mistake. Whether the Constitution or other laws permitted it was a question that would have to wait for another time.

My campaign negotiated to accept the party's spending as counting toward our cap and to pay $100,000 or so on top of that in fines. The total impact was about $600,000. I held a press conference at the capitol—standing room only and packed with the kind of drama that anyone in my shoes would have wanted to avoid. But facing the matter square-on was my choice.

At the press conference, I said, essentially, "I don't necessarily agree with the decision, but my campaign will respect it, and I will take responsibility for the error."

At the time, I fully presumed that this would mean the end of my campaign. I thought it was over. I concluded I was going to lose. But I was willing to accept that as a consequence. At least I had dealt with the biggest event of the campaign head-on.

That press conference would wind up being a turning point in the campaign, all right, but not a negative turning point. Handling that controversy directly by taking responsibility actually turned into a net plus in the polling in the following days. It wasn't something I had expected, but it was something I would never forget.

Boldly, but short of funds, we soldiered ahead. Because of the settlement with the Campaign Finance Board, we could not afford to advertise for several crucial weeks leading up to the election. In the final weeks of the campaign, we used what money remained to toss up simple ads, hammering home the common sense platform I had been running on for years, going all the way back to my very first campaign for the legislature in 1992. The linchpin was my steadfast pledge: "No new taxes." I meant it. Our citizens paid too much in taxes, and I absolutely would not budge on that belief. There were other issues, too, of course. For example, I wanted to see performance-based pay for teachers and tax incentives for job growth. We also needed to put the state back on a more reasonable course after decades of runaway spending and liberal policies.

In the end, all I could do was hope my message had been heard.

★ ★ ★ ★ ★ ★ ★ ★ ★ ★

ON ELECTION DAY, Mary and I decided, among other things, to stop into Holy Trinity Church in South St. Paul. It was time to reflect on all we had been through—the incremental steps along the way, the twists and turns, and the very idea of running for Governor, which had become a reality. It also served as a moment to express gratitude and request guidance in prayer. Whatever the outcome, I was grateful for the opportunity and wanted to remain faithful to whatever path God would set before me.

We voted. We went to dinner with friends. Then we headed to the Radisson Hotel in Bloomington, where the Republican Party sponsored one big election-night event for candidates—including Norm Coleman, who won the U.S. Senate seat later that night.

Each of us had a room upstairs in the hotel, while friends,

family, and supporters gathered downstairs in a ballroom to wait for the election results to come in. Mary and I went up to our room and were visited by a few friends. I went downstairs early on for a short speech and to personally thank everyone I could for coming out and supporting us that night and during the campaign. Then, as is the tradition, I went to the room again to wait for the results.

At some point I realized there simply wasn't anything left to do. There wasn't a phone call to be made or a hand to shake. Staring at the television, watching every tick of the exit polls and early results didn't seem productive. So we took a nap.

We had an inkling of hope because the polls had turned positive for our campaign in the last few days. But still, this was Minnesota, a state that strongly favors Democrats, and my opponent, Roger Moe, was a towering political figure.

The nap didn't last long, and soon we were back to checking the television.

When the results were in, I'd won.

Not only that, but I'd won pulling away. In a three-way race, Moe received 37 percent of the vote, and Independence Party candidate Tim Penny garnered 16. I'd received 44. So in a race that most people, including Mary and me, thought was an uphill battle at best, we'd won by a comfortable margin.

Various supporters and campaign folks started to flood the room. I received the concession calls from my opponents. It was all a bit surreal. It still felt like a part of the campaign. The notion that I was now Governor-elect didn't fully set in until it was time to go downstairs for the victory speech. I hugged Mary before I left the room. What a strange life. We were taking it in, as we always had, moment by moment.

A few days before the election, we'd received a call from the

State Patrol asking if we wanted to start protective service. It was a courtesy they extend to all major candidates during the final days of any election, but Mary and I declined. We had been campaigning for over a year and been fine without it, so we waived it. But now two guys showed up at the door of my hotel room—one in a trench coat—both looking like Secret Service agents out of a movie. They were Troopers with the Executive Protection Detail of the Minnesota State Patrol.

The Troopers escorted me down the back elevator of the hotel, through the kitchen, into the massively crowded ballroom. I was positioned just behind and between them as they acted like a human snowplow, pushing their way into the crowd so I could get through. As I approached the podium, I stared at the backs of the Troopers and thought, *That seems wrong. These guys are blocking people from getting to me.* I didn't care for that. I didn't care for the message it sent. Here were my best supporters and friends and relatives who wanted to extend a hand of congratulations, and suddenly I had people in front of me keeping them at bay. It all happened so fast, there was no time to think or adjust, but I filed that feeling away to make sure my protective detail kept a comfortable distance at events in the future.

Standing up on that stage, in front of that crowd, was beyond what I could have expected. I had never really considered what that moment might feel like, but whatever I'd thought, the moment itself exceeded my expectations. The roar of the crowd, the lights, the banners, the support from hundreds of people in one room, all were amazing. Yet I couldn't enjoy it as much as I would have had Mary been there at my side. There she was, stuck up in a hotel room, minding the rules, watching on television. The one person most responsible for my success, observing from a distance.

So I made my speech, and the security guys escorted me out

of the ballroom, back to the room to get Mary, and out to a waiting black Ford Crown Victoria. They opened the car doors, and Mary and I climbed into the backseat of this modified police car, some stranger driving. *What a strange life,* I thought again. We didn't know who he was or what our relationship with him was supposed to be. We were just rolling with it. "Where do you want to go?" he asked.

We looked at each other and said, "Home."

As I said, no one gives you a handbook for this. There is no advance warning or coaching. We weren't sure whether we could talk freely or if our conversation might be repeated. So we sat quietly in the back of the car. I remember looking at Mary, and it didn't even need to be said. I could tell by her facial expression and her eyes that she was thinking the same thing I was. *This is weird!*

We both sensed our lives were entering an entirely new phase. There was no way to prepare. The only requirement was that we follow, step by step, the path as it was lit before us. The ride in the back of that car from the hotel to our home in Eagan symbolized a transition from what had been a fairly normal life to what would become a fairly unusual one. Without a word, that feeling struck both of us, simultaneously. We had approached the campaign with open hands and a certain casual sensibility, thinking, *I might win or I might not, but I'm sure going to give it my all.*

Now I'd won. Casual time was over.

11

★ ★ ★ ★ ★ ★ ★ ★ ★ ★

A LINE IN THE SAND

WHEN I WOKE UP the morning of November 6, 2002, I had one thing on my mind. I knew I had to live up to the promises I made to the people of Minnesota. I also knew fulfilling those promises would not be easy. The forces in favor of the status quo, the forces opposed to meaningful change—especially when it comes to shrinking the role of government in people's lives—were so large, so loud, and so powerful that any leader who stood up to say, "We're not going to do it that way anymore," would be met with thunderous opposition. It would take spine, resilience, and courage. It would take persistence and an unshakable commitment to never give up.

That, I was prepared for.

In recent years, a few conservative voices have referred to my fighting back against Minnesota's long-standing left-wing policies as "heroic." That's not a word I apply to myself. I've met plenty of true heroes during my time in office. That said, it does take an uncommon resolve to stand up and fight those forces. If you're not steeped in politics, you'd be astonished at the depth and breadth of the forces in Minnesota, and frankly across the country, that are opposed to restraining or reducing the growth of government.

I wish I could say the next few years turned into a glorious bipartisan exercise. Wouldn't that have been wonderful? It would have been so pleasant. I should have guessed from the battles in my life thus far that nothing would be so easy. There *were* a few such moments, and for those I am both proud and grateful. But from a broader perspective, it was a constant battle. The larger story features the value and impact of drawing a line in the sand and saying, "Enough." Enforcing that line was challenging. It was difficult. Frankly, at times it was painful. But that's the kind of resolve it took to get it done.

My eight years in office would be rife with head-on collisions, special sessions, constitutional issues, lawsuits, even a government shutdown. I wish the headlines could have read that Pawlenty mesmerized the liberals with his charm and wit and that they changed their views due to his winsome ways. But hard-fought battles over big issues are never that lovely. Once I drew a line in the sand and said I would not raise taxes—that neither businesses nor individuals are better off with heavier burdens—the options narrowed significantly. I could fight, or I could fold.

And I would never fold.

★ ★ ★ ★ ★ ★ ★ ★ ★ ★

PRIOR TO ACTUALLY WINNING THE ELECTION, I hadn't thought much about what the transition would involve. I never allowed myself to get ahead of the outcome of the vote, so I hadn't prepared too much for the aftermath of victory. The coming days would turn into a quick and complicated climb up the learning curve.

Waking to the strange sight of police cars and men in dark glasses in the driveway of my family's suburban home was step one. Meeting with outgoing Governor Jesse Ventura and hearing his response when I asked if he had any advice ("Nope") was step two. There were so many steps after that, I've lost track.

The day after the election, once the baton-passing press conference was over, Mary and I had a separate press conference together. Finally the people of Minnesota could see in the papers the next day, "Oh! This guy does have a wife!" Then we headed over to the hospital to spend some time with her father.

Perhaps if the transition had been the only thing on our minds, things wouldn't have seemed quite as complicated. But Mary's father was terminally ill.

I'm sure the support I offered Mary during that very difficult time was inadequate. Most of her sisters lived in other parts of the country, and her mom was in her eighties. In addition to caring for our girls and caring for me, Mary was dealing with the slow loss of her father, who was increasingly uncomfortable and in pain.

It felt as if we had been pushed into a high-speed turbowasher. Over the course of the next sixty days, we were spun around in just about every way imaginable. Every time we got a handle on one problem, something new would pop up.

The state gives the incoming Governor some money and some office space near the capitol for the transition, and we used it to quickly assemble a team. I brought in Charlie Weaver, a smart, likable guy whom I've known since law school, as chief of staff. Charlie served in the Ventura cabinet and was a former legislator. For the first few weeks it was basically Charlie and a small handful of others running the whole transition office. We started identifying the slots that had to get filled, and some folks from my campaign and others broke into committees to head up the HR functions. We also needed to figure out a Governor's-office budget, a staffing model, and a cabinet. The transition office and effort grew quickly to a staff of thirty, then forty full-timers, part-timers, and volunteers.

At the same time, we needed to fund and plan an inaugural, which, for a new Governor and a party that had been out of power for a while, was a big deal. We needed a whole separate crew of people to crank up rooms, bands, streamers, lights, and sound systems—not just for the inaugural ball but for an entire week's worth of inaugural festivities. We planned to hold a prayer service at our church, set up a Governor's hockey game to play against the former Governor's hockey team, read to schoolchildren, and more. It was like planning a wedding—times ten—on short notice. Seven days of functions and parties and events to be planned, funded, invited, RSVP'd—only this wasn't the private sector; it was government, meaning that everything was databased, compliance checked, and overseen by lawyers and accountants.

Then there was the Governor's Residence that needed management, a State of the State speech that needed to be written, a budget that needed preparation, and of course there was the $4.6-billion budget deficit that needed immediate attention. Thanksgiving and Christmas came and went quickly.

The amazing thing was, none of it felt like a burden. I felt every bit of what we were doing truly mattered. All of it was done with as much effort and passion and commitment as we could bring to it. It was all hands on deck, all in, all hours, all days. And that's how my administration would run from that day forward. I expected nothing less. That office was bigger than me—bigger than all of us—and I did my best to surround myself with people who understood that.

Even so, you've got to let the steam out of the pressure cooker every once in a while. I appreciated the occasional, much-needed run or, better yet, inline skating with hockey stick in hand. Some people come back from a run and want to collapse on the couch, I realize. But for me, a run is better than a nap. I come back feeling focused and reenergized.

Sometime during the first few days of the transition, I found a moment one morning to slip out of my house in Eagan and go inline skating. Just a few miles from my house, I remembered I was scheduled to do a call-in interview with a local radio station, so I skated into a gas station and hopped on a phone. The radio host asked what I had been up to that morning, and I said, "Well, I got up and I came out inline skating. In fact, I'm calling you from this gas station in Eagan." I hadn't realized I shouldn't be out there alone. One of the Troopers happened to be listening to the interview. He heard me reveal my location and peeled out of the driveway to find me. The routine of the omnipresent Troopers hadn't yet sunk in.

I soon learned the value of a security detail, though. One night about 3 a.m. we were startled awake by the sound of a helicopter hovering above the trees in our usually peaceful neighborhood. Outside our window was a scene of flashing lights and multiple squad cars. Someone dressed in all black and a ski mask had approached our house, but when the Troopers spotted him, he took off into the park across the street. The neighbors, fortunately, were patient with the commotion.

Adjusting to the constant presence of total strangers in the form of State Troopers was particularly challenging because Anna and Mara were still just little girls. We had no way of knowing at the time how much we'd learn to value the Troopers' loyalty, their professionalism, and even their sense of humor. Every day seemed to bring an odd new experience. The first time the girls threw their backpacks into the back of the Navigator I'd inherited from Governor Ventura, I noticed a machine gun. Apparently the gun was at the ready in case of a hijacking or shoot-out. To my knowledge, no Governor of Minnesota had ever been involved in such a thing, so I asked the guys to take it out. I'm not opposed to guns. I'm pro-gun. I own guns. But the machine gun was going to have to make way for flowered backpacks and soccer equipment.

* * * * * * * * * *

THE WEEKEND BEFORE MY INAUGURATION was originally set to become a twofold celebration. The fact that Mary's family would be coming into town meant we could gather everyone for a birthday party for her father that Sunday afternoon before the scheduled swearing-in on Monday. He was terminally ill and fading, but still alert, so we wanted to make sure that birthday was a happy one—he'd be surrounded by those he loved and those who loved him.

But God had something different in mind. The Friday before I was sworn in, Mary's father passed away. So what was to have been his birthday party became, instead, his funeral. Friday was spent writing the obituary, outlining the eulogy, and preparing for the funeral service and burial. We leaned heavily on our pastor, Leith Anderson, throughout The Weekend—as it would come to be known in our family. He was there for us, supporting us both privately and publicly. He presided over the funeral on Sunday. Less than twenty-four hours later, he presided over the prayer service that marked the beginning of inauguration day.

Sixty days. A bullet-train ride on a roller-coaster track. And I hadn't even begun my time in office.

* * * * * * * * * *

WHEN I SPOKE of a line in the sand and took a no-new-taxes stance during my campaign, repeating that pledge again during my first State of the State address, I'm sure some people, especially those on the left, thought it was nothing more than a bullheaded political maneuver—as if the line itself were an act meant to draw attention. As if the gesture were somehow empty, an exercise in sound-bite politicking that would blow away in the gales of the ever-shifting political landscape. They were wrong.

My desire to cut spending and reduce the size and role of government is not driven by polls or a series of check marks on a scorecard of how to win an election. I've simply had enough with the growth of government. And I'm not alone. People all over America have had enough too.

I believed in my heart, my mind, and my gut that Minnesotans had been led astray by liberal policies. In the course of my lifetime, Minnesota had become a place where the government was the primary caretaker for too many people, which meant many people no longer had any incentive to plan and take care of themselves. For example, our transit system's bus drivers were retiring after only fifteen years on the job and yet were qualifying for government-paid health insurance for the rest of their lives. We lived in a state where teachers' salaries increased year after year based on seniority rather than results. Public-employee pensions and well-intentioned social service programs were on autopilot, and their costs were out of control.

Besides those individual examples, the big picture was even uglier. From 1960, the year I was born, until I became Governor, the average two-year spending increase in my state's budget was 21 percent! The state of Minnesota had become so addicted to big government, it needed an intervention. That's what I was here for—fresh off an election and with a Republican majority in the House that shared my views.

I firmly believe government must be limited, effective, and prioritized. It's what our Founding Fathers envisioned. Unfortunately Minnesota had been heading in the opposite direction for many decades. The same is true today at the federal level, and it's frightening. What happens when government grows at an unlimited pace? We all suffer—in ways we may not even perceive until it's too late.

Endless government growth becomes a form of tyranny. When the government takes up more and more space—space that was previously reserved for individuals, families, the faith community, charities, markets, and the private sector—the result is more displacement, discouragement, disincentive, and dependency. As government swells to become nearly everyone's financial nanny, freedom and personal responsibility are diminished. Each day, with one more encroachment, liberal, big-government policies chip away at the pillars of our country, stripping away one more piece of our freedom. Government overreach slowly suffocates our human spirit. And it drowns our entrepreneurial ambition.

Mary and I had lunch not long ago with a young businessman. A few years back, he took a calculated risk and made it big in the new North Dakota oil boom. He described to us his frustrations with the current trajectory of the government's economic policies and the burdens it heaps on him daily. "Governor, I have so many ideas," he said, "so much energy, and the resources to take more risk. I should be going at Mach 5 with my hair on fire, hiring everyone in this restaurant and telling them to start Monday. But you know what I'm doing? Nothing!" He felt he had no way of discerning where the next government burden would fall or what new government program would, yet again, drive up the cost of doing business. So rather than investing or starting and growing new businesses and providing more jobs, he's sitting on his hands.

Government should be in the business of igniting, not extinguishing, the American spirit. When someone faces too many government barriers or has little individual incentive, that person's attitude shifts away from being industrious and hardworking. Away from creating and designing and dreaming and working or taking that extra risk to start a business. That spirit, that drive, is replaced by a kind of lethargy. Even if the spark is there, the incentives are not, and so complacency sets in.

We've reached a troubling point in America. The Associated Press recently reported that 47 percent of Americans didn't pay any federal income tax in 2009. Forty-seven percent! Now, consider also all those whose jobs are not generated by the private sector but by government. I'm talking about all employees who work directly for the government or whose jobs are funded at government expense. That includes the federal government, state governments, townships, cities, school districts, and counties, as well as intermediate levels of government like the mosquito-control district and waste management, plus those organizations that receive public funding. That sure looks and feels to me like a country that has become addicted to government. How can that *not* be dispiriting? The kind of collective lethargy we see now is reminiscent of what we've seen in Greece and other places where large numbers of citizens think of the government as their primary caretaker. We've been drifting in that direction for quite some time, and the Obama administration has fully and enthusiastically embraced that vision for America.

Greece is often cited as the home of democracy. But just because we followed them into democracy doesn't mean we have to follow them into bankruptcy. The get-up-and-go of many of the people of Greece drifted away long ago. The entitlement mentality has set in to such an extent that very few people think they need to work hard—or work at all. They expect wildly ridiculous early retirement and unsustainable social programs. It sounds dramatic, I realize, to think that's where America could be headed. But I see the signs all around us. It's as if we've been slowly letting the air out of the tire. The pinholes are so small at first that you don't even notice. Eventually you start to see the tire sag a little, but you keep on driving. But when it finally goes all the way flat—or, worse, has a blowout—you're going to know about it!

The good news is we can patch those holes and reinflate the tire. But we have to act quickly. We need to firmly reject the government-as-nanny mentality and insist on a proper balance between the private sector and the public sector, between individual responsibility and government responsibility. Minnesota had most definitely mixed up those priorities on a state level by 2002, and we've done the same thing in a major way in America today.

Think back to 1979. Jimmy Carter was President. The economy was in deep trouble. Then up stepped Ronald Reagan, saying, "There is a better way. America has certain values and ideals that have made us great, and greatness doesn't include having the government do everything."

We are not a nanny nation. Free people don't need a nanny. We don't need a big bureaucracy to dictate our every decision. Government in America is meant to be limited, smart, and effective. Government has an important role in our lives, but its role is not to swallow us up. Government, most importantly, needs to respond to, not direct, the will of its citizens. Abraham Lincoln famously championed the importance of *who's in charge* in America when he said, "We here highly resolve that . . . this nation, under God, shall have a new birth of freedom—and that government of the people, by the people, for the people, shall not perish from the earth."

Americans are fundamentally strong, good, kind, innovative, inventive, hardworking, and fiercely independent. We're unlike any other country in the world. The government should be there to give a hand when it's needed and set reasonable limits where appropriate. But then government needs to back off.

* * * * * * * * * *

THAT FIRST LEGISLATIVE SESSION was tumultuous, to say the least. Republicans controlled the House. Democrats held control of the Senate. In my first State of the State address, I reiterated my campaign promises: *"We will not raise taxes. We will reduce spending. We will grow jobs."*

The pressure was on. Some of the measures I suggested were must-do initiatives. Others I knew were long shots. The Senate basically responded to everything by saying, "Go fish. We're gonna do it our way."

As the session unfolded, the Republicans in the House had my back. When the Senate drew up a bad proposal, the House members did their best to kill it or clean it up before it came my way for a signature or veto.

Stepping into the Governor's office in the final months of an existing budget cycle felt like being put in as quarterback in the fourth quarter of a championship game. And the clock was ticking toward the deadline to finalize a budget for the upcoming two-year period. The fact that I hadn't budged on my stance on taxes meant the only possible way to ever meet the budget deadline was to cut and cut deeply. With a two-on-one fight coming from the Governor's office and the House, the Senate would have to find a way to accept the cuts we wanted to make to the budget or risk going into a government shutdown.

As the end of the session approached with no resolution, I convened a special session of the legislature to give the negotiations more time.

I actually learned a bit about the art of negotiation from Roger Moe, my DFL rival in the Governor's race. The man had served as Majority Leader in the Senate since 1981 and clearly knew a thing or two about winning negotiations. When I was Majority Leader in the House, I noticed Moe would often disappear about four o'clock in the afternoon. I always wondered what he was up to. Finally I asked him. He told me he went for a jog or to catch a shower and a good meal. He took that time-out so he could come back refreshed and have a leg up on his unrefreshed rivals if a session were to draw out late into the evening.

The Governor's Residence was a quick five-minute drive from the capitol, so I started following that same routine. After a quick afternoon run and shower, I was good to go, while legislators were often stuck at the capitol. It was a minor advantage, but one that mattered. Staying alert while your opponent is wearing down is one way to gain an edge. I knew it was important to set the tone in that very first legislative session if I had any hope of accomplishing my goals in the next four years.

As the special legislative session wound down, everyone was ready to go home. The members wanted to wrap up their part-time legislative duties and get back to their other lives. There were parents with kids who would soon be home for the summer and workers whose employers expected they would be back on the clock. Summer vacation plans were approaching. The ticking clock was a big advantage. That, along with the will of the people.

Finally I got a phone call. "The Senate Majority Leader wants to see you. He wants to see you alone, face-to-face."

John Hottinger, the new Senate Majority Leader and longtime member of the legislature, walked into my office and closed the door. I came out from behind the Governor's desk as he sat down in one of the visitors' chairs in my office. I sat in the other. And then I listened.

The deal he offered was this: The Democrat-controlled Senate would pass my bills and most of my budget cuts, but he wanted me to be responsible for making sure there was complete Republican support for each measure, and then the Democrats would put forth only the minimum number of votes needed to get those measures passed. The Democrats who would vote with the Republicans were senior members with very secure seats. They wouldn't need to worry much about their votes coming back to haunt them in elections down the road. They weren't happy about it, he said, but they would hold their noses and vote with the Republicans.

I agreed. And I did my part. If I didn't get 100 percent of the Senate Republicans behind a certain measure, I got close. And even though those bills were offensive to the liberals who controlled the Senate, we passed much of what needed to pass to begin setting Minnesota back on a course of fiscal responsibility in an incredibly difficult economic climate.

The press had gotten wind that something was finally happening, and when I walked out of the capitol, I found a swarm of reporters. "We've reached agreement," I said.

Someone in that huge press gaggle shouted, "What's the agreement?"

And I responded, "They'll pass all our bills."

I didn't mean for it to come off as gloating. But it did.

The positive aspects of so much of what we did were immediately overshadowed by oversimplified media accounts of the battle between right and left. It was reported as a near-total political and policy victory for me. As a result, Democrats walked away from that session feeling like they had been steamrolled. Now, I'll admit, our side cleaned up. But I made a mistake in tone in making the Democrats feel so thoroughly beaten. They became very bitter and resolved to never let me win again. Often lessons are learned in defeat. But this one I learned in victory. A measure of grace is always essential. I should have recognized that the manner in which we fought that spring only foreshadowed the depth and breadth of bigger battles to come.

12

AMERICAN HEROES

ANYONE WHO WALKED into my capitol office during my eight years as Governor must have noticed the mementos I had on display. They didn't relate to budget battles or victories over Democrats. They reflected another gubernatorial duty: Commander in Chief of the Minnesota National Guard. That position—especially the opportunity to associate with the men and women in our military—was one of the most meaningful parts of the job of Governor.

By law, Governors act as National Guard commanders in chief only when the Guard is on a state mission, rather than a federal one. Those state missions include responses to natural disasters or providing security in extraordinary circumstances or events, such as the Republican National Convention, which was held in Minnesota in 2008. Once deployed for a federal mission—the Iraq war, for example—a Guard unit is placed under the command of federal officials. A massive number of our finest and bravest Minnesotans were deployed overseas during my time as Governor. They included members of the Minnesota National Guard but also many members of the active military and reserve units.

While I never served in the military, I have enormous respect and reverence for the men and women who do. We would not have the country we have without their service, courage, duty, patriotism, and honor. Mary and I always tried our best to honor the commitment and service of our armed forces by doing all we could to support these outstanding heroes and their families. For example, I made it a personal mission to appear at every deployment ceremony I could during my time in office—as well as every funeral for the fallen.

The mementos I collected and kept in my capitol office were there for a reason. They were a constant reminder to me and my visitors of what real courage and real sacrifice for our country looks like.

A Minnesota flag flown by one of our National Guard units in Iraq in 2005 was one of my favorite mementos. It came back dusty and torn, and it hung in my office in that condition, which I thought was appropriate.

In the conference room just outside my office, I kept a display of military coins—each emblazoned with the individual insignia of the units I've encountered. Military commanders present these coins as a gesture of respect or appreciation. At one point, I was told of an interesting tradition for military members: the person with the coin from the lowest-ranking commander buys the beer. That's my kind of tradition! I haven't tried it, even though I have coins from some pretty high-ranking commanders, because I'm not sure it's really true. Plus, I should be the one buying for these guys anyhow.

In my conference room I hung a signed photo from Bruce Springsteen: "To Tim and Mary—If I should fall behind . . ." (a reference to one of his songs). A friend of mine picked that up for me. I'm a huge fan of the Boss—although he probably didn't know I was a Republican when he signed that photo! But almost all the other wall and display space in that conference room was covered with tributes and remembrances from the moments I was fortunate enough to spend with the members of our military here or overseas. There were photos from Minnesota's 148th Fighter Wing, pictures of our Red Bull Division—the modern offspring of what used to be the Minnesota First, which played a pivotal role at Gettysburg—and a bird's-eye shot of more than three thousand Minnesota National Guard members in full battle gear at their deployment ceremony in Camp Shelby, Mississippi, just before they shipped out to Iraq. In the middle of all that, I kept my father's burial flag and the dog tags that he wore as a member of the Air Force during World War II.

My dad passed away in 2000. Even throughout the course of his last few months, when our family came to understand how badly his health was declining, he never complained. His upbeat nature and sense of humor remained largely intact. It was difficult to watch him decline. Here was a man who loved life and brought so much happiness to those around him. He had remarried when I was in college, and he enjoyed his later years, relaxing at the cabin, telling stories, and visiting with friends and family. I miss him.

He didn't have a chance to see me become Governor, and neither did my mom, of course. It would have been great to have them at events like the inauguration and other big moments. My dad did have a chance to see much of my work in the legislature, though, and he was incredibly proud. That I know.

Like many World War II veterans, my dad didn't speak much about the war. It would take an effort to get him to open up about it. But even as a kid, I knew his service to our country impacted him deeply. I often thought of that as I tried my best to encourage and support our military members.

* * * * * * * * * *

I REMEMBER MY FIRST deployment ceremony vividly. I flew up to Camp Ripley with the Adjutant General (TAG) at the time, Major General Eugene Andreotti, and we walked into this 1960s vintage gymnasium. The Guard had earlier presented me with a leather flight jacket with a patch on the front that read, *Tim Pawlenty, Commander in Chief.* I rarely wore it. Not because I didn't like it. Just the opposite. I was really honored to have it. But I didn't want anyone to think I was trying to pretend that I had been in the military at any point or that I was trying too hard to look like a member of the military. I thought such a conclusion could be disrespectful to military members.

The deploying soldiers were in a two-column formation on the right side of the stage, and the audience, made up of family members and friends, sat in folding chairs on the gymnasium floor. After remarks and a short program, the General and I did a pass in review, where we walked behind the soldiers, then walked in front of them and eyeballed them in a ceremonial review of their readiness. They stood at attention as we gave them the once-over. It was a ceremonial nod, as if to say, "You're ready."

I was tremendously moved by the ceremony and the chance to see and meet these soldiers. I can still feel the lump in my throat from that day, especially from some of the comments shared. It marked the beginning of a long series of military-related events that would carry me around the world, allowing me to repeatedly and sincerely express Minnesota's respect and appreciation for these outstanding men and women, whenever and wherever I could.

It's one thing to hear about military service. It's another to go eyeball to eyeball with soldiers going off to war—to hear their family stories and their hardships, to hear what they believe, and to hear why they're making this sacrifice. Like everything else in life, you can read about it or you can watch it on television, but when you look into the eyes of a man or woman who's about to deploy or who has been through a life-changing experience, it's a whole different level of human connection and understanding. As Governor, I was the state official most responsible for making sure these brave men and women were treated right when they left and, just as important, treated well when they came home.

I came into office at an unusual time in the history of the National Guard. TAG laid it out for me on the plane on the way up to that first deployment ceremony. "Look, you are a wartime Governor," he said. "In the history of the state, there've been wars, but there've only been a few times when the National Guard has been this massively and this intensely deployed." It didn't happen in Vietnam, and it didn't happen in Korea. It happened to some degree in World War I and World War II, but only a few times in the state's history had the governorship featured this much involvement with the military.

From the invasion of Iraq in March 2003 to the end of 2010, eighteen thousand men and women from Minnesota's National Guard were deployed. That number doesn't include the reserve or active military members. Minnesota has the fifth-largest National

Guard in the country, and those brave men and women have been called upon to fight the War on Terror in extraordinary numbers.

As Commander in Chief of the Minnesota National Guard, I knew a good deal of my time and attention needed to be focused on them and on military issues. They deserved that and much more. In addition to showing up at events, I also made sure that military and veterans' issues were on the top of the legislative priority list. My administration modernized, enhanced, and improved the support for men and women in the military and their families in a nation-leading way during my time as Governor. I am most proud of the work we accomplished in that regard.

* * * * * * * * * *

MY COMMITMENT TO OUR MILITARY grew deeper as months and years passed and the sacrifice these heroes made became dramatically and painfully apparent for so many Minnesota families.

On July 3, 2003, Army Pfc. Edward J. "Jim" Herrgott, a twenty-year-old from Shakopee, was killed by a sniper while on patrol outside a Baghdad museum. He was the first Minnesotan to die in Iraq that year. Two more would follow: thirty-five-year-old Staff Sergeant Brian Hellermann of Freeport and Army Staff Sergeant Dale Panchot, twenty-six, of Northome.

I remember flying north for Dale Panchot's funeral. Northome is way up there. It was a forty-five-minute drive from the small airport we flew into. It's rural. Really rural, actually. They held the service in the high school gymnasium, and it was packed. The whole town must have been there. It seemed everything in the town came to a standstill for his service.

The flag-draped coffin was in the front of the gymnasium when I arrived. I paid respects and sat down. Later I offered words of condolences to the family and to those in attendance. Words in those circumstances always seem so inadequate, but I tried my best to convey sincere appreciation and gratitude for what his service represented. The community outpouring of respect and affection for this soldier, this young man, was magnificent. He was killed in the Sunni Triangle while on patrol near the city of Balad. Most Americans have never heard of these places. Most couldn't point to them on a map, but this twenty-six-year-old gave his life in that strange, far-off place because his country asked him to do it. The truck he had been riding in was ambushed, according to reports—fired upon by automatic weapons and rocket-propelled grenades. Dale enlisted in the reserves at age seventeen. He had already served nine years, following in the footsteps of his father and his grandfather. He had plans to finish college and to someday start a family. Now those days would never come.

Dale's family and friends buried him on a hillside just outside of town. It was cold, and the wind was whipping. Everyone was bundled up, standing in this stark landscape, surrounded by leafless trees, laying a soldier to rest in small-town America.

Nine more would die in 2004. Eighteen lost their lives in 2005. By the end of my two terms as Governor, I would attend more than fifty soldiers' funerals.

As time went on, I came to know more and more of the soldiers and their families. At deployment ceremonies, Mary and I stayed afterward, no matter how long it took, to greet every single one who wanted to shake our hands or take a picture. It was important to us to let them know how much their service was appreciated. It was our way of saying, "Thank you." Of letting them know that their Governor and the citizens of their state were grateful for their sacrifices. It wasn't me, Tim Pawlenty, that mattered in those moments. It was the office I represented, the office of Governor, the position of their Commander in Chief.

It was not uncommon at funerals for the family to display photos of their son, and they periodically included one taken of the two of us at his deployment ceremony. In those cases, I was present for one of the last photos a family took of their child before losing him to the war. The impact of that was not lost on me.

Those of us who have not experienced this type of loss can only imagine what family members of fallen soldiers feel, but I know their sadness is accompanied by great pride in the service their sons and daughters provided.

I learned long ago that different people grieve differently and that different things comfort them. At times it felt appropriate to share some insight, perhaps from our common faith, and I would. Other times, I think just my being present helped some grieving families recognize how much their loved one's sacrifice meant to our state.

Of course our nation's commitment to members of the military must go beyond our words and attendance at events. Our deeds must also match our words. That's why I worked so hard to make sure Minnesota's military- and veteran-support programs were nation-leading.

An example is our Beyond the Yellow Ribbon program. It was first envisioned by Major General Larry Shellito, who took over as TAG in November 2003, and Chaplain John Morris. It provides needed programs and services for returning military members and their families to ease the transition and reintegration back into civilian life. It is the best reintegration program in the country. The federal government routinely recognizes it as the model for other states to follow.

* * * * * * * * * *

IF YOU'RE EVER FEELING SKEPTICAL about whether our country is still producing great, patriotic, strong people, just go spend some time with the amazing men and women of our military. They'll put you in the right frame of mind in a hurry. When you think about the sacrifices they make, the way they are willing to lay their lives on the line for our country, our freedoms, and each and every one of us, it is absolutely inspiring.

They don't have to do it. They volunteer. They raise their hands. They step forward. They say, "If my country needs me, I'll go do this." For a year or more at a crack, they leave their families, their communities, their hobbies, their recreational pursuits, and their places of worship behind. You will never meet finer people.

They understand service beyond self—and they live it. They conduct themselves with decorum and respect. Their service and the values that service represents exemplify why this country is so great, why this country is so good, and why this country can continue to be great and good in the future.

Seeing our military men and women in action and witnessing up close the conditions they endure only drives home that point.

In the early months of 2004, just before the one-year anniversary of the Iraq invasion, I received a call from the Department of Defense in Washington, asking if I would like to take part in a trip to Baghdad to visit the troops and learn more about the situation in Iraq. These trips are a fairly common occurrence now, but back then, it was unheard of for Governors. I said, "Of course!" and was instructed to secretly send them some paperwork and to keep the whole trip under wraps. The only people on my staff who knew about it beforehand were my chief of staff and my press secretary. They really wanted to keep this thing quiet for security reasons.

Six Governors met in Washington to begin the journey. The first stop was the Pentagon, where we received a number of briefings, including one from Defense Secretary Donald Rumsfeld. We then headed to Andrews Air Force Base to board one of the planes that serves as Air Force Two—a 757—and flew to Amman, Jordan. From there, we hopped a C-130 to Baghdad.

We were given helmets and Kevlar vests, and we traveled a route along the Syrian border. At one point, one of the crew yelled out over the rumbling sound of that big old plane, "We're now in Iraqi air space." I looked out the little window near the back, but I couldn't see much of anything. Just the notion of being in Iraq seemed surreal. The war was about a year old at that point, and after a quick and relatively smooth invasion, hopes were high it would go reasonably well.

Our approach into Baghdad underscored the significance of ongoing security concerns. We were told the plane would not land in a normal way. Instead, the plane would do a corkscrew landing. We were told, "Sit down and strap in!" We were about to drop from our high, out-of-shooting-range altitude all the way down to Baghdad International Airport in a big hurry.

Before the trip, another Governor who knew about the corkscrew landings had bought me some brown underwear as a joke, saying, "Just in case you soil yourself." A corkscrew landing is just what it sounds like. The plane suddenly drops toward the ground, going round and round and round in the shape of a corkscrew, mixing up the pattern now and then so the plane would be harder to shoot down. Even in a cargo plane as big as the C-130, we were pulling g's, which is interesting but kind of unsettling. A different plane we used later on that same trip actually got shot at, and that experience repeated itself on a future trip to Iraq when I was in a helicopter. Also unsettling.

When we landed that first time, someone dropped the back gate of the C-130 into the dusty, sandblasted landscape, and one of our greeters yelled out, "Welcome to Baghdad!"

Civilian and military leaders met us. We piled into armored SUVs and drove at high speed down Ambush Alley—then one of the most dangerous roads in the world, between the airport and the Green Zone—where we met Paul Bremer, the administrator charged with overseeing Iraq, in one of Saddam Hussein's old palaces.

It was all a whirlwind and a completely new experience for a kid from South St. Paul. And yet, it's extraordinary how much information you can process when you're thrown into a new situation like that. I came away from the trip with a fuller understanding of our intentions, capabilities, mission, and resolve than I could ever have received from watching the news, reading a white paper, or even talking to our soldiers upon their return.

Here's one funny story from that trip, just to give some sense of the complex rebuilding effort we faced in Iraq. At one point, our guides took us to downtown Baghdad and gave us a chance to walk around a bit and chat with Iraqi shopkeepers. (I wouldn't say we *freely* walked around, since there was a fully armed Apache helicopter hovering seventy-five yards overhead and a perimeter of heavily armed American soldiers keeping an eye on us at all times.)

I was chumming around with Governor George Pataki of New York during this part of our exploratory trip. Imagine two tall white guys walking around the streets of Baghdad, approaching old guys with cigarettes and other strangers on the street and saying, "Hey, how's the war going for you?" Though the responses came through a translator, we heard everything from, "Saddam's horrible. I'm glad he's gone," to "This is awful! You Americans aren't doing enough!" We asked one shopkeeper what his main beef was with the Americans, and he complained, "I only get twelve hours of electricity a day." We said we'd relay his complaint.

Then, just before we walked away, Pataki had the presence of mind to ask, "How many hours of electricity did you get when Saddam was here?"

The man replied, "Eight!"

Pataki and I had a laugh over that. Look, if I were that shop-keeper, I'd want twenty-four hours of nonstop electricity too. It's hard for most Americans, even some of the poorest people in this country, to imagine going half a day, every day, without electricity. At least we were improving the situation incrementally.

Another Defense Department trip to Iraq allowed me to accompany John McCain to Fallujah as he began to lay the groundwork for his push for the visionary and daring surge that would help turn the tide on what many felt was a losing battle in Iraq.

In the coming years, I would wind up traveling to Iraq five times and Afghanistan three, with side trips to Kuwait and Jordan in between, plus separate military trips to visit Minnesota's National Guard contingent in Bosnia and Kosovo. There were many incredible moments.

En route to visit our Minnesota National Guard peacekeeping troops in Bosnia, our commercial flight out of Budapest was canceled due to bad weather. Mary and I had already flown from Minnesota to Amsterdam and then to Budapest. We were on a tight timeline and were only going to have a couple of days with the troops as it was, and we didn't want to miss our chance. So our small team rented vans and drove through the night across Croatia in thick fog to the Bosnian border. There we met a unit of our Minnesota soldiers in the middle of a bridge that connected the two countries. It was like a prisoner exchange scene in an old movie. We drove to a midpoint on the bridge. They greeted us in full gear with a convoy of armored vehicles behind them. It was still dark and foggy. "Governor Pawlenty," Colonel Gutknecht said in his deep, gravelly voice, "welcome to the Balkans."

It was our first stay on a forward operating base (FOB) in

Bosnia, and we got a few hours' sleep before an early morning briefing and a good visit with the troops. Peacekeeping in Bosnia and Kosovo mattered, and our Minnesota National Guard personnel understood their mission. Unlike the U.N. Dutch "peacekeeping" force whose inaction allowed the atrocities at Srebrenica, the worst massacre in Europe since World War II, our troops were prepared to act. As we stood at the Srebrenica-Potočari Memorial and Cemetery on a chilly, gray day, it was a grim and heartbreaking reminder of the purpose of the mission.

Year after year, I had the great honor to witness, firsthand and up close, the great work of our troops and the ability of the United States of America to project its presence around the world. America's capacity to mobilize is stunningly impressive.

Every trip made me appreciate our military even more. But seeing our great country's capabilities (including the ability to guide a bomb through the roof of one of Saddam's bedrooms with such precision that it left the remainder of the palace untouched and intact) and the great resolve of our troops did not diminish my understanding of the human cost of war.

On a trip to Basra in 2009, I arrived on base just a couple of days after a crudely made rocket landed in the middle of a group of American MPs—taking the lives of three Minnesotans in a single blow. I met with the chaplain who was with those servicemen in their final moments. He handed me a piece of metal about three inches wide and long. It was thick, dark in color, and textured to the touch. It was jagged and broken at its edges. I didn't realize what it was at first. Then he explained that it was a piece of the very rocket that had killed those fine young men.

I keep that piece of metal on my desk at our home in Eagan. I see it almost every single day. It's a cold, hard, jagged reminder. We should never forget their sacrifice.

★ ★ ★ ★ ★ ★ ★ ★ ★ ★

AFTER THAT FIRST TRIP to Iraq in 2004, the other Governors and I were scheduled to stop at the Pentagon to share our thoughts with stateside military leaders. Before we had a chance to do that, right after we landed, we were invited to visit with President Bush in the Oval Office to give him a firsthand briefing about our experience on the ground in Iraq.

I have an official White House photo of that moment. I didn't realize until I saw the picture afterward that I was suffering a serious case of bed head that morning. The Governors sat on the sofas. The President and Dick Cheney sat in the chairs by the fireplace, and behind us, milling about, were Colin Powell and Condoleezza Rice. Stories from our interactions with the shopkeepers and citizens on the streets of Baghdad were certainly part of the conversation, as were our observations about troop morale, which was really high.

The occasion reminded me of the previous time I met with the President in the White House just before the start of the war in Iraq. Shortly after my inauguration in 2003, I was in a meeting at the Old Executive Office Building next to the White House with some other Governors. A few of us were invited to the White House to meet with the President. I assumed the meeting was a courtesy meeting, and I appreciated the President's taking the time to say hello.

But almost as soon as President Bush settled into his seat in the Roosevelt Room, he began talking about Iraq. He was fully engaged, and it was clear Iraq was at the top of his mind. His determination on the topic was evident. As I left the Roosevelt Room and walked down the White House driveway after talking to the President of the United States about the possibility of the nation going to war, I knew that my job as Governor was going to be broader in scope than I might have imagined.

* * * * * * * * * *

THE MORALE OF OUR TROOPS is one of the most amazing and inspiring aspects of their service. It's a great lesson for all of us: no matter how big the challenges we face may be, it is possible to overcome significant obstacles if we keep a positive attitude.

Let me give you two dramatic examples.

I first met Staff Sergeant John Kriesel during a visit to Walter Reed Medical Center. I walked into his room, and his hospital gown was half-off his body—instantly revealing to me the pain he'd been through. This young man had lost both his legs and two of his friends, Specialist Bryan McDonough and Specialist Corey Rystad, to a roadside bomb in Iraq. He had a scar that ran from below his navel all the way to his upper esophagus. His wife sat beside him as he told me about what he had been through. What we know now is that a group of soldiers refused to let him die, and his recovery has been extraordinary. He's been shipped to four different hospitals and believes he actually died on the operating table three times while enduring a series of surgeries.

As I spoke with him that day, he told me how fortunate he felt, how blessed he was, how thankful to God he was. He told me how proud he felt to be an American soldier and serve our country, and how he would do it all over again and go back right now if they'd let him. He spoke about how much he loved his wife and what an angel she had been throughout his recovery. He could not have been stronger, more positive, or more committed. At one point during our meeting, he blurted out, "I'm gonna come back to Minnesota and run for Governor!" I told him without hesitating that I would help him if that ever happened.

Guess what? He's back in Minnesota today, and in the fall of 2010, he ran for state representative in a tough race.

John also released a book about his life story. It's called *Still Standing*. I wrote the foreword to that book. I think I turned down every other request during my time in office to write forewords for various authors. But for John, I made an exception. He is an amazing guy. Go to his Web site. Read the book. You'll see what I mean.

The second example is Staff Sergeant Chad Malmberg, a man who demonstrated "gallantry in action" while deployed to Iraq. Assigned to the 2nd Battalion, 35th Infantry, Chad was the first Minnesota National Guardsman since World War II to be awarded a Silver Star. It's an extraordinary achievement. I was called on to pin that star on his uniform during a ceremony in St. Paul Civic Center in September 2007. The ceremony was held in a large auditorium filled with members of the military, along with their friends and family. During the program, we all learned the details of Malmberg's heroic acts.

On January 27, 2007, Staff Sergeant Malmberg departed Baghdad International Airport commanding a convoy escort team of five gun trucks and twenty logistical vehicles. As they traveled through Ambush Alley, the convoy in front of his was struck by an improvised explosive device, requiring him to stop his vehicles. What he didn't know at that moment was that his convoy was being ambushed by an anti-Iraqi force of thirty to forty fighters. When his convoy came under attack by rocket-propelled grenades and small arms, he took full command of the battle. For nearly fifty minutes of heavy and direct enemy fire, Staff Sergeant Malmberg directed the actions of his five gun trucks and continually moved his truck to the area of the heaviest fighting. He coordinated fire, situational reports, communications between the three units on the ground, and air support. Under heavy fire, Malmberg repeatedly exited his vehicle to protect his convoy and engage the enemy. As the hostile forces drew closer, he recognized that his convoy could be overrun. He selflessly stood in the "kill zone" and threw a hand grenade into a nearby ditch, killing several insurgents. Far outnumbered, Staff Sergeant Chad Malmberg exercised leadership at the highest level, risking his own life and ultimately saving the lives of every one of the soldiers in his convoy.

As I placed the Silver Star on Chad Malmberg's uniform, you could hear a pin drop. But the moment the medal was on, an ovation erupted. Sergeant Malmberg was invited to the podium for what we all expected would be a speech. Instead, he simply said he wanted us to know who was with him that day—who the team was. He said they deserved just as much credit as he did. He had each of them stand up. Then he said thank you and sat down. A simple but powerful lesson: "It's not about me. We're a team, and they deserve it too."

The military is all about teamwork. And isn't that what our country is all about too?

Military members are tremendous role models for our nation. In spending time with our troops and seeing how the public supports them, I see something else. I see how the country still yearns to support the values the members of the military represent: service, courage, strength, pride, patriotism, and honor. Americans still get it. We know what made this nation great, and we know what will keep it great. We still honor and embrace those values.

Now, we just need more leaders who will do the same.

13

UNEXPECTED TURNS

MY YEARS AS GOVERNOR came during an extraordinary time for the state of Minnesota and our nation, as we watched an unprecedented number of Minnesota National Guard members deploy to fight the War on Terror while back home we struggled with a rocky economy, budget shortfalls, and more. All of it required my attention and leadership.

But these things don't happen in tidy sequence. They often overlap, and some you don't see coming.

On the night of November 22, 2003, news came of a missing persons case along Minnesota's border with North Dakota. Dru Sjodin, a student at the University of North Dakota, had disappeared after working her shift at a store at the Columbia Mall in Grand Forks, a town right on the border. Investigators immediately suspected foul play. The image of a vibrant, smiling, joy-filled young woman who was nowhere to be found soon filled the airwaves.

As the search spread, I offered my help to Dru's family. I told her mother, Linda Walker, I wanted to do whatever I could to help.

Authorities soon zeroed in on a suspect, Alfonso Rodriguez Jr., a repeat sex offender who had been released from the Minnesota prison system a few months earlier after serving out a twenty-three-year sentence for a prior crime. They also quickly identified what looked like clear evidence that Rodriguez had stabbed Dru and abducted her in his car.

The search for Dru grew more intense. The thought that she could be hurt and abandoned but still alive understandably led to urgent requests for help from her parents and friends and eventually from local authorities. They were searching fields spread out over thirty or forty miles. I joined forces with Governor John Hoeven of North Dakota, and we authorized and mobilized National Guard soldiers to join in the search. I went up to the area to thank the volunteers, offer consolation to the family, and check on the status of the search operation.

Rodriguez was taken into custody on December 1 but gave no clue as to where Dru might be. So the search continued, straight through the holidays and into the new year.

Unfortunately, politics found its way into the mix. A Minnesota politician tried to exploit the situation by asserting in the press that Rodriguez's release was somehow caused by my administration's budget cuts.

The suggestion that unrelated budget cuts somehow impacted a decision to release Rodriguez—a decision that was made before I was elected Governor—was, of course, illogical. But once such terrible assertions are made, truth and logic too often lose out to perception, politics, and an avoidance of journalistic rigor.

At that time, if a sex offender served out his entire prison term and was still deemed to be a threat, the county attorney could make a decision to refer that offender to what's termed "civil commitment." Prison administrators, psychiatric professionals, and other state officials were tasked with overseeing each sex offender's case in order to make a recommendation whether to refer someone to civil commitment based on various clinical factors. If a commitment was ordered, the offender would be housed in a different level of lockdown facility. Rodriguez was scheduled for release in 2003, and his evaluation panel had convened back in 2002. That panel decided not to recommend civil commitment for Rodriguez. He should have been committed, but he wasn't.

There was another meeting on Rodriguez's case that did take place in 2003. A committee convened to determine Rodriguez's post-release living arrangements. But that group was not responsible for addressing whether Rodriguez should be released. That decision had already been made. The 2003 group made a decision that Rodriguez, then fifty, could be allowed to move in with his mother in Crookston, Minnesota, where he was properly registered as a level-3 sex offender under Minnesota law.

I was horrified that Rodriguez had been released. He should not have been let out. But the attempts by some to politicize this tragedy were eye-opening for me.

Politics can get nasty and really low. There are unwritten rules of fair play, just as in hockey, and most people in public service play by those rules. Baseless cheap shots are normally off-limits. There are better ways to win a fight.

But some people in politics play by different rules. So I've learned to keep my guard up enough to recognize when an attack may be coming.

* * * * * * * * * *

DRU SJODIN'S BODY WAS FOUND on April 17, 2004, in a secluded, snow-covered ravine in Crookston, Minnesota. I did my best to express my deepest sympathies—and I did everything I could to make sure other horrible offenders like Rodriguez would remain behind bars for the rest of their lives.

Because he brought Dru across state lines, Rodriguez was tried in federal court. That opened up the possibility that he could receive the death penalty—and he did. I strongly supported the sentence, and I went on to advocate reinstating the penalty in Minnesota for the most heinous criminals.

Even though Rodriguez's release decision predated my time as Governor, I came to understand that the system had failed and that it needed to be much stronger. I issued an executive order ensuring that all level-3 sex offenders would be referred for civil-commitment proceedings automatically. My administration also increased funding to lock up sex offenders and make Minnesota's laws relating to sex offenders tougher in a variety of ways.

Dru's parents were incredibly strong and steady figures through-out the entire ordeal. Her mother, Linda Walker, turned out to be an inspirational figure in the wake of her daughter's tragic death. She and the family pursued passage of federal legislation requiring that sex offenders like the one who killed her daughter would show up on a sex offender registry no matter what state they lived in. She dubbed the legislation "Dru's Law," and in 2006, President Bush signed into law the Dru Sjodin National Sex Offender Public Registry—ensuring that residents would never again be left in the dark about sex offenders living among them.

Here were parents, in the midst of unimaginable heartache, exemplifying courage and serving as a source of inspiration for many. Those who model grace and strength through difficulty make the world a better, and often safer, place for others. Can you think of a better example of the American spirit than that?

14

★ ★ ★ ★ ★ ★ ★ ★ ★ ★

BATTLING BIG

BALANCING BUDGETS is just one piece of the fiscal-responsibility puzzle. More battles come when people realize the bloated policies of the past have to come to an end in order for real change to occur. Everybody is for a balanced budget in concept, but people push back if something near and dear to them is impacted.

The biggest examples of this are so-called entitlement programs. America has finally reached the point where entitlement reform *will* get done, simply because it must. If we don't change our trajectory, the country will go broke. Entitlement reform doesn't necessarily mean the programs have to end, but it does mean they need to be fixed.

The people of Minnesota learned just how big these battles could get, and how tough these fights could be, in the middle of my first term.

* * * * * * * * * *

MINNESOTA HAS A BUS SYSTEM that's run by a regional government organization called the Metropolitan Council, or Met Council for short. The brand name for the bus system is Metropolitan Transit, or Metro Transit, and it's staffed by public employees—some full-time, some part-time—who over the years have negotiated a series of union contracts with the Met Council. There was an early version of the contract, negotiated before my time in office, that allowed bus drivers to retire after as little as fifteen years of service and qualify for full health-care benefits for the rest of their lives, even if they retired while they were still young enough to get another job.

Imagine how much that was costing the Met Council, which was funded by tax dollars, year in and year out. By 2002, it was facing hundreds of millions of dollars of unfunded liability because of this extraordinary benefit, and that liability was growing rapidly. The leaders of the Met Council were worried about it and believed the shortfall would soon impair its credit rating and destabilize its future financial outlook. The problem needed to be dealt with head-on.

Over the years, the Met Council tried to fight back in contract negotiations with the union. But the fights were unsuccessful. In 2004, when the contract came up for renewal, it was clear we needed to address the problem aggressively. The Met Council—and more specifically the taxpayers—simply couldn't afford the status quo. So my office stepped in to help.

Staffers and mediators began the process, but as expected, the union leaders dug in their heels. They didn't realize that negotiating with me would be different from what they had experienced in the past. So when March rolled around, we reached an impasse, and the bus drivers decided to go on strike.

The press loves to cover some issues more than others. The mere mention of any plans for a new Vikings stadium, for example, is certain to result in a big news story. And any problem with the transit system is another story the press loves to cover. A Metro Transit strike, if one were to occur, could affect nearly seventy-five thousand people who use that bus system every day, not to mention countless commuters if congestion piled up. All this was fodder for endless big news stories. Some in the media predicted chaos—cities filled with traffic jams and overstuffed parking garages. For those transit riders who didn't own cars, the media trumpeted the dire possibility that they wouldn't find a way to get to work, which could potentially cost them their jobs. There was particular attention paid to the Twin Cities' Somali population, one of the largest in the entire country. Many worked overnight shifts, when carpooling would be less of a possibility. The question of whether a strike would unfairly affect the Somali community was the basis for even more news stories.

The union depended on these doomsday scenarios becoming a reality. Cities in chaos would force the government's hand at the bargaining table. The public would demand a return to normalcy as soon as possible. We would have to give in, or so they thought.

There are basically two types of negotiations. There are those based on good intentions and common goals, with very little in the way of philosophical differences. In those cases, negotiating isn't about leverage or who can really turn the screws to somebody else. Rather, it's a matter of working together to reach a resolution that works reasonably well for everyone involved. At its best, this type of negotiation can be an exercise in trying to do the right thing for the right reason, yielding good results.

On the other hand, when you get into issues that are deeply philosophical, where the chasm between different perspectives is extraordinarily challenging and sometimes insurmountable, the parties are much less likely to budge. In these philosophical negotiations, sometimes it's necessary to work around the parties' differences, setting them aside in an attempt to discover common ground. But if no common ground exists, and if one side has enormous leverage, the outcome is likely going to be one side prevailing outright over the other. Good intentions and positive personal dynamics will not bridge the gap.

Understanding the difference between the two is important. During the 2008 presidential campaign, then-Senator Obama led people to believe that if he could only *talk* to Iran, things would get better; if we could only *talk* to North Korea, the situation would improve. The premise underneath his comments was a belief that between his personality and his communication skills, major problems could be negotiated away through simple diplomacy. Of course there's a role for diplomacy, but just how large that role is depends on the type of negotiation and who's on the other side of the table.

Talking sometimes works. But more often there are difficult philosophical gaps underneath the hood that discussion alone can't resolve. It's not a matter of trying to better understand the other side. The two sides may understand one another perfectly, but they fundamentally disagree. Knowing what kind of situation you have on your hands is important. While President Obama wants to talk, Iran has played us like a fiddle. The U.N. sanctions against Iran's nuclear ambitions are watered down and do not represent sufficient leverage to change Iranian behavior. Iran is biding its time. It's not that we don't understand their intentions. We do, and they are thumbing their noses at us. More leverage, not more conversation, is what's needed most.

Sometimes leverage surfaces at just the right time. In the case of this bus strike, leverage presented itself after the strike had gone on for about a week.

Like the media, I was worried about potential traffic congestion, lost work time, and the full impact on our citizens once the transit strike started. Not surprisingly, however, the people of the Twin Cities were resilient and creative. The pull-yourself-up-by-the-bootstraps attitude kicked in, and people simply found ways to work around the problem. The result wasn't chaos at all. People were smart, and they found ways to get to work—including the Somalis on the night shifts. That meant my side now had the upper hand.

The union leaders were certainly strong and did not want to give in quickly. And they didn't. The bus strike stretched on for a total of forty-four days—one of the longest major transit strikes in the country's history.

But we had the upper hand in the bus strike for another, more important reason: the union's position was simply indefensible. Because we had so much press coverage, we were able to lay out the merits of the argument. Once the public knew the bus drivers wanted full health-care coverage for the rest of their lives after only fifteen years of service, they were with us.

During speeches, I would ask for a show of hands of anyone who was not in government who could work as little as fifteen years and then qualify for health insurance benefits for the rest of their lives. Not a single hand went up. I then went on to tell them about the bus drivers and how they received such a benefit on the government dime, and how they, the taxpayers, were paying for it. Paying government employees was one thing, but paying them unsustainable, ridiculous amounts was another. I quickly realized that public support, coupled with the lack of traffic congestion, meant we would win the negotiation. It was just a matter of time.

I didn't have anything against the bus drivers. They're good, hardworking people who get up in the morning, put on their uniforms, and put in an honest day's work for their families. They're the same type of folks I grew up with in South St. Paul. They don't make a ton of money. After more than a month of being out of work, I knew the rank-and-file union members were going to tell their union leaders to settle so they could get back to work—and that's exactly what happened.

But despite all the reasons for optimism in our position, we still needed to close the deal. I didn't want the union to feel I was gloating. I had learned my lesson from my impromptu statement to the press after Senate Majority Leader Hottinger agreed to pass my budget cuts. The room where most state negotiations occur is a large, high-ceilinged, historic expanse with big, heavy tables and chairs and massive old paintings depicting scenes from the Civil War. It's right next to the Governor's office, and it can all be a bit intimidating. In this case, intimidation was not what I was after. I knew we were going to prevail, and by now, they knew it too. So I went back to my roots; I set us up to negotiate in the Croatian Hall in South St. Paul—the same place where I had kicked off my run for Governor in 2001. We didn't meet in the dance hall, and we didn't meet in the basement bar by the tabletop hockey game or jukebox, either. Through Lenny Mankowski, the godfather of that hall, I arranged to meet on the top floor, in an informal space called the Cro's Nest. There we could negotiate in private, away from any press or public distraction.

In the end, we came to an agreement to discontinue the controversial retirement benefits completely for all new hires. It didn't yank that benefit away from current bus drivers after they had been promised it, but new hires would know it would not be part of their benefit package. At its heart, the negotiation wasn't about the bus drivers. The drivers were well-meaning people, but over the years management and labor officials had enabled them, and each other, to create a system with a benefit that was excessive and unsustainable. The gig was up, and it had to change.

The union understood. Crisis over. The buses started rolling again.

* * * * * * * * * *

THIS IS A GREAT CASE STUDY for what needs to happen throughout government today. In countless areas, promises have been made that are mathematically impossible to keep. Something has got to change. The fight must be joined.

I firmly believe the public is ready for a return to personal responsibility. That's not exactly a new concept; historically, this country has flourished on personal responsibility. The American people know the financial situation with government is untenable. And they can handle the truth. Unlike in years past, average people in this country are now concerned with deficits, debts, spending, entitlement programs, and the need for reform. Nobody wants to see their own benefits cut off, of course. Who would? But there's at least more understanding of the need to taper some of these things off over time. Plus, we really don't have a choice. It's no longer simply a political debate; it is a matter of basic mathematics. The programs can't continue in their current form. It will be hard, but we can do it. Americans can manage difficult things. It's just like when my dad and I dealt with the tangled, messy meat hooks on that hot summer day back in South St. Paul. We may not like it, we may not want to, but we have to do this.

* * * * * * * * * *

AS THE 2005 LEGISLATIVE SESSION came around, it was once again time to develop and pass a brand-new two-year budget. One big difference was that the Democratic Party had fully regrouped and reloaded. This time, they knew what they were up against.

John Hottinger was out as Senate Majority Leader. Dean Johnson was in—pushed to the top-dog position on a platform of "Never again. Never again will we capitulate to Pawlenty like that." In fact, the Senate was so determined not to capitulate the way Hottinger had in 2003, I was told they changed the negotiating authority so the Majority Leader could no longer make decisions without approval by the Senate's three most-senior members: Larry Pogemiller, Dick Cohen, and Linda Berglin—all of whom had served in the Senate for decades.

To give you an idea how entrenched these Senators are, Berglin, who's extremely liberal and believes in government-centric everything, was in my office one day early in my first term. We were discussing health care. I was arguing for an approach she didn't agree with, and we were clearly getting nowhere. I finally said, "Well, I think we just disagree on this."

She looked at me calmly and said, "That's okay. I can wait you out." I think it was only my second year in office. She'd been there so long, in such a safe district, that if she disagreed with a current Governor, she could afford to just wait it out—two more years at that point, or a total of six more years if I got reelected. It didn't matter to her. She would still be there. At that moment I realized the depth of entrenched power and longevity in the Minnesota Senate.

Pogemiller and Cohen are the same way. They might as well be part of the paint job on the wall. They're just plastered into the place. Those three haven't seen a new idea they liked in years—maybe decades. Now they were prepared to set up a fortress in their attempt to guard the status quo. They were digging in. This was not a good development.

Even-numbered years are cleanup years in the Minnesota legis-lature. You make some adjustments, and you pass the bonding bill, but there usually isn't a big budget fight. The two-year budget is set every other year, so the 2005 legislative session was round two. Only this time, we didn't have a $4 billion–plus deficit to wrestle over. The budget shortfall was projected to be only a few hundred million. That's still a lot of money, but in the context of a $30 billion–plus state budget, it was manageable. So this fight wouldn't really be about dollars and cents. This fight would be about the blood and guts of our two parties' differing political ideologies and differing visions for the future of our state. Where would we be spending our money? What priorities would rise to the top? What old priorities would take a hit?

I proposed legislation that would improve education in our state—including some increased funding for grades K–12. We pushed tax changes designed to spur economic growth and pushed aggressively for more renewable energy. But we also proposed to cut spending in other areas.

The Democrat-controlled Senate didn't like the proposed tax cuts or the spending cuts. They wanted to raise taxes and restore every one of the spending cuts we proposed, plus restore spend-ing cuts from the previous two years. They had five months to sort it all out and pass a budget the House and I could agree to. They failed.

The clock was ticking again. The Minnesota constitution calls for the legislative session to end in May. The Governor can call a special session to extend negotiations, but in any event, a bal-anced budget must be in place for the next two years no later than July 1.

The DFL decided to dig in hard this time, and they dragged the budget negotiations all the way through the end of the regular session—which meant I had to call for a special session. I ordered it to begin at one minute after midnight on the final day of the regular session to keep everyone working toward a resolution. That gave us until the end of June to come up with a budget. Unlike many other states, we don't have continuing resolutions that kick in if a new budget isn't in place. If there's no new budget, the government, to put it in simple terms, shuts down.

In the last-minute scramble, we came together and agreed on some of the noncontroversial bills. We passed a parks bill and legislation to fund many of the second-tier departments and agencies. But when the clock struck midnight on July 1, most big-ticket, big-budget items were unresolved. Health and human services, K–12 education, higher education—all unfunded. No bills signed. No budget. No choice but to shut the government down.

In 150 years of state history, it had never happened. This was uncharted territory. But I simply couldn't allow tax increases that would kill jobs, and I couldn't allow spending to keep bloating up again after having fought so hard to hold the line in 2003. And the Democrats had resolved that they weren't going to let me win again. So the fight was on.

In terms of the negotiation, I knew a shutdown would not be good for me. It wouldn't be good for anyone. Public sentiment would surely swing down, and I would take a hit. But I thought the legislature would take a bigger hit; I believed the public would understand and support my position. Unfortunately, that's not exactly the way it happened. As far as the press and the public were concerned, we were *all* to blame for what was perceived as a stalemate. There were no political winners or losers. It was a plague on both our houses.

Part of me thought of handling this negotiation the same way I had handled the bus strike the year before. We had some of the basic government functions up and running, so perhaps we could just wait this thing out. But there was one big problem with that plan—schools. August is when schools do all of their hiring, planning, financing, contracts, and facilities preparation. All of that has to get done in August, or the schools don't open in September. I knew that if schools didn't open, patience with a government shutdown would evaporate in a hurry.

In the meantime, the Attorney General started filing lawsuits left and right to get the courts to order that certain programs stay open. The court appointed a special master, a former justice of the Minnesota Supreme Court, to oversee it all. The Attorney General and others went to the court almost daily to say, "Order this program kept open; order this other program kept open," and the court largely granted those requests. We watched as our government was gradually taken over by the courts.

My team and I were actively considering our options. The government was partially shut down, the courts were taking over, and here we were in the middle of the long Fourth of July weekend. Legislators were more than nervous, and the press was going full tilt. We finally reached an agreement in which I achieved key initiatives, such as a nation-leading, performance-based pay plan for teachers. However, my victories came at a price.

The Democrats kept insisting on job-killing tax increases. I told them, "No chance." Stalemate resulted. To break the logjam, I agreed to a seventy-five-cent health impact fee on cigarettes, as a compromise. I really disliked it, but it was the least-economically detrimental plan that would get us to an agreement. The fee was designed to offset the costs the state incurred in providing health care to smokers.

There was some snickering around that fee, and on a public-relations front some people claimed it was actually a tax. It wasn't.

The court heard arguments on the issue and agreed it was, in fact, a user fee and not a tax. But even as a fee, it's something I regret agreeing to. For Democrats, that wasn't really the point. They could lay claim to having generated more revenue to protect some of their cherished government programs from cuts. After a nine-day shutdown, the first in Minnesota history, we did eventually reach a compromise between competing factions.

To this day, I still wrestle with whether I should've let that shutdown run longer. But the process had run its course, and at least I had stood up to and thwarted the efforts of Minnesota's Democrats. Like a goalie prevailing in a play-off hockey game, I had stopped the constant shots on goal. I'd held the line on their insatiable appetite for more government spending.

And I'd scored some goals as well, including the teachers'-salary initiative I mentioned earlier. The legislature passed into law a new program I had proposed, called Q Comp, linking teacher compensation to student achievement. Now teachers could be paid based on actual results rather than simply seniority. Minnesota became the first state to offer a statewide system for performance pay for teachers. Similar policies are now sweeping the nation in even more aggressive forms, and I am proud that Minnesota led the way. Achieving that goal was not easy. The powerful teachers' union and their legislative allies were wildly opposed to the idea. But in the context of the overall compromise, we were able to overcome that special-interest group and begin to place the interests of students ahead of the interests of the unions.

During these years we also made progress on other important issues, including health care. As every person in every state in this country knows, health-care costs have been rising at an astronomical rate—for individuals, businesses, and government alike. My goal was to push for real changes to the health-care system in

My parents, Virginia (Ginny) and Eugene
(Gene) Pawlenty, on their wedding day,
April 17, 1948.

I've always loved playing hockey—still do, in fact.
This is me with my youth hockey team in grade school
(front row, 2nd from the right).

Nice tie, for a
kindergartner.

Our wedding day, September 26, 1987.

Anna and Mara at the Governor's Residence, 2010. (Photo by DaleStudios.com)

Our first dance as the First Couple of Minnesota at the Inaugural Ball in January 2003.

◄ At a family wedding with Mary, Mara, and Anna in 2003.

Enjoying beautiful ►
northern Minnesota
with Anna and Mara.

The Pawlentys

Anna and Mara with the First Dog,
Mazy, in 2006.
▼

Showing off a walleye I caught during the Governor's Fishing Opener on Lake Kabetogama in May 2010.

The Great Outdoors

Enjoying a relaxing ride on a beautiful fall day.

Running in the Twin Cities Marathon, October 3, 2004.

Former New York City Mayor ▶
and fellow Republican Rudy
Giuliani came out to support
me during my campaign at
the Minnesota Professional
Fire Fighters headquarters
in St. Louis Park, MN,
November 6, 2006.

Campaigning

◀ Addressing supporters after being
elected Governor of Minnesota,
November 6, 2002.

Addressing CPAC ▶
(Conservative Political Action
Conference) in 2010.

Sharing some quality ice time with Minnesota's finest!

Celebrating the 100th anniversary of the Tenvoorde Ford Company in St. Cloud.

There's a reason they call me T-Paw!

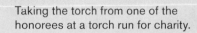

Taking the torch from one of the honorees at a torch run for charity.

If you're going to make it in politics, you've got to have a good sense of humor.

Sharing a few laughs in the locker room at the inaugural hockey game in 2003.

On August 1, 2007, the I-35W bridge over the Mississippi River in Minneapolis collapsed during rush hour, killing 13 and injuring 145.

President George W. Bush ▸ visiting Minnesota in the days following the bridge collapse.

◀ Northern Minnesota's farmers took a terrible hit in the summer of 2006 when an extreme drought devastated the corn and soybean crops.

In the spring of 2006, a massive ▶ tornado cut a twenty-mile path of destruction through southern Minnesota, destroying homes, farms, and livestock.

Dark Days

But the silver lining in all of this is that Minnesota has an extremely proud tradition of always rallying around individuals, families, and victims of natural disasters. We may get knocked down from time to time, but we always come up fighting.

◀ In May 2008, Mary and I visited Dru's Garden in memory of Dru Sjodin, a college student who was kidnapped and killed in 2003.

Talking with the Minnesota National Guard soldiers stationed at COB (Contingency Operating Base) in Basra, Iraq, in July 2009.

◀ Getting a guided tour of Kosovo in 2004.

Visiting with troops ▶ stationed at Camp Shelby prior to their deployment to Iraq in March 2005.

Getting a bird's-eye view of the situation in Afghanistan, 2009

Thanking a returning soldier at Fort McCoy in 2007.

Honoring those brave Americans who gave their lives in Vietnam.

Paying final respects to Army Staff Sergeant Dale Panchot, who made the ultimate sacrifice for his country in 2003.

◄ Mexican President
Vicente Fox

Israeli Prime Minister ▶
Ehud Olmert

Senator John McCain
▼

General
David Petraeus
▼

President George W. Bush
▲

Famous Faces

Afghan President Hamid Karzai
▼

Paying our respects at the Srebrenica-
Potočari Memorial and Cemetery in Bosnia
while visiting Minnesota National Guard
soldiers in December 2003.

Playing a little foosball at Best Buy (a
Minnesota-based company) in Shanghai
on our trade mission to China in 2005.

Foreign Travel

Remembering the victims of the
Holocaust at Yad Vashem during our
trade mission to Israel in 2008.

At the Taj Mahal during the first-ever Minnesota trade mission to India.

Foreign Travel

◄ Speaking to a gathering at the U.S. Ambassador's Residence in Santiago, Chile, during our trade mission to South America in 2009.

Moving Forward

Rise up; this matter is in your hands.
We will support you,
so take courage and do it.

EZRA 10:4

Minnesota. I wanted changes that would drive down costs while improving results, changes that would encourage competition by engaging consumers in the decision-making process.

The reforms we made in health-care choices for our state employees are one good example of this new approach. It works like this: State employees are given easy-to-understand information about providers' costs and quality measures. If the employee chooses to go to a higher-quality, more-efficient provider, they pay less out of their own pocket. If they choose a more costly alternative, they pay more. You can easily predict the results of that plan: State employees overwhelmingly chose care from lower-cost, high-quality providers—and premium increases in the program have been relatively small or flat for five years.

As that one program illustrates, it is possible to stop the rising tide. Not by increasing the bureaucracy but by getting government out of the way and putting power back in the hands of the consumer, making sure consumers have some skin in the game financially, so they're given the incentive to make better choices. People like to have choices. We shop around for the best price and quality of television sets and clothing and car repairs. It makes sense that we should want the same options when it comes to health care. In the end, having that choice means everybody wins.

For decades, our health-care system in the United States has been set up like an open bar at a wedding. People consume goods and services without knowing or caring about the price or quality, with no regard to who is paying the bill. Bill? What bill? The bill magically disappears to a third party. Obviously no such system is sustainable. Our government programs, including health care, need to look more like a cash bar than an open bar. Any system that creates the illusion that something is free, when we know it's not really free, is doomed to fail. Such systems defy what we know about markets and what we know about human nature.

The results of our changes to state-employee health care are but one example of this principle in action. Minnesota also has one of the highest percentages of citizens using health savings accounts, which are like 401(k)s or IRAs for health care. They work because consumers have powerful financial incentives to be cost conscious and make wise choices. Simply put, consumers are better off with choices, and they will always spend money more wisely when at least some of the money is their own.

* * * * * * * * * *

MANY OF THE GOALS I ACCOMPLISHED in office required drastic measures. I could only assume that further drastic measures would be needed to accomplish more. At times, I wondered what the price would be along the way. More tough negotiations? More government shutdowns? By the time that 2005 shutdown ended, the 2006 election season had already started heating up, and I wondered, with only sixteen months left before going to the polls, was I finished?

There was another question weighing on me too: Did I really want to run for reelection? The constant battles with the legislature had been tough and far more grueling than I had anticipated. Then there was the obvious time away from my family. On the other hand, we had accomplished real change in Minnesota. There was much more to do, and I was standing strong; I knew the cause was worth the effort. But where my family and I were concerned, were these battles truly worth fighting?

As much as I'm a Viking fan, I'm also a fan of one of the greatest football coaches of all time, who just happened to coach the Green Bay Packers. Vince Lombardi once said, "A man can be as great as he wants to be. If you believe in yourself and have the courage, the determination, the dedication, the competitive drive, and if you are willing to sacrifice the little things in life and pay the price for the things that are worthwhile, it can be done."

As I wrestled with those big questions, I kept moving forward. I wanted to make the most of whatever time I had left in office. Besides, I knew that my strength, as always, came from somewhere else. I found myself reflecting on Joshua 1:9, which says, "Have I not commanded you? Be strong and courageous. Do not be terrified; do not be discouraged, for the Lord your God will be with you wherever you go." That passage was a source of inspiration and peace. Courage, it seems, is something God expects from all of us.

15

★ ★ ★ ★ ★ ★ ★ ★ ★ ★

DOLLARS AND SENSE

"WHAT MATTERS TO YOU THE MOST?" If you ask that question of people around the country, after faith, family, and friends, they will often list activities that bring them joy or meaning. Some might list sports or recreation; others may mention traveling or the arts. But with very few exceptions, those activities require money. It's pretty tough to go hunting if you can't afford a shotgun, or biking if you can't buy the bike, or even to a movie if you can't pay for the ticket. And access to money means access to a job.

One of the best and most important things we can do for people in America in order to continue to improve their quality of life is to focus on things that will increase, not decrease, the likelihood that people will start or grow businesses that will provide jobs. What my Democrat friends don't understand very well is that it is hard to be pro-job and anti-business at the same time. That's like being pro-egg and anti-chicken. It just doesn't work.

A relatively small percentage of American citizens have the desire, capacity, and risk tolerance to start or grow a business. But these are the folks who hire employees, buy capital equipment, innovate, invent, build buildings, commercialize research results, and keep the private economy going. If the people in that group lack confidence in the direction of our country, they will sit on their hands. They will not invest. If those individuals determine that the burdens placed on them by government are unreasonably discouraging, they will do less than they would if such burdens were reduced.

* * * * * * * * * *

IN ORDER TO SHIFT Minnesota in a pro-chicken, pro-egg direction, I had to find ways to improve our business and job climate. We started a program called the Job Opportunity Building Zone (JOBZ). It's a program that allows companies who start or grow their business in economically depressed areas of the state to essentially enjoy tax-free status. JOBZ ignited 306 projects, with commitments of 4,563 new jobs and retention of 9,582 existing jobs that would otherwise have been lost. It also produced more than $705 million in new capital investments.

But specialized tax breaks and government incentives aren't enough. We needed to make the whole state more competitive and job friendly, not just parts of it.

Minnesota's taxes were too high, its government spent too much, and its bureaucracy was too slow and lumbering for the state to be deemed pro-business or pro-jobs. Every Governor for decades had said it was important to get Minnesota *at least* out of the top ten highest-taxed states. None of them ever did. I did. Many Governors in Minnesota have talked about the need to contain state spending. None of them did. I did. As I've mentioned, the average two-year increase in Minnesota state spending from 1960, the year I was born, until I became Governor was about 21 percent. We brought that down dramatically, to an average of 1.7 percent per year during my time as Governor. And for the first time in the 150-year history of Minnesota, we reduced state spending in real terms.

We also passed lawsuit reform and regulatory reform, merged and streamlined government agencies, deployed technology to save costs, sped up the time spent waiting to get permits, and much more. Importantly, we also focused on growing jobs by growing exports.

Minnesota has a relatively small trade office in terms of staff and resources. So we asked ourselves, "Do we want to do a little bit all over the world and have nobody notice? Or would we better off targeting a few places that have higher potential and focusing on those?" The latter seemed the stronger strategy.

With that in mind, we began to prioritize and put much of our trade focus on China.

Minnesota is home to more Fortune 500 companies per capita than any other state. (I think a lot of people are surprised when they hear that fact!) Many of those big companies—3M, General Mills, and others—either already have relationships with China or have the knowledge and ability to put together their own trade initiatives whenever they choose. What I wanted to focus on was fostering the kind of relationships that could bring meaningful results for small and midsize companies in the state while at the same time encouraging investment in Minnesota from Chinese companies that were looking to expand into the U.S.

So we created a China-Minnesota partnership, a sustained reprioritization of the trade office that disproportionately emphasized China in our state-encouraged trade and international activities.

In 2005, we took a group of 250 people to China on our very first trip as part of the initiative. It was the largest state-based trade mission to China ever.

China's so big, I wasn't sure even 250 people would get noticed—but we arrived to a very significant reception. Among other stops, we traveled to Beijing, where the senior leaders of the government hosted a dinner for our delegation and their Chinese counterparts in the Great Hall of the People. It's a gigantic, historical Communist government building near Tiananmen Square, and the banquet hall was filled. We celebrated our friendship around those many tables, and the banquet was a success, with toasts and speeches recognizing the importance of the moment. We had made great progress.

There were many such moments during my time as Governor. We would wind up going back to China again and making other trips to Poland, the Czech Republic, Canada, India, Israel, Japan, Chile, and Brazil, fostering business relationships and deeper understandings of the cultures and climates of each of these countries. The day-to-day activities and business relationships formed were valuable, as were the lessons I learned along the way. The world needed to hear more about Minnesota and its businesses, and our businesses could benefit from any doors we could open.

One of the lessons I took away from these trips was a better understanding of how different cultures and countries view history and what they consider to be a long-term perspective. During one trip to Israel, I mentioned our pride that Minnesota was celebrating its 150th anniversary. I described our plans for a celebration to the Mayor of an Israeli town. He listened politely and smiled a little bit. "Well, that's interesting, Governor," he said, "and thank you for sharing. You'll probably be happy to know that our city is celebrating our two-thousandth anniversary!"

The Chinese also have a very different view of history and time. In the United States we tend to think in terms of next year, three years, maybe five years from now. But the Chinese have such a long history that they take the intermediate and long-term view more seriously into consideration—thirty or fifty or a hundred years down the road. That doesn't mean they are not moving fast, though; they're moving at blazing speed, with a big appetite for growth and change.

Shanghai and Hong Kong feel like New York on steroids. You cannot be there and experience the tempo and intensity of development, study, investment, and entrepreneurial activity and not come away impressed. Mary and I took a helicopter tour over Hong Kong and the surrounding areas. As we walked away from the helicopter, I turned to Mary and said, "We're gonna get our cans kicked if we don't get going in the United States." The pace and intensity of China's growth and future plans are almost unfathomable.

Of course China has huge challenges as well, including human-rights issues that need to be addressed. The question is not whether China will continue to grow. It will. The question is not whether we will focus on our ongoing relationship with China. We will. The question for the United States is whether we will be able to maintain a relationship with China that is strategically beneficial for us. Our relationship with China is currently fraught with imbalances, including trade imbalances between our countries, that work to China's advantage.

★ ★ ★ ★ ★ ★ ★ ★ ★ ★

PEOPLE UNDERSTANDABLY WORRY about outsourcing, but we can offset that in part by achieving more "insourcing" in our country by global companies.

You can't put the horse back in the barn. There is no going

back to an America-only trade policy. It's not possible, it's not realistic, and it's not even wise from a macroeconomic standpoint. As you might guess, I'm a pro–free trade person—but it also has to be *fair* trade. And unfortunately, manipulation of trade is rampant around the world. This manipulation can't be dealt with on a state level or a business-to-business level. The federal government needs to take the lead role and forcefully advocate for our interests.

We also need to fully grasp the challenge we are facing. People think about manufacturing and how inexpensive it can be to produce goods in China. But when it comes to education, Asia is racing us to the top. Today's conversation may be about who can make tennis shoes cheaper, but it will soon be "Who has the brightest and the most engineers and scientists?"

These days you hear a lot about American exceptionalism— whether America is unique and ideally suited to be the world's leader. President Obama has suggested it's all a matter of opinion, that America is no more exceptional than nations like Britain or Greece. I disagree. America *is* exceptional. That's a historical fact, not simply a point of pride.

But we can't be so confident that we rest on our accomplishments. For example, we cannot price ourselves out of the market and believe there's not going to be a consequential effect as to where people decide to deploy capital, construct buildings, add jobs, buy equipment, and more. We need to step it up. We need to be more competitive.

I've also learned on my trade missions that the world is not automatically in awe of the United States. Businesses in other countries are discerning, and they are increasingly confident about their own standing in the world. You see it in China; you see it in Brazil. More and more, countries all over the world are willing to look beyond or away from the United States to further their alliances and interests.

We need to act in order to keep America strong. And we need to be strong in order to make America work in a global marketplace. Because our strength affects more than just our economy. It affects our national security.

I saw an example of this up close in Minnesota, when Essar Steel—part of the massive global conglomerate of Essar companies, based in India—put plans into motion to build a $1.6-billion steel-manufacturing plant in our state's Iron Range. Minnesota has a rich mining history, but until recently all of the iron ore we dug out of the ground was shipped out of state. None of the steel was made here. For generations, Minnesota's mining communities dreamed of this opportunity, with many jobs attached, coming into the region. I was thrilled for it, too, and on a trip that brought me from Minnesota to Delhi to Bangalore and finally to Mumbai, I met with the family that owns and runs Essar. But just as I drove up to the gate, I received a phone call from a U.S. official informing me of some troubling news. "Essar may be involved in petrochemical development and investment in Iran. We have reason to believe it's an active deal. In fact, we have reason to believe the people you're about to meet were in Iran last night."

The information wasn't yet solid enough for me to immediately confront Essar with the problems caused by such plans, if they were true. So I met with the family, appreciated their hospitality, and continued to follow the itinerary they had set up. In the meantime, people began investigating the possibility that Essar was actually investing in Iran. I boarded a plane to Amsterdam before heading back to Minneapolis. During the trip, I received word that Essar's intentions had been confirmed.

We simply couldn't do business with a company that was

involved directly with Iran, particularly in the energy sector. I convened a press conference. My message was, "Great news the other day about Essar coming to Minnesota. But here's what I've learned." I described the problem with Essar investing in Iran. Then I said, "They can't do both. They have to choose between their investment in Iran and our help with their investment in Minnesota."

It was blunt. The Iron Range has at times gasped for economic air. This Essar deal was the biggest thing the region had seen in decades—or longer. And I took a lot of flak over this. Many took swipes at me, accusing me of making a political decision at the expense of jobs.

After the press conference, I sent a letter to Essar, noting something I think they may have overlooked: "If these news accounts and the other information I have are accurate, you may be in violation of the Iran Sanctions Act." I was in contact with the State Department, and the possibility was not something that could be taken lightly. And to their credit, Essar didn't. I was impressed by the diplomatic skill, knowledge, and integrity of the Essar executive, who handled the matter responsibly.

After taking some time to consider the choice I had put before them, he called and said, "Governor, we've thought about this, and not only do we want to avoid violating any laws, we don't want to violate the understanding and relationship we have with Minnesota. We agree to stand down from any further activities with this petrochemical plant in Iran."

That was a good outcome.

I didn't feel like I'd won some kind of victory; it just felt like the right thing to do, for the right reasons, for everyone involved. It turned out to be a win-win. Legitimate concerns had been raised, and it made sense to push the clutch in until we got this figured out. I wish the press would do that more often instead of taking the easy way out. Some issues are complicated, and the American people are smart enough to understand them if they're reported with accuracy. This was one of those cases where, once thoughtful people heard the facts, they agreed we needed to put the deal on hold until Essar backed out of investing in Iran. This was about something much bigger than one project in Minnesota.

Of course, the whole world is considering how to address concerns relative to Iran these days. The U.N. has passed sanctions, but they are watered down, and I don't think they will work. They will not change Iran's behavior. I believe Iran's intent is to get a nuclear weapon, and if it does, I believe we need to take its leader at his word when he says he wants to destroy Israel. It's extremely concerning, and all the more so because Iran is not being fully held to account; nor are Iran's enablers and accomplices.

My trade missions underscored for me that business, foreign policy, and even matters of national defense are now often merged to the point where Governors and business leaders in every state need to be keenly aware of the repercussions and ramifications of their actions on a global scale. In Minnesota, we passed one of the first and most aggressive pieces of Iranian sanctions legislation in the country. Our federal government needs to lead the charge and foster America's economic growth in the new global marketplace while assuring that our allies and business partners are actively reinforcing our common interests.

16

★ ★ ★ ★ ★ ★ ★ ★ ★ ★

LITTLE PINK HOUSES

SERVING THE PEOPLE as the Governor of Minnesota was serious business. But it was also a heck of a lot of fun.

There are many reasons I loved being Governor, but one of the greatest things about the job was that nearly every day I had the opportunity to meet new people. It's the nature of the business. Wherever I went, whether to an official meeting, to a speech somewhere, or just popping into my favorite Vietnamese soup joint—Pho' Ca-Dao in St. Paul has sticky, red-tile floors, but it serves up the tastiest chicken and rice-noodle bowl you've ever tasted (#17!)—conversations with interesting people were a daily, often hourly occurrence. One hour I'd be talking to an educator; the next hour, to a scientist; the next, to someone who's got an engineering problem or a brilliant idea or an issue they wish I'd address; and the next, to some farmer telling an old joke. My staff had a hard time keeping me on schedule at times because I'd drop in to a shop on Main Street during a visit to a town in greater Minnesota, and I'd strike up a conversation with the shopkeeper just for fun. It was a wonderful, enriching experience to talk with creative, thoughtful, fun people all over my state.

Sometimes, I had the great privilege of talking with people who've done really impressive things—like, for example, writing songs millions of people can sing by heart.

A few years ago, Mary and I bought four tickets to a John Mellencamp concert at the Xcel Center and invited my sister Rose and her husband, Rick. The two of them are huge Mellencamp fans, as Mary and I are, but for Rose, he's a rock hero. An icon. My security team called the arena ahead of time to let them know we'd be there. Word got to Mellencamp, and he invited us all backstage before the show.

I assumed it would just be a quick handshake in the corridor. I had seen him in interviews and he had a reputation for being sort of a prickly guy, especially when it came to politics, and his political leanings are way on the other side of the fence from mine. But when we went back, it quickly turned into much more. Rose was speechless—which was fun to see in my older sister—as John stood up to greet us. I said, "I'm Tim Pawlenty, the Governor of Minnesota. Glad to have you back in the state; we're all big fans." The usual kind of stuff. But then for some reason I added, "Oh, by the way, I'm a Republican."

He said, "Now, why would that matter to me?" He completely dismissed the political part of it and instead asked if we wanted some dinner.

In a room backstage, they had a whole buffet set up. John's wife was there along with some band members, and his dad was there too. John told me his dad had recently been fitted for a new hearing aid by Starkey, a Minnesota company. So I thought I'd tease his dad good-naturedly, moving my lips as if I were talking but without saying anything, so he'd think something was wrong with the new hearing aid he'd just picked up. John and his dad both seemed to think it was pretty funny (if perhaps unexpected from a Governor), and we all had a good laugh. I discovered John Mellencamp is a genuinely great guy, completely unassuming and welcoming.

Sometimes we get the idea that people of a certain talent or position are somehow different than we are. But time and again I've found that most people, no matter how famous, are just regular people once you get to know them.

I've realized over time that whether it's folks at the annual Governor's Fishing Opener (that's the first day of fishing season— a really, really big deal here in Minnesota and something Mary and I always loved participating in) or Toby Keith or Bill Clinton, people are just that—people.

My lunch with Bill Clinton came during a big anniversary celebration with the National Governors Association. It was what you might expect, a meal around a table, with the added benefit of some really interesting conversation. I was the chair of the NGA and introduced the former President when he spoke, so we sat next to each other. As much as most conservatives can't stand Clinton's politics or policies, five minutes in his presence and you can't help but at least like him. He has a sort of old-school, joyful personality coupled with a series of stories and shticks. He's interesting to be around.

Through the years I've had the opportunity to spend time with a wide variety of people whose places in history are both divergent and fascinating. Henry Kissinger, Afghan President Hamid Karzai,

Rwandan President Paul Kagame, Mexican President Vicente Fox, and so many others. Spending time with people who have such varied and rich life experiences has in turn enriched mine. While there's a certain level of initial formality that comes with some of these meetings, what you realize pretty quickly is that, for the most part, they're more down-to-earth, engaging, and approachable than you might expect.

That is most certainly true of President Bush.

I first met President George W. Bush while I was running for Governor. He gave most of the major Republican candidates around the country a little face time and a photo op at the White House. It was an honor, but understandably brief. I'm sure it was one of many such encounters he had with candidates that week, but I found it encouraging.

I'll never forget the first time he called me. I was at the Wooden Nickel bar in Marshall, Minnesota. We were in transition following the election in 2002; I wasn't even Governor yet. As part of my get-to-know-your-new-Governor visits, I had stopped into this old-style bar with booths and a popcorn machine and draft beer. I was sitting there eating lunch and some guy came out of the back room and said, "President Bush wants to talk to you."

I said, "Yeah, right," but he insisted.

"No kidding; it's the White House on the phone back here."

Seriously? So I went back into the little office and picked up the phone and heard the White House operator: "Hold for the President." He was calling to wish me good luck before the start of my first term. How he tracked me down at the Wooden Nickel is a bigger question.

After my first couple of meetings with the President in the White House after I became Governor—one right before the war in Iraq began in 2003 and one after returning from the Baghdad trip in '04—I had the good fortune of spending time with him in my home state. In '04 he ran for reelection, of course, and I accompanied him on a bus tour across Minnesota, starting in St. Cloud. He seemed to enjoy the bus rides, talking on the microphone, broadcasting through speakers outside the bus, greeting bewildered onlookers as we drove down the road.

Over the years, he came to Minnesota a number of times for various events. Typically I met him at the airport and rode into town with him. Whether it was helicoptering down to Mankato or talking over chips and pop in a trailer on the side of a cornfield set up as a holding area for an event, I spent a good deal of time with the President over the years, traveling from one place to another or in meetings. Mary and I even stayed overnight at the White House three times, once in the Lincoln Bedroom.

When you're a guest of the President, you're handed an all-access pass, which permits you to look around everywhere (within reason). If anyone looks at you strange, you simply hold up your card, like you're backstage at a rock concert. I wound up having to work most of those days, but Mary had some time to wander the grounds, go into the kitchen, visit the floral shop—everything you could imagine seeing in the White House.

It's remarkable to experience up close a place so steeped in history. The way the living quarters are laid out in the White House, the President and First Lady have their bedroom down at the end of a wide and well-appointed corridor near an arched window that has been famously photographed throughout the years. They have a private dining room, sitting areas with historically significant furnishings, a glorious room that is three or four times the size of a normal living room and can seat a small army of people for luncheons, plus other historic rooms that have been the sites of incredible moments in U.S. history. At the far end of that same corridor are two more rooms, the Lincoln Bedroom and the Queens' Bedroom. Both rooms are more accurately described as suites. Other, equally lovely bedrooms sit yet another floor up.

The first year we were overnight guests, Mary and I were dropped at the South Lawn entrance and came up the elevator with a porter, who showed us to our room. It was about three in the afternoon, and we decided to wander around a bit. As we did, we noticed a guy wearing a baseball cap, sweatpants, and a T-shirt down at the end of a corridor. I thought maybe he was a maintenance guy. But as I looked at him, he noticed Mary and hollered, "Judge!" It was President Bush. He came over and couldn't have been more friendly and welcoming as he placed us fully at ease. He was thoroughly gracious and genuinely happy to see how much it meant to us and others to be in that historic home.

We have great memories of those visits. During one of them, Mary and I arrived separately, which led to an awkward, if funny, moment. The porter took me to my room, opened the door, and there stood another Governor—in his underwear. I thought, *What the heck is he doing in my room in his underwear?!* About half a second later, the porter and I both realized he had brought me to the wrong room! Whoops.

As overnight guests, we, along with the other Governors and their spouses who were "sleeping over," had dinners with the President and First Lady in their personal dining room. They both had a remarkable way of making everyone feel fully comfortable and genuinely welcome. Dinner conversation was always lively. On one of those occasions, the President himself led us on a broader tour of the White House, including the Oval Office, telling stories in that great Texas accent of his along the way.

What I saw in President Bush, up close, was a funny, decent, disciplined, strong guy. When I saw him at the White House or in those bus rides or helicopter rides, we might shoot the breeze or talk some sports, but more often than not we talked politics and policy. He would ask about Representative Michele Bachmann or Senator Norm Coleman. And when it came to Iraq, he was fully engaged and attentive in every way.

Once I attended a wake in Little Falls for one of Minnesota's fallen soldiers. This young man had died in Iraq, and his father was grieving terribly. He was standing by his son's open casket when he pulled me aside. He grabbed hold of my shirt and my arm, and he said, "I want you to tell President Bush something for me. Tell him to finish the damn job. I don't want my son to have died in vain. I don't want him to have died and have the United States just fold and leave. Tell him to finish the job!"

The next time I saw President Bush, I delivered that message. I told him exactly what that father had said. It was a sentiment he had heard before, I'm sure, and it's one that's quite common among military parents. But in the President's eyes, I could see an understanding of that father's words. When it came to the war, the need to keep our country safe, and his resolve to see that none of those soldiers died in vain, he obviously felt it and believed it deeply. I'm confident history will remember President Bush very differently than the pundits of 2008 did.

★ ★ ★ ★ ★ ★ ★ ★ ★ ★

GETTING THE CHANCE to spend time with Presidents was certainly a great privilege. Two of my more-memorable experiences in Washington, however, involved saying good-bye to two Presidents. As a sitting Governor, I was invited to attend the funerals of President Ford and President Reagan.

Ford was a legendary congressional figure in his own right before he became Vice President and then President, and as such, his mourners gathered at the U.S. Capitol. A military honor guard brought his casket up the steps and into the rotunda. The room was filled in 360-degree fashion with friends and dignitaries from bygone eras as well as Governors and officials from the current era. It was remarkable to be in the presence of these American titans, past and present, all paying deference to one of their own.

When he became President, Gerald Ford obviously didn't inherit the best circumstances. But by all accounts, he was a thoroughly decent man, and he most certainly was a healer of the nation's wounds. That probably was his most important role, the reason he was called to the presidency at that time in history. The respect in that room as the country said good-bye was overflowing.

President Reagan's funeral was similarly awe-inspiring. I remember wandering around toward the front of the National Cathedral before the service started. Walter Mondale, who's from Minnesota, was there, and he was kind enough to introduce me to a few people. At one point, I was standing with Mondale, George Bush Sr., and Jimmy Carter, and I remarked on how Americans appreciate that they all, despite their differing political views, were consistently civil and decent. Just then, Al Gore walked over and joined the conversation, and I said to him, "Mr. Vice President, I was just commenting to the gentlemen here that even though they have different views, they've always conducted themselves in a remarkably civil way."

Gore looked at me and quipped, "That hasn't been my approach." It was a little moment of levity on a very sad occasion.

Ronald Reagan, the man who first inspired me in politics, was gone. From where I was sitting in the National Cathedral, I could see President George H. W. Bush, President George W. Bush, and President Bill Clinton, all sharing this moment of respect and admiration for one of the nation's greatest Presidents.

I have been to a lot of funerals, but as I watched the joint honor guard carry the casket down the center aisle, I felt the significance of that moment. *One of the greatest American Presidents ever, one of our greatest leaders ever, is gone,* I thought. *A chapter in history has come to a close.*

I was honored to be a part of that moment, honored to have the opportunity to pay my respects. The entire occasion served as a potent reminder of Reagan's legacy—a legacy of greatness.

★ ★ ★ ★ ★ ★ ★ ★ ★ ★

ALTHOUGH I'VE HAD THE OPPORTUNITY to do some amazing things and cross paths with some impressive and interesting characters along the way, I will really miss many of the ceremonies that were just plain fun. Like the time Governor John Hoeven of North Dakota invited me up to kick off a big hockey game at the state-of-the-art Ralph Engelstad Arena in Grand Forks. North Dakotans love their college hockey. On this particular night, they were playing the Minnesota Gophers. It's a big rivalry, and Governor Hoeven and I decided to do a little pregame taunting at center ice. He wore a Sioux jersey, I wore a Gophers jersey, and we both walked out of the tunnel into that massive arena with the sound and lights. It was packed to the rafters. They introduced Hoeven to uproarious cheers. Then they introduced me, the Gophers' Governor—to boos and jeers. Hoeven grabbed the microphone and told the crowd we had a bet, and that Minnesota was sure to lose. Then I grabbed the microphone, and with all the gusto of a professional wrestler, said, "That's right; Governor Hoeven and I have a bet, and as far as I can tell, there's no way Minnesota can lose this bet. That's because even if you win, half your team is from Minnesota!"

The crowd went nuts. "Boo. Boo!"

Then just as the crowd died down a bit, I added, "And the other half is from Canada!" That made the crowd go completely wild. As we walked to the tunnel, North Dakota fans were really in a lather yelling at me.

Another time, at another arena, I was invited to join a bunch of kids and skate through a red ribbon at the opening ceremony of a brand-new rink. I wanted to up the ante a little, so I gathered the kids before we hit the ice and shared an impromptu plan. "Instead of just skating through the ribbon, at the very end, we should all dive and slide on our bellies across the finish line." The kids loved the idea! Of course, if you're going to try to hog-pile with skates on, chances are someone's going to get cut in the head, so maybe that wasn't very good planning on my part. Then, as I tried to really ham it up in front of this whole community, I dove a little awkwardly and wound up slamming my chin and cheek into the ice. I didn't lose consciousness, but I came darned close. The room was spinning, and I was nearly seeing stars as someone handed me a microphone and expected a few coherent words from the Governor of the state.

These moments were fun, of course, but the real joy in being Governor was the opportunity, alongside wonderful people from Minnesota, to make a positive, lasting difference. The politics in my home state are really challenging for a conservative. But it's a good state, a beautiful state, and it's filled with really good people. If you take a walk down Grand Avenue near the Governor's Residence, you're going to get a perspective that's very different from the one you would get if you walked into a coffee shop in a farming community in southern Minnesota. And what you'd get at that coffee shop would be different from what you'd find if you walked through a town on the Iron Range in northern Minnesota. There are a lot of differences from one region to the next. But there are a lot of similarities, too. Minnesotans personify the heartland of America. They're modest people, they're not real loud, and they have a quiet strength about them. They don't feel the need to attract attention or proclaim the way they're making a difference—they just get it done.

There are farmers who work the land and take care of their livestock, and they work and live in small communities where everybody knows everybody. There are Scandinavian jokes like "I love my wife so much I almost told her." Dinner out in Minnesota small towns is at the café, where you get the open-faced hot turkey sandwich with some gravy, green beans, and a glass of milk for five or six bucks. We live a simple life in many ways, but it's a good life. Our focus is on family, community, and the outdoors. Even in the metropolitan areas, there's a great appreciation for the outdoors here. People in Minnesota hunt, fish, hike, bike, go to a park, and best of all, we go to "the lake." I think part of it is because we all get so cooped up in the winter. When we can get outdoors, we relish it. I know I do. I try to be outside as much as possible.

Minnesotans have heart, and it shows in measurable ways. Caring for one another is simply an expected part of how we live. Minnesota is at or near the top of the nation in things like voter turnout, charitable giving, volunteerism, civic involvement, church attendance, and education levels. It's a great state because it's filled with very good people, people who remain down-to-earth and who remind me, always, of the importance of being that way too.

17

★★★★★★★★★★
▽

FAMILY

ONE IMPORTANT ASPECT of being a successful Governor is the ability to multitask at the highest level. But for me, never was multitasking more essential than when trying to balance work and family.

Our first daughter, Anna, wasn't born yet when I was first elected to the legislature. By the time I was elected Governor in 2002, Anna was nine, and our second daughter, Mara, was six. When we stepped out of the Governor's Residence for the last time, Anna was within a semester of graduating from high school, and Mara was in ninth grade. Essentially the entirety of their growing-up years had been spent with Dad in public service. Yet although they had come to understand my work and my schedule, just as any children do, they escaped what could have been a far-more-complicated existence. Some combination of instinct, protection, and good judgment caused Mary and me to do everything possible to keep both girls out of the public eye. We tried to surround them with "normalcy" as much as possible.

But nothing was quite normal for the girls—or Mary and me—during those first days and weeks after I was elected Governor. Anna and Mara watched the election results as long as possible at Grandma's house until they could stay awake no longer. We spoke with them the following morning, and they seemed reasonably pleased with the outcome. At ages six and nine, "win" sounds better than "lose," of course. Dad had won. That seemed nice. "Are you happy, Dad?" I was, and that was enough for them.

The weekend before the election, Mary tried to describe to Mara that if Daddy won, people would give Mommy a new nickname. "Mara, if this happens, people will sometimes call me the first lady."

Mara was defiant. "Mommy, you can't be the *first* lady. Eve was the first lady."

A child's perspective is simply different. Their concerns were much more immediate. But none of us really knew what this meant or what it would look like for our lives. It was impossible to prepare them for more than Mary's new nickname when, in fact, we didn't know what to expect. Would Mom quit her job? Would we move to a different house? Why are there so many cars in the driveway and why are they black? And most of all, "Who are these people?" While these were the questions of two school-age girls, they were Mary's questions as well.

Mara, our six-year-old, responded to all the added uncertainty by choosing not to speak. She went selectively mute. Anna was exactly the opposite. A perennially outgoing child, she would introduce herself while holding Mara's hand. "Hi, my name is

Anna. This is my sister, Mara. She doesn't talk." People would look at Mara and nod sympathetically, as if she had some kind of ailment.

But at least some things stayed the same. Once we decided that Mary would continue with her work as a district court judge, other decisions flowed easily from that. We kept our home in Eagan, as she needed to reside within her judicial district, so we only lived in the historic Governor's Residence part of the time. That meant school, friends, sports, and most of the girls' routines would stay the same.

The Governor's Residence was an adventure for the girls, but for all the sleepovers and endless games of hide-and-seek, it was still not our home. For one thing, the presence of the incredibly helpful staff meant there were always people around us. We grew to value and appreciate all the hard work it took for them to care for that lovely old home, especially when simultaneously juggling the periodic presence of our family with the requirements of preparing for and hosting large events. But the staff was highly flexible, making scrambled eggs for the girls one morning and serving a world-class breakfast for eighty foreign ambassadors who arrived in St. Paul for the Republican Convention the next.

The dark wood, the vast distances between rooms, and even the occasional bat served as a reminder that this historically important home does not exist merely so children can do cartwheels in the large entryway (although that was common when our children were little). The Governor's Residence, an architecturally significant place on the National Registry of Historic Places, has a museumlike feel and functions as a ceremonial building too. It's a place for the public to tour and for Governors to host everything from formal dinners to receptions to breakfasts with legislators. Breaking bread together can lead to breaking the ice during tough negotiations. The state of Minnesota is fortunate to have such a beautiful building that welcomes people from throughout the state as well as around the world.

Our real home remains in Eagan. There, we live within easy shouting distance of the neighbors' houses—shouts that can only be drowned out when the neighbors two doors down fire up their Harleys. Most of the rooms within our home are all within sight of one another. And given everything else a Governor has to do, it felt especially good to come home for a few hours on a weekend and cut the grass. I love getting that lawn looking really good. When the sun is out and I see how the trees have grown over the years and how the flowers are blooming, that house is our little slice of heaven.

We have one computer in our Eagan house that the whole family shares (and sometimes fights over). If I'm on that computer and the girls are watching television, they're doing so just around the corner, and all three of us are within easy earshot. Upstairs, our bedrooms are all mere steps away from one another. And my only office at home is a desk tucked into a small alcove off the master bedroom, where I can look over the railing to see who's coming up the stairs.

Sometimes it's Mazy, our little black Yorkie-bichon-Maltese-shih tzu with one white paw, coming up those stairs. In 2006, Mara, through her persistence, convinced us to get this dog, and we've been delighted with her. We're convinced she's officially the greatest dog in the world (of course) and not sure which of the four of us loves her the most.

We live a pretty modest life, and there's a certain togetherness that comes from being in that space. In contrast, when we were in the Governor's Residence, I could be in the kitchen rummaging through the refrigerator while Anna was three floors up in what was essentially her own private apartment. It's so spread out, it was easy to miss her when she came and went with her friends. We all learned to use the pager system, which was an upgrade, I suppose, from hollering. It was not uncommon for us to call each other on cell phones from inside the same house, just to communicate. For someone who grew up the way I did, it never felt normal. And I'm glad it didn't.

The girls adjusted reasonably well to the change. They even learned to handle the back-and-forth between the Governor's Residence and our Eagan house, and they became content to be in either place. Kids are resilient. It helped that we welcomed their friends as often as possible and made their rooms in the Residence into places they could consider a bit of "home away from home."

Mara got over her decision to stop talking. It's fair to say she's made up for lost time. She and her girlfriends talk endlessly, and we've been pleased to see how mature she's been in the few public events we've asked her to attend. She wows 'em. As a naturally kind and thoughtful child, her ability to make others feel valued is always apparent. She's intent on her schoolwork and brings her organizational skills to every other area of her life, including her faith.

Anna, a girl with a quick wit and a clever mind, has become a remarkable young woman. Although she naturally doesn't hesitate to express her strongly held opinions, she's learned to gauge when to speak up and when to be a bit more measured. I brought Anna with me to the White House for the National Governors Association's annual dinner when she was sixteen, Mary having relinquished her ticket with the White House's permission. Anna can easily move from her volunteer work with disadvantaged schoolchildren to pulling weeds in our backyard to playing Scrabble with her grandma to a state dinner at the White House. That's a fairly strong range for any teenage girl.

Both children have been athletes since early childhood, a result of one of the best choices we've made as parents. Early on we decided that keeping the kids constantly busy with physical activity—whether it was first-rate swimming lessons at the Family Swim School, playing in countless soccer games on traveling teams, or enduring the rigors of varsity volleyball—was a good plan, and sports have been a passion for them ever since. When I first became Governor, I still coached the girls' soccer teams. That would be sacrificed with time, but Mary and I always made sure to keep them involved in sports, where they could learn the lessons of team play and sportsmanship in addition to the great exercise. Mary refused to let the girls play hockey, though. The youth hockey lifestyle in Minnesota is too all-consuming and held the potential to be the straw that could break the camel's back. She had to draw the line somewhere. But overall, sports, combined with school and friends, have meant our girls are in constant motion.

It surprises people to learn that for the most part, the fact that I was the Governor was simply of no consequence to the girls. They were just never caught up in it. Anna tells me her boyfriend didn't even know the Governor *had* kids when they first met. In short, never did my job as Governor, or any job Mary or I have ever held, define our children.

I've been blessed by a wife who has put in Herculean efforts to make sure our kids stay on track. Mary decided to step down from the bench following my reelection in 2006, which made a tremendous difference in our family's ability to manage the many moving pieces. She's a mediator and arbitrator now, with the flexibility to decide which cases to handle and when. The bench lost a great judge, but our family gained her steady presence.

People ask me, "Is public service worth the sacrifice?" I think it is. Committed people, including those who have children, are needed in the public arena. Busy careers, regardless of their focus, will always push up against the needs of a family. Maintaining some measure of balance, however that balance is structured, is essential to keeping the family strong, grounded, and committed to one another.

* * * * * * * * * *

CARING FOR THE KIDS part-time is one thing. Caring for a marriage part-time is a whole different story.

What's remarkable about my relationship with Mary is that never once, never in all these years of difficult schedules and time apart, has our marriage felt like a part-time endeavor. We've been married more than twenty-three years, and the backbone of our marriage is still firmly in place. Like soldiers who have been in the trenches together, our bonds have strengthened. Through the battles, the challenges, the obstacles, and the joys, our love has grown. Whatever sacrifices we've made in the area of our "normal" lives have been more than outweighed by our shared view that God has given us the opportunity and the skills to serve. So we do.

Mary's support of my political career has not always been as dramatic as that Rocky Balboa speech that helped launch my run for Governor. More often it's been her quiet, consistent encouragement that has given me strength. When I'm down and need that extra push to get back in the ring, she's there. When I need the calming comfort of family, she's there. When I need a passage from the Bible to lift my spirit, she's there. When I need to be reminded that the answer to the challenge of the day is prayer, she's there. She grabs my hand, and we pray together.

My busy schedule has not kept us apart as much as one might expect. She traveled with me to Bosnia and was there on that dark, foggy night when we were greeted by our troops on the bridge. She went with me to Kosovo and has accompanied me to countless National Guard deployment ceremonies throughout Minnesota, speaking warmly with the soldiers' families. She's as comfortable riding in a Black Hawk helicopter as she is riding in a car. She has been at my side when we've entertained dignitaries and leaders from all over the world at the Governor's Residence. She was with me through all the many White House visits and was an active participant on our Minnesota trade missions all over the world. But my favorite was her cheerful ability to weather the elements every spring at the Governor's Fishing Opener in northern Minnesota with a smile. She froze and caught fish and smiled and ate shore lunch and visited schoolchildren and often baited her own hook. She's an amazing woman. But she, like me, always found the most comfort when we could get home and sleep in our own bed in Eagan.

Our marriage is a source of calm and happiness for both Mary and me. I'm not an expert in why marriages last, but I think it helps to marry your best friend. It also helps to maintain a sense of humor and a broader perspective.

Mary and I share common interests, too, including running. We encouraged each other through the summer of 2005 to get in better shape and train (again) for the Twin Cities Marathon. Mission accomplished on October 2, 2005. The race went well, but the day wasn't over when we finished. It was filled with National Guard deployment ceremonies all over the state. Neither of us had any intention of letting those guys down, so we hit the tape at the end of that marathon and kept on "running." Sometimes together, sometimes apart, one or the other of us managed to get to every one.

I tried my best to pour the same amount of effort into each of those ceremonies, but as the day wore on, standing on the stages became harder on my knees than I had bargained for. Same for Mary. But somehow we made it. When we said good-bye to the very last soldier on the last deployment ceremony we attended together that day, we put our arms around each other, leaning in, literally holding one another up on the way back to the car.

The two of us, walking together, holding each other up—that's a pretty good metaphor for all we've been through. It's been a long and sometimes difficult journey, but it's been an unbelievably rewarding and meaningful one as well.

We would need that support to carry us through the challenges that lay ahead. Challenges that in 2005 we could hardly imagine.

18

★★★★★★★★★★

RUNNING ON EMPTY

MY DOUBTS about whether I could win a second term in my highly blue state, coupled with my questioning whether or not I even wanted to run again in the 2006 election, continued into 2005. We went ahead with fund-raising and planning, not wanting to be caught off guard or fall behind should I decide to go forward. It takes time and money to win an election, no matter what. But that year there was no Rocky moment when Mary said, "Yes, this is it; now get in there and fight!" The decision came incrementally.

Nationally, the landscape was starting to look bleak. Frustration with the war in Iraq had turned to frustration with the Bush administration and was bubbling over and hurting Republican chances on many fronts. In the Minnesota sea of liberals, I knew that national sentiment wasn't exactly going to help my chances.

I knew my opponent would be the man who had been gunning

for me the past three years, Attorney General Mike Hatch. He was hard-charging, aggressive, and not averse to throwing political punches. I knew it would be a difficult campaign. So when I made the decision to run, I knew I'd have to run hard and be all-in.

The race unfolded as I expected; it was a hard-fought battle in a political environment that was tough on Republicans.

By mid-October, the polls indicated that Hatch had pulled slightly ahead. I had advisers around me saying we had to "go negative or go home." Negative campaigning, as awful as it is, often works. But in those final weeks of the campaign, I decided against it. Instead, we went out and shot a series of incredibly positive ads. If I was going to lose, I much preferred to go out on a high note.

I was dressed in an old jacket and blue jeans, and I looked right into the camera as I walked toward it and spoke about what we had accomplished over the past four years. I talked about what a great state it was—not because of the politicians but because of the people—and I said there was more to do. I told Minnesotans that it had been an honor to serve them and that I hoped I'd earned their vote for a second term.

In the last days of the campaign, there was a bit of a dustup. Hatch's running mate, Judi Dutcher, who normally seemed to be a knowledgeable person, took a question somewhere on the campaign trail about E85. Her response, essentially, was, "E85? What's that?" E85 is the term that refers to an 85-percent-ethanol blend in gasoline. Ethanol, of course, is made from corn, and to the farmers and workers in the Minnesota ethanol industry, it was a gaffe. Nobody who spent any time around farmers and biofuels would have been stumped by that question. Even so, the whole thing probably would have come and gone in the press in a few days without much consequence, but for the fact that it caused Hatch to overreact. A reporter asked him about the Dutcher situation, and he called the reporter, among other things, "a Republican whore." Hatch is a seasoned politician, and I assume he seriously regretted the comment.

Despite that incident, I still didn't know what Election Day would bring. My campaign's internal polls showed I had opened a very small lead on Hatch even before the E85 flap. But most public polls showed Hatch with a lead. Election Day was unseasonably warm, and I took most of the day off. Mary had me looking at paint samples, as the basement needed to be painted whether I won or not. And we went to Holy Trinity in South St. Paul, to sit still for a while and to pray. We know that God is happy to meet us anywhere, but on that day I felt like I needed that connection to my roots. The church was quiet, and someone turned on a few soft lights. As we left the church, we were fully prepared for any outcome.

After returning to our home in Eagan, we went for a run, and as we turned to head east on the homestretch of our usual route, we faced a strong east wind. In that moment, Mary said, "You're going to win." She later said it wasn't merely hopeful thinking, and she didn't say it to boost my spirits. She said she could just tell. Which was interesting, because I could not.

It was just Mary and me in the backseat of the Suburban as we headed back to the same Radisson where we'd waited out the election results four years earlier. When we finally turned on Minnesota Public Radio to check on the early results, they weren't good. The announcer said something to the effect of "It's not going to be a good night for Republicans." Then he added, "And it's not going to be a good night for Governor Pawlenty. The exit polls are showing him down by eight points."

But neither of us was down about it. We appreciated the fact that we had been given the opportunity to serve for four years and make a genuine difference. We were going to be fine with the result either way. Still, after checking into our suite and heading to the ballroom to greet my supporters, I could feel the weight in the room. Everyone in the place tried to put a nice face on it, but you could feel the concern.

Back in the hotel room, I started writing my concession speech. I told Mary I wanted to be ready. I had spent four years in office, and I wanted to point out some of our successes and be gracious in defeat. So I grabbed a writing tablet and sat at the desk. She sat very quietly so I could concentrate on writing.

At some point later in the evening, she turned the television back on, and I was still behind, but I was down by only a few points. As time elapsed, that number dropped . . . and continued dropping. Mary said, "Stop writing. Come and watch this." But I didn't. I told her I knew how these things went, and I wanted to be prepared.

It was getting late when a close friend of ours came into our room. He had initially decided to head for home but turned around and came back. Something, he felt, was changing. At one point I finally put my pen down and sat next to Mary. As we continued to watch the returns, the picture on the news channel flipped. Where my photo had been on the bottom, it now was at the top. I was ahead.

It was an incredibly tight race, even then, but finally, well after midnight, the AP called it in my favor. I had pulled it out by one percentage point.

The tradition is that the other side calls the winner at that point, but in light of how close it had been, Hatch wasn't conceding. He went to the microphone and told the cameras that he would sleep on it and see how it all shook out in the morning. Even though it seemed a bit strange to make an acceptance speech before my opponent had given his concession speech, my supporters deserved the boost. So I went downstairs about 3 a.m. and stood in front of the few hundred who'd stuck it out after every other Republican candidate had lost, and I did my best to fire them up.

The results for Republicans nationwide that night were dismal.

Mary was still a judge in 2006, and once again she was barred from joining me for the victory speech. But I wanted to pay her special tribute this time around, and I remembered the perfect line to do it.

Mary and I love to go to the movies. Once our kids were a little older, we found we were able to sneak out and catch a flick from time to time, just the two of us. I'd come to enjoy comedy actor Will Ferrell. Something about that guy just makes me laugh. That year a friend with a similar base sense of humor gave me a big thumbs-up on *Talladega Nights: The Ballad of Ricky Bobby*. Mary and I went and saw it, and it instantly became one of my favorite comedy movies.

There's a scene in that film where Will Ferrell (as Ricky Bobby) offers an impassioned prayer of thanks at the dinner table. He thanks God fervently for everything he appreciates, including the always-delicious Taco Bell. And as he completes his list of blessings for which he is truly thankful, Ricky Bobby thanks the Lord for his "red-hot smokin' wife."

So on that night, as I enthusiastically thanked my supporters for getting to the polls and asking me to serve another term as their Governor, I gave special thanks to the woman who made it all possible, who saw me through it all. I gave thanks to Mary, "my red-hot smokin' wife."

I still use that line now and again in speeches when describing Mary, and we both laugh.

* * * * * * * * * *

THE TRANSITION INTO THE SECOND TERM was nothing like the first. The team was already in place. Our family had already settled into a routine of splitting time between Eagan and the Governor's Residence. We still had to plan an inaugural celebration, but in comparison to the first time, it was easy.

One enormous change that made this transition and the months to follow a whole lot better was an improved state budget. My approach had worked. The budget office prepared a presentation as part of the November budget forecast. Lo and behold, the number was $2.17 billion.

Not a $2.17-billion deficit. A $2.17-billion *surplus*.

Our state was back on track. Our economy was improving, and after four years of nonstop wrestling with the legislature, we didn't need a special session or government shutdown to finalize a balanced budget. It seemed my policies were working, and my second term looked like it was off to a promising start.

19

★ ★ ★ ★ ★ ★ ★ ★ ★ ★

THE BRIDGE

BY THE TIME the summer of 2007 rolled around, I felt for the first time in a very long time like I could take a few moments to catch my breath. We had made it through the end of another long and tumultuous but successful legislative session and budget fight. My governorship felt stable and on course. With no election on the horizon, I actually found a bit more time in the schedule for exercise.

On the afternoon of August 1, right before suppertime, I decided to go for a run.

It was a picture-perfect Minnesota summer day. Hot, but mostly clear skies. Perfect conditions for me to get outside and work up a sweat. It was an unspoken rule that when I went for a run, even the ever-present State Troopers would leave me alone, hanging back and ready at a distance. So I knew something was wrong the moment the black Suburban rolled up alongside me. I was still under the leafy canopy of Summit Avenue, only a mile or so from the Governor's Residence, when Trooper Tony Policano pulled over and lowered the window.

"Governor," he said, "a bridge fell."

I stopped running. "What do you mean? Like a piece of a bridge fell off somewhere?"

"No, we think the whole bridge fell."

"What bridge?"

"The 35W bridge in Minneapolis."

My heart nearly stopped. It was staggering to even think about. A massively busy interstate crossing the Mississippi River. A span traveled by more than a hundred thousand cars each day. A bridge I had crossed myself countless times throughout my life. It was just after six. Rush hour. My mind spun with images of that bridge filled with traffic. So many cars. So many people.

I jumped in the back, and we sped to the Governor's Residence. I didn't even walk the few extra steps it would take to get inside the main part of the house. Instead, I ran into the Troopers' office, where they have a bank of televisions and monitors, and I saw the devastation for the first time. The news helicopters were already circling. Imagery of the huge bridge crumbled like a toy became all too real when they zoomed in. I saw cars perched precariously over edges of twisted steel and concrete. *Is that a school bus?* Rescue workers tried to reach those trapped in their vehicles. The entire midsection of the bridge was submerged in the Mississippi.

All those people. All those families. It was catastrophic.

I moved into the library and spoke by phone with members of my senior leadership team. We assembled quickly and started assessing our course of action.

Six short years after 9/11, the first thought on many minds was the worst thought imaginable: Could this have been an act of terrorism? The answer would turn out to be no, but none of us knew in those opening hours.

We could only be thankful that the lessons of 9/11 had been learned. Our first responders knew what to do. Our agencies knew how to coordinate with one another in a worst-case scenario. We had trained for catastrophic events. We previously passed budgets that included the equipment necessary to allow our first responders to do their job as effectively as possible no matter what the situation—including high-tech communications devices that would allow rescue workers to communicate even if normal means of communication went down, as is often the case in a major disaster. We were as prepared as we could be for an event like this, and I knew that the people who had survived the crash and were clinging to life on that bridge and in the water were in the best hands possible to bring them to safety.

Yet I knew that people would be looking for answers as soon as I showed up on the scene. The media would ask the questions on everyone's mind: *Was it a bomb? Was it terrorism? Was it neglect? Had this bridge been inspected? Did it fail? Did it have anything to do with the construction work taking place on the bridge that very day? How many people were injured? How many are dead? What will be done for the families? Are the rest of our bridges safe?*

As we headed to the scene, I asked my chief of staff to look into the maintenance and safety records of that bridge, knowing I would get questions about it as soon as the press had an opportunity. I did not want to misstate it. All of this was happening very quickly, but I knew I would get briefed if there were any signs of terrorism. We had first responders on the scene that would keep us updated with up-to-the-minute numbers of injured and dead, and I had quickly authorized the National Guard to assist in any way they could. My team also reached out to Minneapolis Mayor R. T. Rybak to coordinate efforts, putting the ball in motion to create a gathering place for families and scheduling a joint press conference later that evening. And we already had a team working on rerouting traffic so that those not directly affected by this horrible tragedy could get where they needed to go in the days to come.

Driving up to the 35W bridge was horrific. Seeing it on the news was one thing, but witnessing the massive devastation up close is something that's difficult to put into words.

There was a security camera nearby that actually captured the collapse on film, and no matter how many times you watch it, it just doesn't seem possible that something that big could fall that fast, that completely, into oblivion.

Nothing could have prepared me for seeing and hearing and feeling the catastrophe right in front of my eyes. Ambulances, police cars, flashing lights. The buzzing pulse of news helicopters and public safety helicopters circling overhead. National Guard Black Hawks landing on nearby bridge decks. A rubbery, metallic smell of destruction was in the air. A command center was being quickly assembled in a nearby parking lot. Citizens who had initially responded to the crisis had given way to the professional first responders, who were still in the midst of pulling survivors from cars stranded on collapsed sections of bridge, some dangling at precarious angles down close to the river, and up higher, suspended over the crumpled roadway below. In many cases, six more inches and cars would have slid into the water. So while some cars fell, some were still hanging on in these strange, seemingly impossible angles.

Shortly after arriving on the scene, I met up with Mayor Rybak. The two of us boarded a State Highway Patrol helicopter to get an aerial tour of the scene. The size of the catastrophe was astounding, and seeing it from above just hammered home how large of a task lay before us—not only the immediacy of rescue and recovery and demolition of the remaining structure, but the need to rebuild as quickly as possible to sustain this major commuter and trucking route through the Twin Cities.

Although Mayor Rybak and I are firmly planted on opposite sides of the political fence, anyone in a position of public service and leadership knows we all care about and want the best possible outcome. And on this day, rescuing and doing whatever we could to ease the pain and suffering of the victims and their families was the only task that lay before us. In the coming days and weeks, the two of us and our staffs would work together—and work well—as a team. Together we attended a massive nondenominational memorial service for victims—a healing moment for Minnesotans—as well as many other events, side by side.

Of course, nothing Mayor Rybak or I did that day or in the trying days and weeks that followed could hold a candle to the level of support and sheer heroics the people of Minnesota showed to one another on that bridge. There were some remarkably heroic stories that unfolded in the aftermath of this sudden disaster. Dozens of average people who were in the area rejected the common first instinct to run away and instead ran toward the danger in order to help. That alone speaks volumes about human nature and the depth of the American spirit.

One construction worker was standing on the bridge when his section of roadway collapsed and fell the full sixty feet to the Mississippi below. He essentially rode the bridge down like a surfboard through the air, and his piece of the bridge fell relatively flat. He was knocked off the slab and into the water, but somehow he came to the surface both conscious and basically uninjured. When he climbed back up on that piece of the bridge, he saw and heard other people pleading for help in the water. The Mississippi River at that point is very wide, with a strong current. Put that much blockage in the water, and suddenly the current concentrates and begins to circulate in strong, unpredictable ways. Whirlpools develop, and later on people would describe the experience of getting sucked down or pushed up by the current in those murky waters.

The construction worker was dazed and hurt, but not seriously, so he looked around for anything he could grasp and spotted a broom handle that had fallen with him. Ignoring his own precarious situation on his little island of pavement and steel, he started using the broom handle to pull people from the wreckage, lifting them out of the swirling current.

There was also a school bus on one of the collapsed sections of bridge. The bus, returning from a day trip to a water park, was filled with children. The bridge collapsed in pieces, and the piece the bus was on fell about thirty feet but didn't fall into the river. It stayed up, on a slant. And what was right next to that bus when it fell? An 18-wheeler. That big truck's cab was smashed so severely in the fall that it caught fire and the driver was killed. Yet it didn't affect the bus at all.

As the bus clung to the pavement at a dramatic angle on a fallen bridge with carnage all about, everyday people began climbing over the wreckage to get to those kids—ignoring the risks to their own lives in the interest of helping others. A twenty-year-old volunteer on that bus had the wherewithal and strength to kick open the rear door and help carry the children out, one by one, into the arms of waiting strangers. A tremendous story of heroism. Dozens and dozens of similar stories would emerge over the course of that evening.

Mercifully, the main headquarters for the Minneapolis Red

Cross was very near the site of the bridge collapse. The biggest, highest-functioning, most well-staffed, best-resourced Red Cross facility in the state, maybe even the entire upper Midwest. Just across a parking lot. Thirty seconds from the scene. That facility instantly emerged as one of the epicenters of rescue, relief, and support during those first critical hours. All of those kids walked across the parking lot into the Red Cross to be greeted by a staff of caring souls. Those same caring souls would greet many others as the night went on. Best of all, those loving Minnesotans helped to make sure that every one of those kids was reunited with his or her parents as soon as possible.

Terrorism or an explosion of some kind was ruled out very quickly and was essentially dismissed that evening on the national level by Secretary of Homeland Security Michael Chertoff. Because this was an interstate highway, federal officials were involved from the start and coordinated with city, county, and state offices during the recovery efforts and the subsequent investigation. So we all knew the question of why the bridge collapsed would loom large at our press conference, for sure.

I connected with my chief of staff via cell phone as I headed to the press conference. Everyone wants to know everything instantly in a situation like this, and he had contacted Mn/DOT (the Minnesota Department of Transportation) staff, who indicated the bridge had been inspected in recent years and no major problems had been discovered. It was the only information we were able to gather in that short amount of time.

Standing alongside Mayor Rybak at the press conference a few minutes later, when the expected question came up, I repeated that information.

That information would turn out to be inaccurate.

In the coming days, further research would uncover that in

a series of inspection reports over the years, concerns about the bridge had been expressed by various people. In the end, none of those specific concerns turned out to be the reason why the bridge fell. It was an older bridge, built in the 1960s. It had been inspected, reconstructed, and widened over time, and it would take the National Transportation Safety Board (NTSB) a full year to get to the bottom of what went wrong.

But I relearned an important lesson that night. With that much history, that much complexity, and that much information yet to be sifted through, the answer should always be "We need to do a thorough review and gather all the facts," not, essentially, "My chief of staff just talked to some harried bureaucrat who assured us the bridge didn't have any problems." It was bad information that added confusion to the situation rather than clarity. In a crisis situation, no matter how great the pressure from the media and public to have instant answers, a leader has to acquire the facts and take the time to get them right.

Starting the next morning, the story of the rush-hour bridge collapse became an absolute media frenzy. We had countless national and international media outlets on-site, broadcasting live pictures for days. Anderson Cooper, Katie Couric, Matt Lauer, Brian Williams—you name it. They all wound up doing at least a few days' worth of broadcasts with the fallen bridge as a backdrop. The media attention only added to the chaos. My team and I were trying to manage the crisis, plus respond to the media's requests for information and perspective, and everyone was operating on incomplete information about the history of the bridge. The story was partly about the tragedy and the rescue and the loss, but over the next few days the story understandably began to turn to what happened, why it happened, and the inevitable question "Who's to blame?"

I suppose this is as good a time as any for me to step back for a moment and mention another sad thing that happened in the middle of all of this—a moment from the arena of politics that exemplifies the worst of the worst when it comes to the motivations of some politicians.

In the frantic hour or so of information gathering and planning at the Governor's Residence before I headed to the scene on the day of the collapse, I had big decisions to make and needed to set a course of action for the coming hours and days. I needed to focus on the task at hand. Yet within that very first hour I experienced one of the most disgusting examples of low politicking I've seen in my entire career.

As more of my staff arrived, a group of us moved to a different room, where we sat around a table, most armed with cell phones and BlackBerries, working frantically to get every bit of information we could before heading to the bridge.

It was about that time when one of my staff members received a troubling phone call. A DFLer—whom I won't even name because what he did was so awful—called to indicate how he was going to use this tragedy politically to carve me up. This while people were still being rescued, while first responders were just beginning to recover the bodies of those who had died. At that moment, when no one knew anything about what had led to this bridge falling, his first instinct was to call a member of my staff and threaten to attack me politically—saying so in dramatic and ugly terms.

We'd had a long-running battle with this legislator, so criticism from him would have been expected in the weeks following the bridge collapse. But I remember thinking, *What kind of low point as a politician do you have to hit in order to lash out like that? While the rescue effort is still unfolding, you've already made the choice to politically exploit a tragedy for some hoped-for political gain?*

Unbelievable.

Serving as Governor, not only during this incident but at countless other moments throughout my eight years, afforded me a crystal-clear opportunity to witness the full spectrum of human motivation, emotion, and character across a wide range of circumstances and among a large variety of people. I've seen the most inspiring, most courageous, most heartwarming, most affirming traits you can imagine. Yet I've also seen some of the most petty, politicized, unfair, uninformed, ill-motivated behavior. On that day, it was the last thing I ever expected—and the first thing I had to push aside.

As the first night went on, more people were accounted for. More people who had looked death in the face on that bridge were reunited with their families.

I didn't go to bed that first night. I didn't sleep much for the next few days—or really the next few weeks. There was so much on my mind and too much to be done.

Mayor Rybak and I visited the recovery center at the hotel both together and individually throughout the ordeal and spoke with as many of the families and individuals as we could. And of course, that meant speaking with families in the hotel ballroom who were hearing about happy reunions between husbands and wives, parents and children, while still waiting with every hope in their heart for good news about their own loved ones. We met with those who were praying with everything in their being to get some positive word that the person who meant the world to them had been found. Yet as they watched the clock and noticed the emptying room, we saw the awareness of the inevitable growing inside them.

To some degree, the fact that there was construction on the bridge that day, reducing the number of lanes and slowing rush-hour traffic to a maddening crawl, may have saved lives. In the end, there were not as many cars on the bridge as there might have been on a typical day. And with rescuers on the scene within minutes, the loss of life was contained.

Of course, none of that would matter to the families whose loved ones were still missing as the hours ticked past that first night. Especially when it became apparent that a number of vehicles had been trapped in the wreckage under the murky waters of the Mississippi in a tangled web of concrete, steel girders, and rebar that made it impossible for any rescue or recovery team to get to them.

By the time all was said and done, rescuers and hospital workers would help 145 people injured on that bridge. And families, friends, loved ones, and caring neighbors across the state would be left to grieve for thirteen of their fellow citizens whose lives were lost that day without warning. But that night, we didn't know how many were lost. We simply couldn't get to those vehicles beneath the wreckage. And until that was done, we couldn't provide any relief or closure to those waiting families.

We needed help.

* * * * * * * * * *

BY THE AFTERNOON OF AUGUST 2, five bodies had been recovered from the wreckage and the river, and President George W. Bush had shared his condolences under the increasing glare of the national media spotlight, while simultaneously pledging to help the city of Minneapolis and the state of Minnesota rebuild the I-35W bridge.

Try as they might over the next few days, sheriff's divers still could not get through the wreckage to reach the vehicles tangled beneath the surface of the Mississippi.

On August 3, First Lady Laura Bush toured the bridge site and spoke publicly about the parallels she felt to the devastation she'd witnessed after Hurricane Katrina. She was warm and gracious as always, and she offered public support and comfort. I found Laura Bush to be a remarkable woman who consistently exhibited an extraordinary measure of calm strength throughout her years as First Lady.

On Saturday, August 4, Air Force One touched down at the Minneapolis–St. Paul International Airport. As was my custom, I went out to meet the President on the tarmac.

The President took a lot of criticism during his second term, but in that moment, I couldn't help but think back to the President Bush we'd watched during the immediate aftermath of 9/11. The man's focus and determination helped rally New York City—and the country—in a kind of national solidarity that hadn't been seen in generations. The way he spoke to the rescue workers at Ground Zero and the way he addressed the nation inspired hope and provided a rock-solid resolve.

I was well acquainted with President Bush by that point, so there was an ease to our interactions. As he exited Air Force One and reached the bottom of the steps, he put his hand on my shoulder and said, "Let me see your eyes. I want to see if you've been getting any sleep." I was taken aback by the gesture. Worrying about how much sleep I was getting in the midst of all this wasn't exactly my first concern. But he continued. "I want to see if you're tired. In a crisis, a leader needs to have a clear head and clear thinking."

Mary was with me. Mayor Rybak was there too, along with a couple of members of Minnesota's congressional delegation. We walked from Air Force One over to Marine One, the President's helicopter, where we boarded to take another aerial tour of the scene before heading into a meeting to discuss what needed to be done. As we took our seats, the President said, "People are gonna look to you for answers, for comfort, for strength . . . and you're up to it."

The fact is, I wasn't getting a lot of sleep. I wasn't eating right. I found it nearly impossible, given what everyone else was going through, to stop and worry about seemingly small inconveniences. No lack of sleep, no amount of stress I was under could possibly compare to the stress and worry those families were feeling, knowing their loved ones might still be stuck under that wreckage. I did realize, though, that I had to keep my head on straight and stay focused in order to do all I could to help those families. I had some help in that department—help that has always been there when I needed it most.

First, I prayed a lot during this time—for wisdom, for discernment, for judgment. I asked God for the strength that only He can provide. Whether during ordinary days or times of crisis, I turn to God for strength and hope. Psalm 18:2 assures us, "The Lord is my rock, my fortress and my deliverer; my God is my rock, in whom I take refuge."

Second, Mary, predictably, pulled alongside me. She was quiet, but I remember her just appearing at my side in the middle of this tragedy, a strong source of support and encouragement and comfort. I valued it. Although it was unplanned and all-too-often unacknowledged, her appearing and staying by my side helped bear me through those days.

And they were extraordinarily long days. The rescue, dealing with the grief and the sadness that come with the loss, managing and leading the ensuing operations, and communicating not only the specifics of the operations that were under way but also the emotion and the raw feelings of the event. It was challenging. But it was nothing compared to what the grieving families endured. It was nothing compared to what the great heroes of that day went through.

And now, I had President Bush's ear. It was up to me to ask for the help we needed.

When Marine One landed, we entered the Army Corps of Engineers building just downstream from the bridge site for a closed-door meeting with the President and others, including Lt. General H. Steven Blum from the U.S. National Guard Bureau and Hennepin County Sheriff Richard Stanek, whose team had been trying to extricate the vehicles beneath the wreckage.

Sheriff Stanek and I spoke of the recovery efforts and how a number of families were understandably distraught, as the bodies of their loved ones had not yet been recovered. We spoke about the potential availability of a highly specialized, highly trained unit of demolition-and-recovery divers that were part of the U.S. Navy.

Just upstream, the bridge was in a state of suspended animation. We toured the scene with the President. We walked over to the wreckage of that truck, so precariously close to the yellow school bus. We shared the stories of heartbreak and heroes. The President spoke to the media, pledging his support to the people of Minnesota. Before his visit was over, he met with some of the families who had lost loved ones in the tragedy. Then we accompanied him back to the airport, saw him onto Air Force One, and watched as his plane took off.

Shortly afterward, I received a call from Mary Peters, the Secretary of Transportation. I reminded her we needed to get at the cars that were still under water and that we didn't have the capabilities. We needed that expert underwater demolition team who could get through the debris, in water so thick with mud and silt that divers couldn't see their hands in front of their masks.

She gave me the number for the Secretary of the Navy. Moments later, I had him on the phone. "We need some specialized help here," I said. He was working out of Washington at the time, and he agreed there were only a limited number of people in the entire world capable of doing such work. Specifically, he referenced a highly trained team of Navy divers who could get into that water and accomplish the task at hand.

With the President's help, we managed to slice through any red tape and had that dive team on-site within days. One by one, the team found and recovered every single one of those bodies. By the time they were done, almost three weeks had passed since the collapse. Imagine having a loved one trapped under that wreckage for so long. It's unbearable. But they found them all.

Inevitably and sadly, the bridge collapse would play into the political landscape for the entire next year. In short, claims were made that the bridge fell because we shortchanged the transportation budget. In particular, it was alleged that we should have made certain improvements but didn't because we didn't have the money. It was untrue and of course overlooked the reality that we were spending millions of dollars to improve the decking, railing, and lighting on the bridge when it fell. To suggest we would spend money on those items but not on another, even less expensive repair made no sense. But ultimately, after an exhaustive investigation, the NTSB concluded the bridge fell because of an original design flaw dating back to the 1960s.

Time-tested lessons in leadership emerged in this crisis, as they always do during such events. First, when faced with a disaster or crisis of any kind, a leader needs to show up. A leader needs to be visible. Second, a leader needs to take command or control of his or her operations. And third, if there are extraordinary measures that need to be taken, take them. Usually a leader has been given authority ahead of time to act within proper parameters of executive powers. Don't wait. Act.

When the I-35W bridge collapsed, I made a series of these sorts of decisions. For example, Mn/DOT, somewhat understandably, didn't want to have any outside firm or government organization review the historical safety and inspection records of that bridge. They wanted to conduct an internal investigation. But I knew that would reek of bias, so I ordered the hiring of an outside firm to conduct an arm's-length review, top to bottom, stem to stern, of all the decision making from the 1960s up to the day the bridge collapsed. I also ordered an immediate review and assessment of every bridge in the state of Minnesota and undertook that on an emergency and prioritized basis. That review revealed some concerns and resulted in a few of our bridges being temporarily or permanently shut down. One bridge on the Wisconsin border had the very same design as the I-35W bridge, so we were particularly interested to know if that one was similarly at risk.

We also needed to make sure people could move on our roadways. The I-35W bridge was one of the busiest in Minnesota, a main artery for getting in and out of Minneapolis. The impact of having that bridge down was potentially devastating. The bridge fell on a Wednesday, and between that Friday night and Monday morning, crews rebuilt and laid down an entire new lane of freeway on a couple of alternate routes. We added specialized bus routes, rerouting, redirecting, and reprioritizing buses over the entire map. Within days, I think most people would have agreed the traffic flow through Minneapolis was less than ideal but more than manageable—something no one could have imagined on the day the tragedy occurred.

These were just a few of the things we did from an executive level. I also firmly believed there was no room for politics to slow down the construction of a replacement bridge, and we worked to speed up every process we could to get that job done quickly and safely. We decided to put the new bridge in the same footprint as the old bridge so as not to trigger extraordinary environmental reviews. We received immense help from the federal government in the form of emergency replacement funding. We used a dramatically accelerated design-and-build process and paid a premium for the contractor to work around the clock, straight through the winter.

Just ten months after the redesign process began, a brand-new, $350-million, state-of-the-art bridge was in place, and at 5 a.m. on September 18, 2008, the I-35W St. Anthony Falls Bridge opened its massive ten-lane span to traffic.

Two months later, the NTSB released their final report on the cause of the collapse. As I mentioned, the primary problem was a design flaw stemming all the way back to the 1960s, when the bridge was built. Gusset plates on the bridge were only half an inch thick—a flaw that could have brought the bridge down at any point in its four-decade lifespan. The additional construction and expansion over the years, adding additional lanes with the massive weight of additional layers of concrete, only exacerbated the impending disaster. And on the day the bridge fell, the weight of construction equipment and materials centered over one particular area of weakness was the straw that broke that mighty old camel's back.

None of these details would emerge in the immediate aftermath of the collapse, though. In fact, just as the national media turned its attention to other matters and the rescue and recovery efforts came to a close—just as I thought I might be able to turn my attention to some of the other matters a Governor needs to address in an average month—storm clouds were gathering over the southeast corner of Minnesota.

20

* * * * * * * * *

HEAVEN AND EARTH

ON THE NIGHT OF AUGUST 18, 2007, just seventeen days after the bridge collapse, the skies opened up over southeastern Minnesota. More than a foot of rain fell in what seemed like an instant. Rivers rose. Flash floods ripped through this beautiful area, and towns like Caledonia, Rushford, Houston, and La Crescent were hit hard. One couple, along with the woman's seventy-two-year-old mother, climbed to their roof and rode their house like an unstable, over-size boat as the current ripped it from its foundation and carried it downstream past neighbors who stared in horrified amazement, unable to help.

Roadways washed away, sweeping cars and their unsuspecting passengers into the dark waters. Seven people died. Lucky survivors huddled on kitchen tables just beyond the water's reach for hours before rescuers arrived.

The rains kept coming on August 19. A Sunday. People all across Minnesota prayed for the tragedies to end, for God to comfort those who, now in two parts of the state, had lost loved ones with no warning in this single, horrible month.

I sent Black Hawk helicopters as well as three hundred National Guard soldiers to aid in the search and rescue and to guard the populations of whole towns that had been evacuated to higher ground. I toured the area, spent time with the people, and pledged to do what I could. It seemed almost too challenging for even strong Minnesotans to handle. But as usual, they rose to the occasion.

The response needed to be immediate. People on the ground, almost as soon as they got over the initial shock, pledged to help each other—neighbor to neighbor—as they stayed, rebuilt, recovered, and overcame. The Red Cross, along with local churches and charities, got in gear immediately.

More than 1,500 homes were damaged across six counties. Businesses were washed out; damage estimates were massive. Through swift action on the part of many good people, we put a state aid package together and passed it in an emergency special session of the legislature by September 14.

But effectively dealing with disasters and heartbreak takes more than money. It takes more than preparedness. It takes leaders who can connect with the people affected and provide them some level of reassurance and hope when they need it most.

I'm always amazed at the outpouring of relief from communities themselves. I've mentioned the Red Cross, but there's also the Salvation Army, local churches, and other nonprofits that come rolling in, schools that open for emergency shelter, neighbors who help neighbors in their time of need. No matter how many tornadoes and floods I've seen, the people of Minnesota—just like people all across this great country—step up when the chips are down.

Some of the most meaningful moments for me as Governor were the most unplanned and unexpected.

On a fall day in 2006, I had two stops on my schedule: a funeral and a visit to a storm-damaged area just west of the Twin Cities.

The funeral was for a young Marine who had been killed in Iraq. At these terribly sad events, where the bravest young people of our community are laid to rest, a verse of Scripture is often read. At this service, the verse shared was John 15:13, where Jesus told His closest followers on the night before He died, "Greater love has no one than this: to lay down one's life for one's friends." It's a great comfort to the families to see their loss in that context. After the service, the mom and dad told me that their son had chosen to have that verse tattooed on his back. Amazing.

After the funeral I headed to Rogers, where the night before, a tornado had touched down without warning. Tornadoes are a regular occurrence in our state. In the spring of 2010, for example, we had close to forty tornadoes touch down in a single day, causing massive devastation. On this particular day back in 2006, news reports talked about a young girl who had died when a house collapsed during a tornado. At the time, she had been under the care of her teenage brother, who had tried to save her but failed.

My first thoughts were of the horror the girl's parents must have felt. But my second thought was with her brother and the sadness he must be feeling.

The neighborhood was cordoned off. We drove past the barricades and pulled up to the house. The Mayor of the town was there, along with the police and fire crews. The family's pastor and dozens of members of their church had come to lend support as well.

Standing off to the side, by himself, was the teenage boy, who looked shell-shocked. I asked his mom and dad if I could have a word with him, and I took the boy aside.

I asked him how old he was, and then I told him, "When I was about your age, a terrible thing happened to me. My mom died." I shared how much it hurt, how lost I felt. But I also relayed a bit about how the pain had eased over time. I assured him that his sister's death was not his fault and that he was a hero for trying so hard to save her. He probably didn't remember a word of what I said, but I hoped he understood that I cared about him, and so did a lot of other people.

His parents were close enough to hear me, I think. They had a look of gratitude on their faces. Without thinking about it, I called the group around us and asked if we could have a prayer together. With the teenager in the middle of this loving circle, I asked God to bless and comfort this boy who had gone through such a horrible ordeal, to bless the memory of the girl who had died, and to be with their parents, who were going through the worst time in their lives. I prayed for the Mayor and rescue workers and for the other residents who had lost homes in the neighborhood. I prayed for healing and restoration.

A funeral and a neighborhood visit. Nothing that would extend beyond those little circles of individuals, trying to help each other through incredibly difficult circumstances. A couple of moments in time when my role as Governor, my faith in God, and my own personal story came together, hopefully in a positive way, to offer some hope where hope seemed to be slipping away.

21

★ ★ ★ ★ ★ ★ ★ ★ ★ ★

ROCK 'N' ROGUE

VERY EARLY IN MY FIRST TERM as Governor, people started to ask me if I had any national political aspirations. My answer always went something like this: "I don't know, but what I do know is the best way I can gain a good reputation is to be a good Governor."

Compared to, say, my predecessor, Jesse Ventura, I was a relatively unknown Governor as far as most people in America were concerned. That changed a bit during the 2008 presidential race, though, when my name was suddenly bandied about in the media as a potential vice presidential running mate for Senator John McCain.

Many years passed between that first meeting when Mary and I drove the Arizona Senator around and the time when I formed a friendship with John McCain. I'd sent him notes offering support and congratulations at various points in his career in Washington, and he sent me back thank-yous. But it really wasn't until I was elected Governor and got involved in a few issues before Congress that he and I became more familiar with each other.

For instance, before Medicare Part D came along, back when many senior citizens didn't have access to prescription drug coverage, the issue of whether to allow U.S. citizens to import prescription drugs from Canada came before a congressional committee on which McCain served. One way seniors were finding a solution to the skyrocketing cost of prescriptions, especially in northern states such as Minnesota, was to drive over the Canadian border and purchase the prescription medicine they needed from our neighbor to the north, where medicine was often less costly. McCain was very interested in the issue, and much to the dismay of some Republicans, I testified in favor of the practice in a couple of committees. I had a chance to visit with McCain regarding this issue and other matters.

We gradually became better acquainted. Every once in a while he'd pop me a phone call. In 2006, as I was approaching the end of my first term as Governor, he offered to come up to Minnesota to campaign for me. It was a nice offer, and I found it extremely generous and encouraging. I was extraordinarily proud to have John McCain, a national hero, campaign with me.

He wound up coming to Minnesota on two different trips in 2006, and the two of us tooled around together in a small plane from the Twin Cities to Rochester and from Blaine to St. Cloud and Moorhead, with car rides to events in between. I genuinely liked the guy. Not only because he was a strong leader and had served our country so remarkably during the Vietnam War but because, as a bonus, I discovered he was a really good guy. Full of life. Full of energy. Ageless, in a sense. He'd wake up and hit the road with a big Starbucks coffee in his hand, and he'd have a story or a wisecrack for everything. He'd tell these corny old jokes, and it was clear he'd been telling some of the same jokes for twenty years, but he'd laugh the same at each one of them, whether it was Irish drinking jokes about the O'Reilly brothers or the one about two Governors who meet up in the chow line at prison. (One of them says to the other, "The food was a lot better in here when *you* were Governor!")

Campaigning for statewide office, and all the rigors that go with it, was a lot more fun with someone like John McCain along-side. I witnessed a genuine patriot who loves this country and who I thought could lead it courageously. And I let him know it. "Look," I said at one point, "I don't know what you're planning to do in '08, but if you decide to run, I'm with you. Count me in early and definitively." I had no thought about being asked to be a vice presidential candidate. It was not what I was thinking at all, and I'm sure it was not what *he* was thinking. I just really liked and admired him and wanted to help.

At one point I took it a step further. I was sitting in his office in Washington, talking with him about a variety of issues, and I flat out encouraged him to run for President in 2008. I know I wasn't the only one. I told him the country needed him. I told him he was in a unique position in his career, with a unique set of experiences and insights for this moment in history, and that he could bring the country back together with his willingness to be courageous. I believed it strongly. I thought he was an American hero and that he'd lead the country in a bold and courageous way.

He didn't reveal his intentions, but I could tell he was think-ing about running. If you watched his travel schedules, whom he was hiring, what he was doing, it was clear he was getting ready to run. I believe all the campaigning he did around the country for Republican candidates in the 2006 elections—including what he did for me—served as a warm-up, a testing of the waters, for his presidential bid.

After the '06 elections, the Republican Governors assembled for a conference in Florida. I saw McCain there, and once again I told him I was willing and ready to publicly commit to him anytime it was helpful to him. We attended some events together, and by that point it was clear he was going to run.

Even though I wasn't particularly well known publicly, I was in a position to bring some immediate help to the campaign—starting with spreading the word at that Governors' convention and recruiting others to support John McCain. I also served as an adviser to McCain on a variety of domestic issues. My on-the-ground experience with health care and education made it easy for me to provide some ideas and suggestions to him in those areas.

Experience is invaluable. John McCain knows that. John McCain lived it. A lot of people would forget, or at the very least discount, the importance of experience when they went to the voting booth in '08. There are bumper stickers all over this country now expressing the regrets many people feel about voting for someone without any real depth of experience. Change is good. Change is necessary. The problem is, you can't bring about meaningful change that is right for the country if you don't have the skills and experience necessary to pull it off. But none of us had a crystal ball at the end of '06, and no one, including the pollsters, was able to accurately foresee the future.

When John McCain started to get things rolling at the end of that year, he looked like a clear front-runner in the Republican Party. He very quickly staffed a gargantuan and expensive organization.

It's impossible for any candidate, even a candidate with as

much energy and drive and enthusiasm as John McCain, to be everywhere at once. So as time went on, the campaign used me a fair amount on the cable news circuit to represent the campaign as a surrogate speaker—often head-to-head with whatever surrogates the other side put up to represent the Democrats.

I sometimes also hopped on his campaign bus and served as his warm-up act at speeches. For three to five minutes, I would do my best to fire up whatever audience sat before us with the reasons I believed John McCain should be the next President of the United States.

The line I used to frame the thought for those speeches was, "The best sermons aren't preached; they're lived." I would remind audiences, "There are a lot of people who will come through town who are elixir salesmen, who flap their jaws to sell you some miracle cure. But don't buy it—because you want to buy the real thing, the thing that has been tested and proven and that really works. Let's look at John McCain's record. Let's look at what he's done in his life." I'd walk those audiences through the epic life story of John McCain—a life of dedicated, courageous service not only in the military (although I would certainly highlight that) but in what he's done for the American people in the Senate. For all of his so-called maverick ways, for the most part, he had a conservative voting record, and I urged voters to support this great American.

Most importantly, I reminded audiences everywhere that we live in uncertain times and we need a tested, seasoned, wise, strong, courageous, steady hand on the throttle. "When moments of challenge come, we need an experienced leader to have a firm hand on the controls. That's why we need John McCain."

I'm abbreviating greatly here, but you get the point. It was McCain's record and experience that would allow him to see us through the tough times ahead.

But ultimately, experience wasn't what voters were looking for. In the days leading up to the 2008 election, the only sentiment that seemed to resonate with voters was the desire for change.

In hindsight, perhaps that should have been clearer to some people long before November 2008. By the summer of 2007, the McCain campaign was on its keister financially. The fund-raising hadn't brought in nearly as much as his team predicted, and his gargantuan organization wound up draining nearly every penny. It did not look good.

The thing is, when a man like John McCain is down, there isn't a chance he's going to give up. It's just not in his character.

He was under a lot of stress. A lot of people who were supposed to be helping him went sideways on him, and there was a period where it looked like all was lost. There was open speculation about his quitting the race.

Right then and there, at what was about the lowest point of his campaign, Mary and I hosted a fund-raiser for him in St. Paul. We raised a relatively significant amount of money for a medium-size state during a difficult time in a campaign.

But despite all the challenges, John McCain had a steely resolve. He and Mary and I had dinner following the fund-raiser, and in our conversation he projected that resolve. His tone conveyed strength. He was steadfast. He was not unaware of the challenges, just rock-solid certain he could overcome them. If he was worried, it certainly didn't show. We affirmed that we were with him for the long haul, regardless of challenges or the outcome.

For the remainder of 2007, I was back on the road with him. Traveling with a candidate who is out of money and down and out in the polls might not make a lot of sense to some people. But Mary and I had no intention of walking away from an American hero. The way we looked at it, the hardship he was facing was a test not just of his character but of his supporters' character and his team's character and integrity. We believed in him because of the man he was, not because of his position in the polls or the likelihood that he was going to have more or less money down the road.

Campaign stops in New Hampshire and Iowa, the key early states in the election process, were frequent. In those two places, politics is as personal as it gets. Whatever ideas of a pampered politician you may have go out the window when you're grinding it out with little money and fading polls. McCain and I wound up traveling in a modest van, driving around to people's living rooms. There were times when it would be McCain and me, sometimes with his wife, Cindy, in the room with the host couple, their kids, a few neighbors or relatives, and maybe ten other people. But he slogged it out, doggedly, persistently grinding out the rest of 2007.

I never had a single conversation with John McCain about whether he might quit. In fact, he was adamant that he wouldn't, both publicly and privately. All he ever said was, "We will charge forward" and "It's going to be okay." I never observed even a quiet moment when he showed any doubt whatsoever.

After all, he'd seen fiercer battles than this.

Beyond my resolve to stand by him win or lose, I truly believed he could win. I knew it would be extremely difficult, but his persistent and gritty determination projected confidence. It looked like a tough mountain to climb, but he was the guy to do it.

It became clear early on, however, that he wasn't going to do well in the Iowa caucuses. He was anti-ethanol, and Iowa is a corn state. He wasn't the favorite among the social conservatives. You could feel it in the rooms and see it in the polls. Michigan didn't seem like it was in the cards either. So the last line of defense was New Hampshire, a place where every handshake, every one-on-one interaction with the voters, truly mattered. That was one of the places where he had spent so much time in those living rooms and small-town restaurants, showing the voters who he really was.

On January 8, 2008, the night of the New Hampshire primary, Mary and I watched the results on television. He won—and Mary was moved to tears. She has such a great love and respect for John McCain, and she wanted to see him elected as badly as I did. So to see him pull out that victory after walking a long and difficult road was a thrill. We were elated.

We both thought at that point, *Well, it's still a long, uphill climb, but even if he doesn't make it, this is a remarkable victory.* The New Hampshire victory was a worthy and amazing feat, considering how far he'd come. We talked about it that night. We hadn't wanted this iconic figure who had served and loved his country for his whole life in such astounding and courageous ways to go out defeated. Had he not won New Hampshire, I think the rest would've fallen away from him as well. But when he clawed back and won, we thought, *There's some redemption for him.* Redemption, courtesy of the Granite State.

It was a great comeback story and only the beginning of our seeing just how far McCain could push that throttle with his steadfast determination. Suddenly he was off like a rocket, and it was time for us to hold on for a ride full of twists and turns we never saw coming.

* * * * * * * * * *

AS IMPORTANT AS IT WAS to me to support John McCain, I was in the middle of a legislative session back home during the first half of 2008, and my role as Governor always came first. So I wound up moving in and out of the picture, making appearances without him, going on television shows on behalf of the campaign, and jumping on the bus once in a while. Following the New Hampshire win, I campaigned with him in Florida.

The caucuses and primaries were settled by late March, and lo and behold, McCain emerged as the Republican candidate of choice. Back on top. Right where he started. And that's when the rumor mills started churning.

Bloggers have certainly changed the landscape on the media front. The speed at which news travels—true, false, slanted, indifferent, or otherwise—will never be the same. There's impatience in the blogosphere, an untethering from the political pace that big newspapers and television conglomerates once set. And the blogosphere wanted to figure out and break the news on John McCain's pick for a running mate as soon as possible. But that wasn't McCain's plan.

I don't recall the first place I ever read or heard my name bandied about as a possible VP choice. At first there were a good twenty names or so in the media-invented mix of potential running mates, and I was one—in part because I had stuck with him through the low points of his campaign, I'm sure, and because I had been frequently out there on the talk shows representing him. There were times when they'd mention my name while purporting some inside knowledge: *"According to a source in the McCain campaign, here's what they're thinking. . . ."*

All I can say is John McCain and I had never discussed it ourselves. Not once.

I did not join the campaign as a way to angle for a job. I had no expectations whatsoever. So when it came to media speculation, I simply let it go. As time went by, I stopped thinking about it; there were still something like fifteen names, and mine was just one of them. But the chatter continued to narrow in terms of the number of people mentioned as most likely choices. When the intensity of the speculation increased, I started to wonder. Still, I figured, surely there would be a massive vetting process, and such a decision couldn't be made without significant warning. So with every passing day, the likelihood of it seemed to be more remote.

The speculation grew when McCain asked Mary and me and a few other couples to join him at his ranch in Sedona, Arizona. All we were told was that the trip would provide a chance for a little sightseeing and some campaign strategizing.

The weekend was just that, with good company in a great atmosphere. The McCains have a beautiful property that they've turned into a compound of sorts over the years. There's the main house, and sprinkled around the perimeter of the property are cottages for guests. There were many guests that weekend.

We talked politics part of the time, and the other part we spent relaxing with friends. One night we ate barbecue, which McCain grilled himself, a source of personal pride for him. The next day, in a small caravan of cars, we took in the sights on the way to a little mining town in the hills, where we had lunch. Then we visited the red rocks in Sedona. All the while, campaign ideas and suggestions were welcome.

Not once did the topic of my being a potential VP pick—or the topic of the VP pick at all—come up. Mary and I left the McCain compound appreciative of the great hospitality but without any additional information about his potential choice for VP, including how that selection was likely to be made.

By the time July came around, the possibility of being selected seemed to have disappeared. There was just no way. The convention was scheduled for September 1. I figured, *If they were considering me, they certainly would have contacted us to begin the vetting process before now.*

I figured wrong.

* * * * * * * * * *

AT SOME POINT IN EARLY JULY, McCain's campaign manager, Rick Davis, called me out of the blue. "The Senator asked me to call and tell you that we would like to consider you for the VP slot," he said, "and we wanted to see if that's something you'd be open to."

What does someone say when he's asked if he'd like to be considered for the job of Vice President of the United States?

I said, "Well, tell the Senator I'd be honored if he'd consider me."

The next call came from the office of A. B. Culvahouse Jr., the well-known attorney from the powerful international law firm O'Melveny & Myers, whom McCain had placed in charge of the vetting process. Culvahouse actually served as White House counsel to Ronald Reagan during the last two years of his presidency, advising on such complicated and gravely important issues as the Iran-Contra hearings.

I was told other lawyers in his firm would handle the initial process, and then Culvahouse himself would handle the face-to-face.

The process began with a letter, formally requesting participation in the vetting process. When that letter arrived at our home in Eagan, I held it in my hand and thought how remarkable life is. Unpredictable. Filled with possibilities.

What began very quickly now required a phenomenally huge amount of time and hard work. The first step required preparation of written responses to an extraordinarily long questionnaire that arrived in the mail. This wasn't a census form, mind you. It was page after page of every conceivable question about my personal and family life, as well as my various business and political dealings through the years. Ditto for Mary.

That questionnaire also required us to produce a large volume of documents. Tax returns, real-estate records, investment records. Questions ranged from "Have you ever been disciplined?" to "Have you ever been arrested?" to "Have you ever been unfaithful to your wife?" They wanted to know if I had ever been subject to any controversies while in office. Had I ever written anything that had been published? And if so, copies were requested.

The responses took digging, time, and many late nights. Mary and I were a team of two. No staff. Only us. We didn't have any kind of private, personal assistants in our lives. We couldn't use our official staff—this wasn't official state business. So, as has often been the case in our lives, it was just the two of us.

We didn't have the luxury of time, either. We were counting down to the Republican National Convention. So there was a tightening deadline on the whole process, and I remember being up well after midnight several days in a row. It felt like we were in law school again. In fact, I was thankful we'd had that kind of experience in compiling massive amounts of documentation and information in an organized fashion on a deadline.

I remember the two of us joking one night at some inhumane hour, "No way is Mitt Romney doing this by himself!" We had a good laugh over that—not even knowing if he had been called for the vetting process, as likely as it seemed. Throughout all of this, we were totally in the dark regarding who the other potential running mates might be. All we knew was that if this written part of the examination went well, they would narrow the field and move on to the next stage.

It was kind of comical at times—the Governor and First Lady in the middle of the night organizing stacks of paper now strewn all over the computer-room floor, trying to make tabs and get it all in the right place, checking to see if the three-hole punch worked and then running out to Kinko's for photocopies. It was time-consuming, to say the least, but for Mary and me, it was actually a lot of fun. How often does a couple get to sit down and sort through decades' worth of memories and tough questions together?

So we boxed up and sent in our written materials with no idea what might happen next. All we could do was be patient. In the meantime, September 1 was drawing nearer, and the convention would be held at the Xcel Energy Center in St. Paul. Regardless of what happened next, there was a convention to host.

We were into early August when a call finally came in from one of Culvahouse's assistants. "We want to take this to the next step and meet in person." It was to be surreptitious. They were very clear: no press coverage whatsoever. No leaks. They had given a lot of thought to how to get in and out of town unnoticed, and they pulled it off. Not a single press outlet discovered they were there.

They arrived on a weekend. Like most people, I generally dress a little more casually on the weekends. Unless there's some official business, jeans and a T-shirt are the order of the day. Not this weekend, though. Suit and tie required.

So Culvahouse and one of his law partners arrived. Culvahouse is a seasoned, tall, buttoned-down, Brooks Brothers, Washington lawyer in his early- to midsixties who's beloved and respected by the legal community. He's a counselor and adviser, and that's exactly the aura he projects in person. His firm had already asked me everything under the sun and had the benefit of reviewing all of the written material we'd submitted in advance, so I doubted he'd hit me with any unexpected or surprise questions.

Mary joined me after a point. She would be grilled too.

There were no video cameras. No tape recorders. Just us—

sitting around in suits and ties for no reason other than out of respect for the topic at hand.

We sat down, exchanged pleasantries, poured some coffee. I welcomed our visitors to Minnesota and told them I was honored to be considered. The first question right out of the gate was, "If you were the President of the United States and U.S. intelligence officials came into your office and told you they knew where Osama bin Laden was and that we could take him out in the next four hours with reasonable probability, but there would be a likelihood of some civilian casualties, would you do it?"

Seriously.

I replied without hesitation. "Yes." He prompted me to say more on the subject, and it was immediately clear they weren't here to ask me questions about grade school or whether I'd ever had a DWI (which I haven't). Nope. It was, "Would you kill Osama bin Laden if you had the chance?"

That question set the tone for the interview. Culvahouse needed to determine whether I would get rattled or unnerved by any questioning, whether my thinking was sequential, whether I had a good understanding of the issues of the day, and whether I had flexibility in thought and study. I appreciated the question, I think. Regardless of whether a scenario like that actually unfolds, he wanted to see, in terms of composure, how potential candidates responded—whether they demonstrated sound decision making and articulated clear reasoning. It was a good technique. It was a big question, designed to get me off-balance.

The interview gave Culvahouse a chance to gather a broad impression of my personality, demeanor, and personal history. I'm lucky, I suppose, that the things I've done particularly badly—stupidly, some might say—I've done in public. So my mistakes are known.

As far as I could tell, the interview went well. Mary and I both walked away from the meeting feeling reasonably good. We'd delivered our best effort. But those feelings wouldn't be confirmed in any way after Culvahouse left the driveway. We didn't hear a word. Except for a few follow-up requests for more paperwork, it was complete radio silence.

Days went by. I continued acting as a surrogate for the McCain campaign, speaking whenever asked via satellite on various television shows while the man himself, now the presumptive nominee, crisscrossed the country.

As we all would later learn, McCain was very late in making his choice of a running mate. Various books have detailed the process, and it's pretty clear that his mind was unsettled when it came to whom he should choose.

Mary and I both thought, *You don't pick somebody for Vice President without giving some advance warning.* And as the conventions, both Democrat and Republican, grew closer, we came to the logical conclusion that we were out. It's strange to have such a large, potentially life-altering decision about your future just hang in the balance and then peter out. In some ways, it wasn't terribly different from many of the crossroads in our lives. More often than not, things are out of our hands.

We cannot know what will happen tomorrow, and it's clear God intends life for His followers to be a trust walk. The book of James speaks to this issue. "Now listen, you who say, 'Today or tomorrow we will go to this or that city, spend a year there, carry on business and make money.' Why, you do not even know what will happen tomorrow. What is your life? You are a mist that appears for a little while and then vanishes. Instead, you ought to say, 'If it is the Lord's will, we will live and do this or that'" (James 4:13-15).

So, as we had when the chatter about me started in the press back in the spring, Mary and I wrote it off.

A few days before the Democratic Convention got under way in Denver, I received yet another call, this time asking me to fly out as one of a group of surrogates that would be part of a media rebuttal squad at the other side's big rally, which would start off at the Pepsi Center on August 25 and culminate with Obama's acceptance speech three days later at INVESCO Field in front of some eighty thousand people.

The McCain campaign had already announced that he was going to name his vice presidential pick on August 29 at a rally in Ohio—clearly a way to wedge into the Democrats' big news week and immediately draw press attention back to the Republicans. So I went to Denver to start my spinmeister duties knowing full well I couldn't possibly be the vice presidential nominee. There was no way you'd take your VP pick and have him appear on air in front of the entire press corps the day before the announcement, completely unaware and with no time to prepare. I hadn't met recently with McCain. I didn't have a speech. Given the timing, I knew someone else had been selected.

The media speculation was frenzied, though, and my name was still present in all kinds of media discussions—along with Mitt Romney, Joe Lieberman, Bobby Jindal, and others. On Thursday, I was scheduled to do some morning show appearances—*Morning Joe*, then *Fox & Friends*—followed by an afternoon of press events on Obama's big day. But halfway through those duties in Denver, I received a message from the RNC: "McCain's making his VP pick, and we need to get you out of here." The general feeling was that there was a good chance the name would leak before Friday, and once that happened, the press would ask only about the pick; any other messages we were trying to deliver in Denver would be shoved aside. The rest of the schedule for the day was canceled, and I caught the next flight out of Denver.

The press, on the other hand, didn't quite get the same message. The message they took away from my sudden departure was, "Pawlenty has canceled his schedule in Denver and is on an emergency flight back to Minnesota. He must be the pick!"

By the time I reached the gate in Minneapolis, the press was in a feeding frenzy. One reporter actually bought a plane ticket so he could get through security and meet me at the gate as I stepped off the plane. Much to his disappointment, he wasn't getting a scoop. I told him, "I've not been asked, and I have no reason to believe it's me."

Meanwhile, a national media stakeout had developed outside the Governor's Residence in St. Paul, and a second stakeout was under way in our neighborhood in Eagan. My neighbor called me and said, "Somebody should get out here; this is out of control. There are satellite and news trucks up and down the street; they're in people's yards."

Since there would be no way for me to avoid that media crush in Eagan, I got on the phone with Mary, and we met up at the Governor's Residence. I drove in through the rear gate, through the alley, away from the media pack on Summit Avenue.

Anna had a volleyball game scheduled that night at her high school, and I was glad to be back home early with a chance to watch her play. We didn't want the press corps to follow us to the high school and disrupt the game—talk about an embarrassment for a teenager! So we came up with a simple plan. We sent the State Troopers out the front gate with an official car, while we slipped out the back gate and headed to the high school.

Amazingly, it worked. I sat in the stands with Mary, and we

watched Anna play, completely undisturbed for half an hour or so. Then a photographer showed up. Someone at the game had tipped off the press. He turned out to be an AP photographer, and he snapped photos of us in the stands watching the game. A videographer showed up a few minutes later and soon afterward posted video of us cheering on YouTube—me sitting at a high school volleyball game in Minnesota, with a baseball cap on, maybe fifteen hours before the VP announcement was scheduled in Ohio. You would think the press would get the hint, right? But when we returned to the Governor's Residence, we once again had to avoid the media circus outside the front gate.

The press was there late into the night. Camped out. Waiting. But when I opened my eyes in the morning and turned on the television, the answer they were all looking for was scrolling across the bottom of Fox News: *McCain Picks Palin.*

The official announcement had not yet been made, but if true, I thought it was a surprising and intriguing selection. I had met Sarah Palin, the Governor of Alaska, during National Governors Association conferences. In all of the many months of speculation, her name was rarely mentioned, and the press did not seem to think she was being considered.

My best guess was that it would be Romney. I actually talked to Mitt about that at some point later on, and he said he thought it was going to be *me.*

WCCO radio called me a little after six that morning. I told the morning show host once again that I absolutely was not McCain's pick and that I did not have any personal knowledge about who his pick was—despite what Fox News was already telling the world.

Mary and I went downstairs for breakfast, and as we sat down, the phone rang. John McCain was on the line.

He told me that he had made his pick and that he felt he

needed to "try something different." I told him it was a gutsy pick. A good pick.

Next I made my way to the Minnesota State Fair to broadcast my regular Friday morning radio show at 9 a.m. I talked about the fact that I wasn't McCain's selection live, on the air. Still, a pack of national and local reporters followed me around looking for answers.

When the press finally changed their line of questioning and started to ask me what I thought about his decision, I said very positive things about Governor Palin. "Based on what I know about the Governor, she's a strong leader." McCain, from everything I had seen, was a man of sound judgment, and to me that could only mean that Sarah Palin would make a great Vice President.

There was a funny moment earlier that morning, though. Just after I got off the phone with McCain, I took our dog out for a walk so she could do her dog's duty. We were out of sight of any remaining press. As I put the little bag over my hand and bent down to pick up her poop, I thought to myself, *Well, this is the only number two I'll be picking up today.*

I had to laugh. The whole process had come and gone in a very short period of time. Dwelling on it served no purpose. But I tucked that slightly crass, self-directed joke into my proverbial pocket, thinking it might be fun to share it at an appropriate moment during the Republican Convention the following week.

* * * * * * * * * *

I HAD SPENT a considerable amount of time over the past year and a half planning this convention, promoting it, raising money for it. It's a big deal for any state to host a convention, let alone one that had grown so personal and close to my heart because of my connection to McCain.

The security and public-safety concerns surrounding the event were enormous. So we spent a lot of time dealing with those issues, involving the National Guard both before and during the convention. Command and control responsibility for big parts of the security aspects were a major undertaking. Just look at history—1968 in Chicago, for instance—for examples of what can go wrong if that responsibility isn't handled properly. So in those final days and hours, I was busy.

As it turned out, Mother Nature had plans that were much bigger than anything McCain or the RNC could have predicted. Plans that left all of us scrambling to do the right thing for America at a difficult moment. The convention was set to begin on Labor Day, September 1, just as a hurricane slammed into the Gulf Coast. Countless people had evacuated the New Orleans area, fleeing under the burden of still-fresh memories of the destruction they had been dealt by Hurricane Katrina three years earlier.

Most of the entire first day of the convention was canceled or rescheduled. First Lady Laura Bush, who had been scheduled to speak that evening, gave a short speech alongside Cindy McCain, encouraging everyone to support the hurricane relief effort.

Of course there are endless events planned around any convention, and all of those would be somewhat subdued in the wake of the hurricane.

The change in schedule opened an opportunity for Mary and me to gather together some of McCain's family and closest supporters, so we invited them to dinner. The weather cooperated nicely and we sat on the terrace of the Governor's Residence and relaxed over a casual dinner. It was good to see everyone. Cindy McCain came early and brought their sons. Their neighbors, the Harpers, came, along with Lindsey Graham, Fred Thompson, and Joe and Hadassah Lieberman. Charlie Black, a senior adviser to the campaign, came too. Even among this crowd, there was no talk of the VP pick. Despite what some people might expect, politicians don't all sit around endlessly talking politics. The only mention of any of the twists and turns of the previous week came later in the evening, as folks were starting to leave, when Charlie Black said to me, "You were right in there till the end."

I wouldn't get a chance to spend time with Senator McCain throughout the rest of the convention, and in our future meetings, the topic of his vice presidential selection never came up. Why he decided the way he did is a matter of well-ground public record at this point. It's immaterial to my respect for him and our friendship. I never asked, because I didn't think he owed me an explanation.

By Wednesday, the convention was up and running at full speed just in time for a major speech by Rudy Giuliani, the former Mayor of New York City, the hero of 9/11 who famously questioned Barack Obama's lack of leadership experience in front of that massive crowd at the Xcel Energy Center and a nation's watchful eyes.

The big headliner for that Wednesday, September 3, though, was Sarah Palin. There was a lot of speculation in the air about how Palin was going to do. She did terrific. Mary and I had seats together in the arena, and there was no question Governor Palin showed an ability to fire up that crowd to an entirely new level of enthusiasm. The delegates were clearly pleased.

Minnesotans did an excellent job welcoming the large crowds that week, and we still receive compliments on how "Minnesota Nice" was fully on display. All went as smoothly as could possibly be expected. The convention kept Mary and me busy from early morning to late in the evening each day. We hosted and attended many events, I delivered a brief speech to the delegates, and in the roll call of the states, I announced Minnesota's tally. I even found a perfect moment to share my "number two" joke—with Triumph, the Insult Comic Dog, the puppet covering the convention for the Conan O'Brien show. (Unfortunately my joke never made it on air. I thought it was right up Triumph's alley!)

McCain's speech was powerful, and we hoped the boost from the speech and the convention would carry him strongly into the following weeks.

Over the course of the next two months, however, the election slipped away from John McCain.

Those who blame the loss that November, even in part, on his choice of Sarah Palin as running mate lose sight of the big picture. In truth, it didn't matter whom he would have picked. Once the economy collapsed, Barack Obama was going to win that election. That was apparent. Everywhere you went, you could feel it. McCain could have picked Superman or Wonder Woman and he still wasn't going to win.

At the time, Sarah Palin had more executive experience than Barack Obama. She was the Governor of a state. She had been the Mayor of a city. She had chaired a pipeline commission in Alaska and had cleaned house, kicking out the old boys. On the basis of executive leadership experience alone, she had many times the experience of McCain's opponent. In the fall of 2008, Barack Obama had not held an executive position and had barely warmed the chair in his U.S. Senate office.

Then there's what I call "peering down the glasses" by people who, without carefully considering all the facts, proclaim, "She's not educated in the right schools in the right way; she's not what we expect; she doesn't say just what we'd like." The presumption behind such comments is that if you don't fit a certain mold, somehow you're incapable. Baloney. You don't accomplish what Sarah Palin has accomplished if you're incapable.

For comparison's sake, look at Joe Biden, a sincerely pleasant guy with a bright smile and a winsome personality. He was in the United States Senate for thirty-five years. His entire life, more or less, has been spent in politics. Yet many of the major judgments or suggestions he's made regarding foreign policy have been wrong, and he has a reputation for speaking when he ought to bite his tongue.

What you learn with any politician, just as with any leader or any person of notoriety, is that once you get right up close, you see that everyone has some strengths and some weaknesses.

We all do. So who is it that the media and the supposedly disappointed electorate were comparing Sarah Palin to? Palin versus the ideal? Joe Biden's not perfect, and as we've learned, neither is Barack Obama. The ideal doesn't exist. So this idea that you can only be wise and correct if you are from one of the great educational or political institutions on the East Coast—I just don't buy that.

There are different kinds of smarts. There's street smarts, life-experience smarts, people smarts, book smarts. If you spend a little bit of time around Sarah Palin, you can sense and feel that this is someone who has a lot more capacity than people fully recognize.

Just look at the energy and the passion and the debate and the turnout and the involvement she inspires. She came to Minnesota in 2010, on a Tuesday afternoon, in the middle of a workday, and twelve thousand people showed up to see her. Many of them were camped out by breakfast time so they could get in the door first upon her arrival that afternoon. These people all had tickets. They were all going to get in. The only reason they camped out is because they wanted to sit up front. There aren't five other politicians in the country who could come to town and get half that turnout.

Sarah Palin has become a force of nature in the Republican Party. She inspires people in the conservative cause. She exudes enthusiasm, and that energy is the fuel of grassroots politics. We need that kind of energy and fuel from people all over this country if we want a shot at setting America back on course.

While some might still debate McCain's selection, the undeniable truth is that it took courage to stand up to the critics, the pundits, and the expectations of the media and the Washington establishment and choose Sarah Palin in the first place. The long-term effect of that courageous play in the middle of a historic election was to provide a tremendous platform to this previously unknown Governor. A platform that even today allows her to rally conservatives while the Obama administration continues to fumble the ball with America's future.

22

★★★★★★★★★★

CHALLENGES TODAY

THERE'S NOTHING QUITE LIKE Inauguration Day. The pomp and history that runs through it are unique in American life. Politics aside, the setting and the significance are truly breathtaking.

In 2008, I campaigned against Barack Obama and his party and did everything I could to elect Republicans. But as I sat with the other Governors on the West Front of the Capitol, looking out at tens of thousands of Americans on the National Mall, that didn't matter. The peaceful transfer of power transcends political parties and is always inspiring. It's the realization of the dream of our Founding Fathers.

President-elect Obama had run an inspiring campaign, fueled by optimistic words: *Hope. Change. Yes, we can.* While many of us disagreed with his proposals, I was hopeful he would govern the way he had campaigned and keep his promises to deliver truly bipartisan reforms and stop reckless spending.

Yet from day one, President Obama turned his back on those promises. Rather than govern from the center, he proved to be a partisan liberal. To correct a recession caused in part by government meddling in the economy, the President called for unprecedented levels of . . . government meddling in the economy! $787 billion in so-called stimulus spending. A reaffirmation of the Wall Street bailout and additional bailouts for auto companies, state governments, and unions.

Granted, President Obama inherited an awful budget situation. But rather than hit the brakes, he accelerated spending beyond all imagining. During his first two years in office, President Obama has overseen the first two budgets with trillion-dollar deficits in American history. He has racked up more debt than every President from Washington to Reagan *combined*. His 2010 budget plan will double the national debt in five years and nearly triple it in ten.

Four million jobs have been lost, and millions of Americans who want full-time employment can find only part-time work. Meanwhile, in the federal government (where there never seems to be a recession), federal employees now receive average total compensation of $123,000 a year. Amazingly, government workers now make more than their private sector counterparts. Foreclosures hit an all-time high around the country. Yet in the midst of this Great Recession, the three richest counties in America are suburbs of Washington, D.C.

Contrary to what the President and his advisers promised, investment, innovation, and growth have stalled, even as taxpayers subsidize bailouts, carve-outs, and handouts for the big corporations and unions with power in Washington.

Every child born today inherits a $30,000 share in a national debt that now stands at more than $13 trillion. Do you know how much a trillion dollars is? You could spend $1,000 every minute for 1,900 years and still have money left over. Or think of it this way: 13 trillion seconds ago was 410,000 BC. The point is, when you talk in terms of trillions of dollars, you're talking about numbers so big that we can't fully comprehend them. Yet these are the kinds of figures our government tosses around like it's no big deal. But it is a big deal. It's bankrupting our government and killing our economy.

President Obama broke his promise to pay for "every dime" of new government spending. Of course, that's not the only promise that he has broken. He said that health-care reform would be a transparent, bipartisan effort; instead, the health-care bill was written behind closed doors and passed without any Republican support. He promised to not raise taxes on the middle class, but he broke that pledge.

This is not change we can believe in. This is change we still can't believe.

Shortly after taking office, Obama, who promised during the campaign to crack down on special interests, brazenly began to pay off special interests. He bought two car companies to pay off the labor bosses who ruined them. He bailed out wasteful state and local governments to protect public-employee unions. For the teachers unions, he eliminated a wildly popular and successful school choice program for poor minority families in Washington, D.C.

The candidate who promised to change the way Washington worked has only made things worse as President. On President Obama's watch, Congress has passed thousand-page bills costing trillions of dollars without ever seeing them, let alone reading them. The cap-and-trade energy tax, passed by Nancy Pelosi's

House of Representatives in June 2009, had literally *not even been written!* Chunks of the bill had not yet been printed, and loose copies were strewn about without *anyone* able to know what was kept in and what was left out of the bill.

These practices are so unmoored from America's founding principles, so divorced from economic reality and democratic norms, they threaten the very future of the country.

The President ceaselessly—and gracelessly—blames George W. Bush for running the country into a ditch, but he himself is now driving it off a cliff. Unfortunately for all of us, the current administration and Democrat-controlled Congress have led us further down the road of the socialist, liberal agenda than at any time in the history of this country.

Americans are famously optimistic and confident. Throughout our history, every American generation has taken pride in the knowledge that their sons and daughters would be better off than they were themselves. But today people have doubts. And now surveys show Americans worrying that the next generation will be worse off—that America is in a state of decline.

Listening to the debate in Washington, a pattern seems to be emerging: folks at the bottom of our economy get a handout, folks at the top get a bailout, and the rest of us get our wallets out. The average person is being squeezed from every direction, and the liberals in Washington appear out of answers.

Probably because they never had them to begin with.

And yet, look around today. On the whole, we are an incredibly strong and wealthy nation. It's important to remember, no matter what side of the immigration debate you're on, there's a reason millions of people want to come here every year.

The American Dream isn't a dream. It's real.

President Obama doesn't talk much about the American

Dream. He talks about renewing or keeping America's promise. The difference might not strike you as significant, but it is. *America's promise* suggests something that hasn't yet been fulfilled. It implies that we're always coming up short, and that we need leaders to *teach* us how to reach our full potential as a nation.

That's nonsense.

The United States is the freest, greatest, strongest, most prosperous, and most successful nation in human history. We are the nation of the Declaration of Independence, the Constitution, and the Bill of Rights. We are the nation of Lewis and Clark, Thomas Edison, Henry Ford, George Marshall, and Martin Luther King Jr. We are the nation that built the Panama Canal and orchestrated D-day and V-E Day. We put men on the moon. We liberated millions of people from Fascism, Nazism, and Communism, and our economic engine has enriched the world for two centuries. Our innovators have made leaps in technology, medicine, communications, and security and done it decades— even centuries—ahead of the rest of the world.

Unlike the liberal fantasy of America's promise, the American Dream is not a collective project, but a personal one. This is what President Obama and liberals like him don't understand. They think government runs the country, rather than the people. They think government's proper role is to make people happy. It is this misguided vision of government that has gotten us $13 trillion into debt.

The Declaration of Independence doesn't say we have the right to happiness, but to "the *pursuit* of happiness." The role of government under our Constitution is not to guarantee that people's dreams come true but to guarantee that people are free to make their own dreams come true.

Liberals scoff at this vision. They argue that modern life is too complicated for people to figure out. But in reality, modern life is too complicated for *government* to figure out. Government is not evil. It's just bloated and inefficient, and it permeates everything. But government nonetheless serves vital functions in our national life, such as protecting our borders and curbing threats to our peace and security. So what *can* a limited constitutional government do to get America moving again? Plenty.

* * * * * * * * * *

LIKE DOCTORS, POLICYMAKERS SHOULD ADHERE to the principle of "First, do no harm." Politicians have a professional incentive to always look busy—introducing bills, securing earmarks, and sending out press releases. They think this endears them to their voters and helps win elections. But constantly trying to please voters with more government programs is poisonous to our economy.

The last few years in particular have witnessed national politicians dangling trillion-dollar, thousand-page bills that redefine our economy, all the while scratching their heads about why businesses won't hire and investors won't invest.

The first thing Washington must do is *stop*. Stop the spending, stop the borrowing, and stop the meddling. The federal government is not just too big; it's *way* too big. Every dollar Congress adds to the debt is a dollar that government is planning to tax—either from you or from your kids—down the road. That reality discourages investment, hiring, and business expansion.

Liberal progressives subscribe to the economic theory that government spending has a "multiplier effect"—that every dollar of government spending creates several dollars' worth of economic growth. The theory was first proposed by John Maynard Keynes during the Great Depression in the 1930s; it failed then, and it has failed just about every time it's been tried since. If government spending could create wealth, then the Obama-Pelosi spending spree would have already paid off the debt and made us all rich!

But government spending isn't growth. It's simply tax dollars being redistributed over and over again. And that is the biggest failure of the Obama administration's tax-and-spend philosophy.

You're a taxpayer. Let's say I take a dollar from your paycheck. I bring it into the federal bureaucracy, spin it around, and take thirty cents to pay for overhead, salaries, pensions, and a lot of bloat. Then I redeploy your remaining seventy cents back into the economy. I didn't grow your dollar. If you had kept that dollar, you would have bought groceries or dinner; you would have put it toward your kids' shoes or college; you would've put it toward your mortgage or, if you're lucky, tickets to a Vikings game. Who knows what you would have done with it? To label the phenomenon of the government taking your money and then spending it as "growth" is a joke.

But there's a source of government spending that's even worse. I'm talking about borrowed money. What if instead of taking a dollar from you to redistribute, I go ahead and take a dollar from the Chinese government that your children will have to pay back with interest? This is essentially what happens when we can't pay our bills and foreign countries buy our debt.

Stopping this fiscal insanity means recognizing the hard truth that current levels of spending and debt cannot be sustained. Congress has not only maxed out the national credit card, it has also racked up trillions more in unfunded promises for future entitlement spending on Social Security and Medicare.

The same politicians who are running up the debt on future generations talk as though even modest spending cuts are too excruciatingly painful. Republicans are not blameless in this area. But in truth, fiscal discipline is most painful to the politicians them-selves, who would rather act like Santa Claus than statesmen.

Contrary to liberal rhetoric, spending cuts are not impossible. Take Minnesota, for example. From 1960 to 2002, state spend-ing increased by an average of 21 percent every two years. I low-ered the average growth of annual spending during my time as Governor to just under 2 percent and balanced the budget without raising taxes. In 2009, we cut state spending in real terms for the first time in 150 years.

It wasn't easy; in fact, I used my veto pen 123 times to cut spending and limit government growth and waste. When the leg-islature sent me a bill in 2009 calling for $1 billion in tax increases to balance the budget, I vetoed it and made $2.7 billion of spend-ing unallotments instead. It can be done.

In reality, my administration just did what any family would do. We determined what we could *not* cut, then cut just about everything else. Washington must do the same. We cannot sacri-fice our national security, and we must keep the promises we have made to our veterans, seniors, and near seniors in terms of retire-ment security and health care. But nearly everything else must be on the table.

In the short term, that means declaring a federal hiring freeze and a moratorium on additional spending, period. It means taking back unspent TARP and stimulus money, putting it toward reduc-ing our crushing debt. It means hitting the fiscal Reset button and cutting spending. And it means repealing Obamacare.

The health-care status quo may be unsustainable, but the Democrats' health-care takeover is intolerable. The first step toward true health-care and fiscal reform is repealing Obamacare, period. For my part, I issued an executive order forbidding any Minnesota department or agency from applying for grant funding or projects offered under Obamacare unless required by law or unless it was part of Minnesota's own health-care reform efforts. All of us need to do everything we can to stop this harmful program, delay it, and limit it in any way we can. We must then work toward a reform model that uses market forces to put citizens in charge of their health-care decisions.

But it's not enough to put a leash on Washington. We need to *un*leash America's entrepreneurs, businesses, and investors by extending the tax cuts of 2001 and 2003, then cutting taxes even more. And we must set the corporate tax rate at or below the international average of 26 percent to reduce the incentive for businesses and jobs to move overseas.

Democrats in Washington look at the big deficits and see a need to raise revenue with higher taxes. But raising taxes by hundreds of billions of dollars on small businesses, families, and investors is like hanging a Closed sign over our economy. Regulatory and tax uncertainty under the Obama administration is causing entrepreneurs and small businesses to sit on their cash and not hire new workers. We cannot expect them to hire and take risks if federal policies remain rigged against them, punishing success with taxes and rewarding failure with bailouts.

In Minnesota, during my two terms as Governor, we cut taxes by nearly $800 million. We placed a cap on property taxes and then cut property taxes to impose fiscal discipline on our local governments. We got rid of our marriage tax penalty.

If we can do it in Minnesota—the land of Hubert Humphrey, Walter Mondale, and Al Franken—we can do it in Washington.

The United States is not *under*taxed. As President Reagan said, "The current tax code is a daily mugging." Raising taxes now will derail any hope for economic recovery.

I believe in broader tax reform and additional tax relief.

I support reforms that avoid the classic liberal trap of class warfare, pitting citizen against citizen and worker against worker. I believe we must move toward a flatter, fairer, and simpler system—and a single tax form a small-business owner or family could complete without hiring a team of accountants. *Everyone* should be paying lower taxes—Republicans and Democrats, rich and poor, families and individuals, small businesses and large corporations. And we should eliminate once and for all the un-American practice of double taxation—no more death tax, and no more taxes on dividend income or capital gains.

But first things first. We must stabilize the economic environment by taking new spending and new taxes off the table, as well as lifting President Obama's onerous and unnecessary regulations on small businesses.

* * * * * * * * * *

TODAY, THE FEDERAL GOVERNMENT isn't just broken; it's broke.

And the reason is simple. It does too much. Consider this fact: When the House of Representatives expanded to 435 members in 1913, total federal expenditures were—are you ready?—$1 billion. In the whole year. Today, Washington spends *ten times* that amount *every day*. Can we really expect the same number of people to oversee the spending of 3,000 times as much money?

Of course not.

If we want Washington to start making better decisions, it needs to start making *fewer* decisions. The American people are perfectly capable of making more of their own decisions about their own money and their own lives.

States and communities are perfectly capable of managing most of their priorities without much interference from Washington. I know this from firsthand experience in Minnesota and from working with other Governors. Political decisions should be made as close as possible to where the problems are addressed and where the people who are affected actually live.

In Minnesota, I shut down a cabinet-level agency, Minnesota Planning, because its work was duplicative and outdated. My administration cut government jobs and saved taxpayers millions of dollars. I also launched the largest government reform effort in fifteen years through executive orders and called it "Drive to Excellence." This will save taxpayers an estimated $250 million in my state. It *can* be done.

We need to end federal involvement in bailed-out corporations and government-sponsored enterprises like Fannie Mae, Sallie Mae, and Freddie Mac. We need to stop corporate welfare that simply transfers money from taxpayers to well-connected corporations. And we need to clear out the underbrush of federal regulations that stifle creativity, innovation, and growth in our economy.

When you step back from the trees and look at the forest, common sense forces us to ask some pretty simple questions. Why should the federal government own over half of General Motors? Why are we drilling for oil miles out at sea, thousands of feet below sea level, but not in the safer places on our own dry, unused land to fuel our economy? Why should the United States Congress care what kind of toilet or showerhead you have in your bathroom?

Or consider all the dusty old junk stuffed into the federal attic. Why, in an age of a thousand cable television networks, do taxpayers still subsidize PBS? Why, in an age of countless terrestrial, Internet, and satellite radio stations, do we still pay for NPR? Why does the federal government own a money-losing train company, a bankrupt insurance company, and two failed car companies? The government is like one of those hoarders you see on talk shows— the folks with fourteen dining room tables in their garage and eight boxes of sweaters in their kitchen. The federal government needs to have a yard sale!

Here's another question: why are government employees making 22 percent more than their private-sector counterparts, plus enjoying better benefits and nearly perfect job security? If we leveled out federal employee pay scales, we could save $40 billion per year. Over ten years, that's almost half a trillion dollars that could help pay down our massive debt. And why are private-sector workers five times more likely to get laid off than their government counterparts?

We should never get used to tolerating federal inefficiency and incompetence. Rather than add new programs on top of old ones that aren't working, let's do something bold and get rid of the old ones. We can use the savings to cut taxes and pay down the debt.

We must return to the principles of limited government and put the people, not the government, back in charge. Limited government leads to unlimited opportunities. We have a chance in coming years—as our disproportionately older federal workforce begins to retire—to fundamentally change the way our government functions. We need fewer bureaucrats making fewer decisions and spending fewer dollars.

Are the nation's schools, highways, and financial system really so perfect that *only* Congress could possibly improve on them? Please. Under government-mandated monopolies, we had black, rotary-dial phones with clunky cords. The free market gave us cordless phones, then cell phones, smart phones, and iPhones. When the government controlled the skies, it was too expensive for regular people to fly. Now air travel is often the cheapest part of going on vacation.

The point is that the federal government has its purposes, and those purposes are helpfully laid out in our Constitution. To me, this is the true debate between the two parties: Democrats want America to act more like the government, and Republicans want the government to act more like the rest of America.

* * * * * * * * * *

FINALLY, WE NEED TO REMEMBER that the key here at home and around the world is *freedom*. When Americans are freer, we are also stronger, more prosperous, and more secure. And as America grows stronger, more prosperous, and more secure, so will the rest of the world.

Just as the American Dream is real, so is American exceptionalism. Our values are different, our people are different, and our goals are different from any other superpower in history. We fight to liberate rather than to conquer. We trade as much to make others more free as to make ourselves more prosperous.

America *is* different. And what makes us different makes us great. Barack Obama doesn't see it that way. He readily apologizes for his country while ingratiating himself to our rivals and enemies.

I believe that America is the greatest force for good and stability in the world today, period. Even President Obama's appeasement of Iran's ayatollahs, his betrayal of Poland and the Czech Republic on missile defense, and his treatment of old friends like Britain and Israel—as indefensible as those mistakes are—cannot alter the fact of America's greatness.

And even if our President fails to understand America's role in the world, our people do not. The American people know we're still at war, and why, and against whom. They know the difference between the peaceful religion of Islam and radical Islam. They know who our friends are, even in countries ruled by hostile regimes. When democratic protesters stand up in Tehran, Americans know whose side they're on.

The American people intuitively know that while our relationships with Great Britain and China are both vitally important, one of them is and must remain *special*. They know who men like Hugo Chavez, Mahmoud Ahmadinejad, and Kim Jong Il really are. And they don't appreciate a foreign policy that often seems more accommodating to them than to our allies.

An accommodating American President is exactly what regimes such as Venezuela, Iran, and North Korea want. But others, including our allies and those fighting for human rights and freedom around the world, want a leader in the White House who will stand by them. To them, America should represent no better friend and no worse enemy.

Regrettably, that formulation has been reversed by President Obama. Increasingly, America is viewed abroad as no worse friend and no better enemy. One example in particular stands out. During the 2009 demonstrations in Tehran against the murderous Ahmadinejad regime, Obama's voice was nowhere to be found—a silence so demoralizing that demonstrators held up signs in English asking whether Obama was with them or with Ahmadinejad.

The leader of the United States should *never* leave those willing to sacrifice their lives in the cause of freedom wondering where America stands.

★ ★ ★ ★ ★ ★ ★ ★ ★ ★

I BELIEVE THAT THE PATH to reform, renewal, and recovery is freedom. A free-enterprise economy brings greater prosperity. Limited government will lead to a stronger, safer, and more prosperous society. School choice will lead to better-educated children and higher test scores. But that's not why we should have things like free markets, limited government, and school choice.

We should have those things because we are endowed by our Creator with inalienable rights. We should have those things because decisions about how to spend our own money and run our own lives belong to individuals.

I believe this is true because I believe in the inherent dignity and intrinsic worth of every person.

I believe in a culture of life, protecting the weak and the innocent—including the infirm, the unwanted, and the unborn. I believe in a culture of freedom that gives every individual the right to pursue happiness. I believe in a culture of community that protects us from isolation. And I believe in a culture of responsibility that protects us from dependence.

Many conservatives look at the state of our union, see the yawning deficits and debt, the corruption of our institutions, and the betrayal of our founding principles, and fear we have reached a point of no return. But that fear runs counter to everything we know about the country we love.

Of course reform, renewal, and recovery will demand courage and patience. But so does everything worth pursuing in this world. The path before us will be difficult—but it always has been. After all, if freedom were easy, everyone would be free. But they're not. We are free because, throughout our history, Americans have embraced the virtues of individual responsibility, integrity, courage, and faith in God.

Even in our darkest hours, America has never faced a challenge it could not meet.

Our generation may not be called to storm a beach or tear down a wall. But we are called nonetheless to action—in our own neighborhoods, in Washington, and around the world—to earn what we have been given and to defend what we love. And though fought on different fields with different tools, our struggle is the same as that of every American generation before us: a fight for freedom. Freedom from a future of debt, dependence, and doubt.

The freedom we enjoy today—and too easily take for granted—is a precious gift, endowed to us by our living God and secured for us by our fallen heroes. The only way we can begin to repay that gift is to pass it on to those who come after us, to leave to our daughters and sons a strong America worthy of our mothers and fathers.

The work before us will not be easy. But the work of freedom is the work of our lives. And the price of freedom tomorrow is the courage to stand today.

23

★★★★★★★★★★

THE FINAL SHOWDOWN

HERE'S THE WAY I hoped my eight years in office would go: I'd work with the legislature and cut spending. (Check.) I'd set the state on a fiscally conservative track. (Check.) We'd get our state back in the black. (Check.) We'd pass big improvements in education, economic development, energy, and health care. (Check, check, check, and check.) The economy would turn around and revenues would rise. (Big. Red. X.)

The dramatic drop in the national economy in 2008, coupled with the wallop of the September stock market crash, did more than just KO John McCain's election chances. It knocked Minnesota's revenue train, along with those of most other states, right off the tracks.

When the budget forecast came out in November 2008, it felt

like I'd been thrown in the DeLorean in *Back to the Future* and shot right back to 2002. Despite all the reforms and reductions in spending, the economy had fallen far and fast, and our state budget was in big trouble.

The November projection put us at a $4.8 billion deficit.

The Democrat response was to beat the same old drum, insisting we needed to raise taxes or the state would go completely bust. Never mind the fact that if we had increased spending the way they wanted during the previous six years, our deficit would have been far worse!

Stop and think about this for a moment. The liberal, "progressive" answer to a bottomed-out economy, the worst economic crisis since World War II, was to raise taxes and hit our citizens and employers in the pocketbook. Talk about hitting someone when they're down. How could that possibly solve anything?

As the 2009 legislative session kicked off, I offered cuts and shifts that would balance the 2010–2011 budget without raising taxes. But we also needed to clean up a deficit that had opened up in the current 2009 budget. The legislature refused to act to address that problem. So I utilized my authority to make emergency cuts to ensure that our money wouldn't run out before the end of the fiscal year.

What amazed me, after all this time, after all of these fights, was that the Democrat-controlled Senate—this time joined by a Democratic majority in the House (Minnesota was swept up in the same liberal-leaning tide as the rest of the country in 2006)—simply would not cut spending to any significant degree. They knew I would veto any tax increase that came across my desk. How else did they expect to balance the budget if they didn't make cuts? They simply kept tossing me bills with more taxes or additional spending; all those bills met their expected fate.

The Democrats' plan, as I understood it, was to try to trigger another government shutdown. Procedurally, they sent me all the main bills at the end of the 2009 regular session. They assumed I was going to veto some of them and that a special session would be needed. Then, if I didn't come around and agree to their demands, they would force another government shutdown.

They sent me spending bills that spent too much but were reasonable in most other respects. They also sent me a tax bill that raised taxes dramatically to pay for their spending bills. It was the same old tax-and-spend approach they knew I adamantly opposed.

They thought they were going to jam me, but I wasn't going to let that happen.

The Governor of Minnesota has an executive power at his disposal called unallotment. The unallotment authority is not unlike a line-item veto. Minnesota law basically says that in times of fiscal crisis, when certain conditions are met, the Governor has the authority to cut or delay spending. Traditionally, this authority is rarely used. But in this case, it was necessary.

I vetoed the tax-increase bill. I didn't call a special session; I used my unallotment authority to make the needed additional cuts to balance the budget. The unallotments removed more than *$2.6 billion* from the budget. Their plan to cause a special session and government shutdown was thwarted.

The other side was shocked. They never saw it coming—and they really didn't like it.

* * * * * * * * * *

ONE OF THE LINE-ITEM VETOES drew the most fire by far: I completely eliminated a program known as General Assistance Medical Care (GAMC).

GAMC provided unlimited health care for low-income single adults without kids. Minnesota was one of only a handful of states in the entire country to provide any benefit for that segment of the population. Our program was perhaps the most generous even when compared to the few other states that offered a similar program. And it showed—GAMC's costs were rising over 30 percent per budget cycle! The program was out of control, and it needed to be fixed. It was one of the many programs causing the state budget to be unsustainable. It was an old-style "fee for service" setup that paid providers for how many procedures they performed without much accountability for cost control or quality outcomes.

I had tried to get the legislature to reform GAMC for many years. They refused to listen or act. Now? I had their attention. The veto would not take effect for almost a year, so we had time to work something out. But the clock was now ticking. The pressure was on.

Of course, the press mostly ignored the underlying problem and wrote about how awful it was that I was trying to take poor people's health care away. That press coverage mostly overlooked a separate decision I made to move everyone covered by GAMC to MinnesotaCare, another program that provided health care to the disadvantaged. That program had benefits that were more limited than GAMC, and the switch would be more affordable for the state.

These were not easy decisions. Reviewing spreadsheets in a conference room made it clear GAMC was out of control and unsustainable. But I knew from past experience and from many encounters with people who benefit from such programs, people who desperately need care, that it's different when you look into their eyes and hear their concerns.

One time I was at the small airport in Mankato when a man

approached me in a wheelchair. He had a clear and severe disability. He took my hand, and I knelt down beside him as he said to me in this raspy voice, "Please, don't cut my health care." He explained how he didn't have money, didn't have a job, and didn't have a family to take care of him. You can't experience a moment like that without being emotionally impacted.

I reached a compromise with the legislature regarding GAMC. The program would no longer be a blank check. The new program would essentially pay hospitals and providers a lump sum of money in exchange for treating a fixed number of GAMC patients. Guidelines were also set to ensure the care received would be appropriate. Providers now had incentive to focus on the wellness of GAMC patients and health-care outcomes rather than how many procedures they performed.

Today, Minnesota remains a top-five state in serving low-income singles. The new program reflects a novel approach that may well work. However, it is unlikely to ever get much of a chance. Since all of this occurred, the federal government passed Obamacare, which will provide health care for single adults without children such as the people in our GAMC program. I declined to have Minnesota join Obamacare. However, Minnesota will soon be forced to participate as a matter of law. Unfortunately, Obamacare will forcibly replace our reformed GAMC program. People in that program will once again receive open-checkbook health care, only this time from a federal government that is beyond broke. Unfortunately but unsurprisingly, the federal approach requires no accountability or reform from the system.

* * * * * * * * * *

MY UNALLOTMENTS AND VETOES did not end my fight with the legislature over the 2010–2011 budget. The Democrats insisted

I overstepped my authority in unallotting $2.6 billion from the budget. They decided to take me to court. According to the way my advisers and I read the law on unallotment, I was absolutely within my authority, but I lost the first round in the courts.

The Democrats were jumping for joy, of course, thinking they had me up against a wall and could raise taxes and spending in the wake of the court's decision. The ordeal reminded me again that some Democrat legislators still resented feeling steamrolled in 2003. At one point in the negotiations after the court's decision, I was outlining a proposal when Democrat Senate leader Larry Pogemiller blurted out, "I am not John Hottinger, and this is *not* 2003!"

Seven years had gone by. Seven! And he was still fuming over the way Hottinger gave in to my spending cuts in the first six months of my first term in office.

I appealed the lower court's decision regarding unallotment. Finally, with just twelve days to go in the 2010 legislative session—the last session while I was Governor—the Minnesota Supreme Court issued a decision affirming the lower court's ruling and overturning the unallotments.

The dissenting opinion by three members of the Minnesota Supreme Court was strong and clear. It laid out in detail the reasons why I had the authority to make the unallotments. Unfortunately four members of the court saw it differently.

I was extremely disappointed with the majority's decision, not so much because they ruled against me—though that certainly is disappointing—but because of the message the ruling sent. In my view, the majority decision was an example of judicial overreach. Instead of applying the law as written, they inserted their own requirements and views into the law.

The court could have easily ruled that the unallotment law was ambiguous but that it was not the court's place to impose its own views and requirements into the law. They could have noted that the legislature and executive branch created the law and that those branches of government had it within their own power to clarify or fix the law on their own without the court intervening.

Even if they did not fully agree that the unallotments were appropriate, the majority could have exercised some restraint and avoided such a dramatic split in the court on such an important issue involving the two other independent branches of government. But that's not what they did. They jumped into the dispute headfirst and even added their own new criteria to the law.

In any event, now I needed to address the $2.6 billion short-fall in a matter of days. It normally takes months to sort through a budget problem of that magnitude. Many people jumped to the conclusion there was simply no way we could possibly get this done without raising taxes. Something had to be done and quickly. If the court's decision was the last word on the matter, the state could have been placed in a position of not being able to pay its bills. We didn't even have the option of shutting down the government, because appropriations had been authorized. The problem was, there was no money.

My team and I considered many alternatives, trying to come up with something that would convince the Democrats. I didn't immediately realize it, but I had an ace up my sleeve. It was an election year, and Margaret Kelliher, the Speaker of the House, was running for Governor. She had been endorsed at the Democrats' State Convention but faced a hotly contested primary against two very wealthy Democrats. The primary was set for August 10, and it was already May. She couldn't afford to have this drag out all summer long. Her ability to raise funds for her campaign would be limited if I called a special session through June and July. She also could not afford to be hunkered down at the capitol instead of campaigning. It would suck up all her time; instead of running effectively for Governor, she would be embroiled in an ugly, summer-long debate.

With less than a week to go in the regular legislative session, the Democrats sent me an awful tax bill with a big, fat tax increase. I promptly vetoed the bill. I also decided it was time to turn up the heat with the public. Our team and I aggressively criticized the Democrats' approach by telling people they wanted to raise taxes in the worst economic times in modern history. Then the Democrats tried making another run at me with some health-care fees. I said no to those, too.

Finally, with the clock ticking on the regular session, the Democrats agreed to legislatively approve nearly all of my original unallotments. So by the spring of 2010, despite having lost the legal battle, I had won the budget battle.

The national economy is still a mess, of course. And Minnesota's next Governor will have to deal with significant budget shortfalls—in part because the legislature refused to make my unallotments permanent. They are only effective for the current two-year budget. After that, spending will be reinstated unless the next Governor and legislature take action.

I hope future voters make the right choice and elect leaders who will see this through. Those cuts need to be permanent. Government needs to live within its means just like everybody else. For the sake of the people of Minnesota, I hope the politicians in St. Paul will finally let go of liberal, nanny-state notions and hold the government in check. We need to have a more-limited, more-accountable government that leaves more power, decision making, and money with the hardworking people of Minnesota.

24

★ ★ ★ ★ ★ ★ ★ ★ ★ ★

NEVER FORGET

AMBUSH ALLEY STILL EXISTS.

In the final summer of my second term, I had the opportunity to take one last trip to Iraq and Afghanistan. I jumped at the chance.

The temperature peaked at about 120 degrees when our C-130 landed in Baghdad. We made it in between sandstorms, but more were on the way. Helicopters were later grounded, so our trip from the base by the airport to the embassy downtown was by truck. I looked out the window of our armored SUV as we once again sped down what was once the world's most dangerous road. I thought again how stressful such drives must be for our troops. Nearly everything can be a potential threat. A stalled car or someone changing a tire on the side of the road prompts thoughts of

Could that be a car bomb? The sight of a garbage can or empty box, *Is that an IED?*

It's difficult to imagine the stress of our troops who drive in areas like these every day. Looking for wires laid across the road. Questioning everything. Always on high alert. I just kept thinking of the focus and courage it must take to endure that every single day.

Today, Ambush Alley isn't nearly as deadly as it was during my earlier trips. Iraq has changed for the better. The country still has a long way to go, but during my trip in 2010 it was a safer place all around. The number of incidents, casualties, and injuries were down. Iraqi police forces and military were taking the lead role. There was a sense among the troops that a corner had been turned—and they're the ones who should know. Many of them had been there before and had a point of reference. Nearly all the soldiers I spoke with told me they felt good about how things were going.

The U.S. plan was to draw military personnel in Iraq down to fifty thousand by September 1, 2010, and to zero by the end of 2011. A new Iraqi government would be formed by then, and everyone was anxious to see how events would unfold. Great progress had been made, and we all hoped it would stay that way. But after coming so far, we need to make sure arbitrary deadlines don't supersede common sense. Our men and women in uniform have sacrificed so much to get us to this point. They have given too much of their time, talent, and blood to let Iraq slide backward— even if it means keeping a small number of troops in that country awhile longer.

In Afghanistan, we visited several spots on our tour, including a base near the Pakistan border. Our military presence in that country was "kinetic," as the commanders like to say. It was highly active, with planned and unplanned enemy engagements breaking out all over the map, every day. While we were there, two military personnel were abducted after they took a wrong turn and got fired upon and their vehicle stalled out. They were subsequently killed.

In contrast to Iraq, Afghanistan had become more challenging and dangerous since my earlier trips. Even before the wars, Iraq had more infrastructure and capacity than Afghanistan. Iraq had education, electricity, and road systems in place, even if they were old or modest in scope. Afghanistan had very little of that, and it had other challenges, including a shared border with the tribal areas of Pakistan that harbored individuals and groups who worked actively to destabilize Afghanistan.

Meeting with General Petraeus was one of the highlights of the trip. I had met him on other occasions and it was a privilege to spend time with him. He is already a historic figure for his work in designing and deploying the counterinsurgency strategies that turned the tide of the war in Iraq. He was now in charge of turning Afghanistan around.

We met with him in his headquarters in Kabul. He is a thoughtful person and as an added bonus possesses a good sense of humor. He believed that the momentum of the insurgency had been successfully stalled and that it would take about two years to get things on track.

Success in Afghanistan will require our country to have strategic patience. We have been there a long time, and public patience with the war effort has worn thin. But General Petraeus demonstrated in Iraq that the right amount of troops and the right counterinsurgency strategy can work. He believes a similar strategy can also work in Afghanistan. We need to give him and our troops a full chance to succeed with this new strategy.

For the public to better understand the situation and have the strategic patience needed regarding Afghanistan, the President and others need to persistently remind America why we're there and why it matters. I supported President Obama's decision to surge additional troops into Afghanistan, though I do not think it should have taken him three months to make that decision. I also don't think he should have announced a withdrawal date at the same time.

We may well be able to start drawing down our troops by the July 1, 2011, date announced by the President, but troop withdrawal decisions should be made and measured against our strategic objectives, not an arbitrary deadline. Signaling our intent to leave by a certain date causes friends or potential friends in Afghanistan to hedge their bets. From Afghanistan's national leaders to shopkeepers, translators, informants, and village elders, nearly all Afghanis find themselves making a daily calculation whether it's in their best interest to help the United States, help our enemies, or just stay out of the way. Prematurely announcing when our commitment will end or dwindle has the effect of unsettling and endangering our local partners.

Unfortunately, the Obama administration's reputation for uncertainty in national security matters is well established. Some of our best allies in the world have had the rug pulled out from underneath them by President Obama. Poland and the Czech Republic are examples. His equivocal statements and actions regarding our great friend and ally Israel have caused obvious tension. His efforts to "reset" relations with Russia have resulted in a proposed nuclear arms treaty that favors Russia and all but affirms Russia's decision to help Iran fire up a nuclear energy reactor.

President Obama needs to understand that the goal of our national security policy should not be for the United States to be popular in Europe or the Middle East. The goal should be to make sure our country is safe and respected. President Obama also needs to do a more forceful job of reminding people about the threat of global terrorism. That threat is obviously real, and it's not going away anytime soon.

I spoke to one military leader in Afghanistan who described 9/11 as the beginning of World War III. "It's not like other world wars," he said. "It's episodic; it's transnational. It will ebb and flow. It will be asymmetrical. We have an enemy that is not as easily recognizable, but this is a global, sustained effort to harm the United States." It calls all of us to better understand what's at stake and to have a greatly enhanced commitment to fight against these forces. And we can all do something, starting with giving even better support to the men and women who are actually in the fight.

Sadly, President Obama will not call this effort what it is. He has stopped using the phrase "war on terror." His administration never makes pointed references—or any references—to the real problem: radical Islamic terrorism. Apparently that isn't politically correct. The fact is, radical Islamic terrorism exists. Pointing that out doesn't condemn all Muslims. But there *is* an element of Islam that is radical and that has terrorist intentions. We need to call it what it is. We need to confront it, and we need to defeat it.

★ ★ ★ ★ ★ ★ ★ ★ ★ ★

AFTER RETURNING FROM THAT TRIP to the Middle East, I found myself more inspired, more fired up than ever. My pride in America always seems to swell when I spend time around the men and women who put their lives on the line to protect our freedoms. It's been my pleasure to spend time with them, whether across the world or in every corner of our state.

One of the most inspiring places I had the opportunity to do so was in Luverne, Minnesota. There, in this beautiful Midwestern town nestled in the southwestern part of the state, is a group of World War II veterans who gather daily for coffee at Glen's Deli. Mary became acquainted with the group some years ago after reading about them in the newspaper. She thought she'd invite them for coffee at the Governor's Residence, and they took her up on it, chartering a bus to St. Paul and simultaneously planting the seed of a beautiful friendship.

These men were the subject of a documentary series directed by Ken Burns, called simply *The War*. They are a group of common people who have lived lives of uncommon bravery. A museum filled with World War II artifacts, largely their own, and a veterans' memorial in front of the historic Luverne courthouse have been erected in their honor. The memorial is a place to reflect, quietly and reverently, on the service and sacrifice of all those who fought to defend our freedoms.

These World War II veterans of Luverne decided to form a club called the Last Man Club. Their founding secretary, Warren Herreid Sr., even drafted a booklet, an "articles of incorporation" of sorts, which gives thoughtful purpose to their last, simple gatherings as brothers in arms. In its preamble, he wrote:

> Some may call us heroes, but we are just common men
> who were called to defend our country and our flag, the
> symbol of the hopes and dreams of our people. We were
> willing to sacrifice even our lives to preserve the American
> way of life—freedom, justice, and opportunity for all—
> for future generations.

As a symbol of their friendship, these men bought a bottle (of some sort of liquor; I don't know what) that will remain sealed and unopened until "the Last Man" opens it for the last toast to all his comrades who have gone before him. The articles even make provision for the final banquet and the final toast.

It's difficult to describe how much Mary and I have come to appreciate the men and women in our military. We've come to know so many of them and their stories personally, and we've done everything we could to publicly highlight their service.

During my first State of the State speech, I honored two veterans, Alf Larson and Harold "Snuff" Kurvers. Both served in World War II. Snuff survived not only the Bataan Death March but two "hell ships" on which he was transported as a prisoner of war, followed by forced labor in a coal mine. Against all odds he returned to Minnesota, married, raised a family, and worked for the U.S. Postal Service until retirement. He's a kind and gentle soul.

I felt I owed these and other courageous veterans the very best I had, and I tried to give it, whether by being present for deployment ceremonies, pursuing policies that were veteran friendly, serving on the national board of ESGR (Employer Support of the Guard and Reserve), or just doing all I could to make a difference.

* * * * * * * * * *

WHEN I LOOK BACK on my time as Governor of Minnesota, I'm pleased to say my administration made a positive difference in a lot of ways. The list of our accomplishments during those eight years is pretty solid. Among the big ones:

1. We put into place some of the best policies and programs in the country for the support of the National Guard and members of the military and their families.
2. We drove down spending in the state to a level that's more responsible and sustainable. From 1960, the year

I was born, until I became Governor in 2003, the average two-year increase in Minnesota's budget was 21 percent. During my time as Governor, we brought that down to about 1.7 percent per year. And for the first time in the 150-year history of my state, we actually cut state spending in real terms.

3. Every Governor for the last forty years thought it was strategically important to at least get Minnesota out of the top ten in taxes. Nobody ever did it. I did.

4. Our school results in Minnesota are nation-leading. I am proud that we dramatically improved our school standards and were the first state in the nation to offer performance-based pay for teachers statewide.

5. We showed the way with some fantastic, market-based health-care reforms.

With any luck, and by the grace of God, I hope we have witnessed the start of a sea change in American politics. And I hope some of what I've accomplished in Minnesota can serve as inspiration for more than a few of these new leaders. If there's anything I've learned during my time as Governor, it's that conservative leadership works—even in a sea of liberals.

* * * * * * * * * *

NOW MARY AND I need to determine what's next for us.

I know where my help comes from. God has given each of us time, talents, skills, abilities, and resources. We need to use those gifts for a cause and purpose beyond our individual circumstances. For me so far, that has led to public service.

This moment in history reminds me of how I first started in public service. It reminds me a great deal of when Jimmy Carter was President. Today, like it did three decades ago, the country needs a strong, hopeful, optimistic leader who will honestly and credibly tell the American people, "We can put this back together. We can do this. We're going to return to American common sense. We're going to return to an American can-do attitude. I'm going to shoot it to you straight, and I'm not going to go back on my word."

* * * * * * * * * *

ON THE WAY HOME from the Middle East in the summer of 2010, we stopped at a military hospital in Germany to visit wounded warriors who had been medically evacuated from the war zone. Visiting with wounded soldiers is always an incredibly moving experience. But there was one particular soldier this time whose enthusiasm and dedication reminded me how important it is to never give up.

This young man, a Special Forces operative, was fully alert and awake when I approached his bedside. I introduced myself and asked him what happened. "No big deal. I've been here three times," he said. He went on to tell me that he first landed in the hospital after taking a bullet through the fleshy top part of his shoulder. He got that patched up and went back to Iraq. He was hospitalized a second time when he sustained burns on his chest and back—pretty serious burns to his upper torso. Once again, he got patched up and rejoined his team. Most recently, he had taken a large ammunition round through his calf. The round had miraculously missed his bone but took out a big chunk of calf tissue and muscle.

Even now, after being rushed for a third time from the battlefield to this hospital in Germany, his attitude was "Get me patched up, and get me back to my team." His first priority, his main focus, was how quickly he could get back to the fight.

I was so taken aback by his attitude that I asked a doctor about it at the hospital that day. "Is that unusual?" I asked.

The doctor shook his head. "It's not unusual at all," he told me. "In fact, it's really common." After faith and family, it is typical for wounded soldiers to think not about their injuries but about their brothers and sisters still in the fight and their hopes to rejoin them.

It made me recall meeting John Kriesel in a military hospital a few years ago—how his own team would not let him die, and how he's still standing now, without any legs. It brought me right back to the emotional moment when I pinned the Silver Star on Chad Malmberg's uniform and marveled at his humble thanks as he shunned the spotlight and instead acknowledged his team. These men and women represent all that's good and true in this world. All that's great about the American spirit. Faith, freedom, team, country.

We are Americans. We don't give up on our country or each other. We are in this together. We can do this if we stand together with courage. We know what needs to be done. Let's go do it.

Rise up; this matter is in your hands.
We will support you, so take courage and do it.
EZRA 10:4

ACKNOWLEDGMENTS

WHEN I COUNT MY BLESSINGS, those who have been friends and neighbors throughout the years always top the list. No matter what twists and turns life has taken, I've been fortunate to have been surrounded by people who know me just as "Tim." So a special thank-you to our friends from Eagan, our neighborhood, our children's schools, law school, and our places of employment, all of whom know Mary and me in environments that, for the most part, do not intersect politics. Each of you has been a source of joy and instrumental in keeping our lives truly "normal."

From the beginning of my involvement in elective politics, I've been grateful for steadfast supporters. No one, myself included, accomplishes anything in politics without them. Thank you to each and every one who volunteered during my campaigns, who worked as part of the staff, who provided financial support, who wrote me heartwarming notes at just the right time, and who made all the difference in the outcome of each election. My official office was also filled with dedicated public servants. I am profoundly grateful for all you have done and all we were able to accomplish together.

A special thank-you, too, for all the Minnesotans who approached me along the way, whether at the fishing opener, at a restaurant, in the grocery store, or any other place I happened to be, just to offer a word of encouragement or to tell me that they and their families have been praying for me. We all need prayer, and I appreciate everyone who expressed a genuine interest in the importance of praying for our state, our country, and our elected leaders.

I also owe a special debt of gratitude to all the highly skilled professionals who worked together to create this book. It was a genuine pleasure to work with all of you. Thank you to Rick Christian, my agent with Alive Communications, who had complete confidence in this book before it existed; Mark Dagostino, my collaborator, who spent countless hours learning about, and writing about, more details of my life than he probably could have imagined; Ron Beers, Lisa Jackson, Carol Traver, Maria Eriksen, and all the incredible professionals at Tyndale, including my editor, Jeremy Taylor.

My family, of course, has been the backbone of my support from the beginning. I deeply appreciate all that my mom and dad did for me, but it's been my brothers and sisters who have weathered life with a brother in politics. Thank you for your patience and understanding.

In addition, my mother-in-law, who is a fierce Scrabble player and was always a loyal fan of my radio show, is owed a special thank-you. While Mary and I were busy with countless events, Mary's mother was a dependable caretaker of our children. We appreciate it very much.

To Anna and Mara, my children, who have spent their growing-up years with their dad as Governor, it is my deepest hope that the opportunities have outweighed the burdens. Anna, thank you for sharing my slightly strange sense of humor and laughing at things that at times only you and I think are really funny. Mara, thank you for exemplifying the Golden Rule and showing me, and everyone else in your life, what it means to truly love others. Thank you both for never letting me take myself too seriously. I love you.

Of course this book, and the substance of much of its contents, would not exist if it weren't for Mary, the one who holds my heart and is the love of my life. Luckily for me, she also happens to be a good editor who is disciplined and sequential and kept this project on track. I will never be able to fully express the depth of my gratitude for her consistently optimistic spirit, wise counsel, and sacrificial willingness to walk this road that has been our life together.

And most importantly to God, whose grace and mercies are new every day.